Education as a Human Right

Also Available From Bloomsbury

Education as a Global Concern, Colin Brock

Right to Childhoods: Critical Perspectives on Rights, Difference and Knowledge in a Transient World, Dimitra Hartas

Rethinking Citizenship Education: A Curriculum for Participatory Democracy, Tristan McCowan

Education as a Human Right

Principles for a Universal Entitlement to Learning

Tristan McCowan

B L O O M S B U R Y

LONDON • NEW DELHI • NEW YORK • SYDNEY

Bloomsbury Academic

An imprint of Bloomsbury Publishing Plc

50 Bedford Square	175 Fifth Avenue
London	New York
WC1B 3DP	NY 10010
UK	USA

www.bloomsbury.com

First published 2013

British Library Cataloguing-in-Publication Data
A catalogue record for this book is available from the British Library.

ISBN: HB: 978-1-4411-2277-3
ePDF: 978-1-4411-1888-2
ePub: 978-1-4411-5059-2

Library of Congress Cataloging-in-Publication Data
A catalogue record for this book is available from the Library of Congress.

Typeset by Newgen Imaging Systems Pvt Ltd, Chennai, India
Printed and bound in Great Britain

Contents

Acknowledgements

This book is the fruit of interaction not only with the cited works but with numerous friends, colleagues, students and strangers, in conversation with whom the ideas put forward here have been moulded. A number of the chapters have also been presented at seminars and conferences over the last four years, and have evolved as a result of these discussions. Some parts of the book have been previously published. Versions of the following chapters have appeared as journal articles: Chapter 4 as 'Reframing the universal right to education' in *Comparative Education* (2010), Chapter 5 as 'Human rights within education: assessing the justifications' in the *Cambridge Journal of Education* (2012), Chapter 6 as 'Is there a universal right to higher education?' in the *British Journal of Educational Studies* (2012) and Chapter 7 as 'Human rights, capabilities and the normative basis of "Education for All"' in *Theory and Research in Education* (2011). I am also very grateful to Rosie Vaughan, María Ron Balsera, Michael Hand, Sharon Tao and Chris Yates for their perceptive comments on chapters. Finally, my thanks go to the millions of teachers and non-formal educators throughout the world who tirelessly – and often in the face of criticism and disrespect – work to make meaningful the lives of others.

Abbreviations

AIDS	acquired immuno-deficiency syndrome
BIS	Department for Business, Innovation and Skills
CEDAW	Committee on the Elimination of Discrimination against Women
CRC	Convention on the Rights of the Child
CREATE	Consortium for Research on Educational Access Transitions and Equity
DFID	Department for International Development
ECOWAS	Economic Community of West African States
EFA	Education for All
GDP	gross domestic product
HE	higher education
HIV	human immuno-deficiency virus
HRE	human rights education
ICESCR	International Covenant on Economic, Social and Cultural Rights
IHRE	Institute of Human Rights Education
LMIC	low- and middle-income countries
MDG	Millennium Development Goals
NGO	non-government organizations
OHCHR	Office of the United Nations High Commission(er) for Human Rights
PISA	Programme for International Student Assessment
SACMEQ	Southern Africa Consortium for Monitoring Educational Quality
SIDA	Swedish International Development Agency
UDHR	Universal Declaration of Human Rights
UIS	UNESCO Institute of Statistics
UNDP	United Nations Development Programme
UNESCO	United Nations Educational, Scientific and Cultural Organization
UNICEF	United Nations Children's Fund
UPE	Universal Primary Education
USAID	United Nations Agency for International Development

Introduction:
The Global Education Landscape

Few places in the world are now untouched by the institution of school. And yet many fail to benefit from it. We are living in an era of dramatic expansion of access to education, but disparities between social groups remain as stark as ever, and even now millions never sit facing a blackboard, let alone engage in meaningful learning. The tremendous faith in education, and its central place in the rhetoric of governments and agencies, is accompanied by negligence and narrow-minded thinking, and for most people the extraordinary possibilities of learning are not fulfilled. But does that matter? Should all children – and perhaps all adults – in fact be entitled to education and learning?

This book explores the principles that might underpin a universal right of this kind. It defends the idea that all people are indeed entitled to education, but goes on to address a further question: that of the forms of education that might correspond to the right. Education today is universally identified with school (or university). The diverse forms of learning that characterized the premodern world – whether through apprenticeships, the family, religious rites or coming-of-age initiations – all still exist, but cluster around the edges of the Leviathan of the school system. In the eyes of governments, development agencies and rights instruments, expansion of educational access means the expansion of school systems. But are we justified in seeing the right to education as being a right to schooling? And if not school, then what?

Take these three episodes (fictional but not distant from the reality of many around the world):

Reconnaissance planes flying over the Brazilian Amazon recently sighted a previously unknown indigenous group deep in the interior of Amazonas state. With time, contact was made, initially with rubber tappers, gold prospectors and illegal loggers, and then with the official state agency for indigenous affairs, which provided basic services to the community. As part of these services, a small primary school was constructed, staffed by teachers from the capital city of the state, Manaus. The agency officials strongly encouraged parents to send their children to the new school. One Monday morning, a group of 14 children aged between 6 and 11 sit down for the first time on wooden benches and face a whiteboard; an unknown adult addresses them in an unknown language, setting out the objectives of today's maths lesson.

Uttar Pradesh, India. A boy arrives at school having made the long walk from the edge of the village. He has an empty stomach but knows that at midday he'll be given a bowl of rice and dal together with the other children. He sits at the back of the class – he is a Dalit so is wary of occupying the front rows. He chants the mysterious words after the teacher, 70 or 80 voices together. As he looks out of the window he thinks about all the things he could be in life, an engineer, a doctor – if he studied hard of course. Tomorrow he would have to help his parents in the fields, but the day after, or maybe the day after that, he'd be back in school again, as long as it didn't rain.

Grace Loy stood up from her computer and looked down at the busy Dar-es-Salaam Street. She recalled the red earth track outside her aunt's rickety home where she had grown up. She had lost both her parents as a baby – later she learned they had fallen prey to the HIV/AIDS epidemic. She thought of the stories her aunt would tell her, her words of inspiration, her patient hands guiding her as she learned to write, to read, to tell her own stories. And then one day she made the long trip to the city to go to university, and here she was. She looked across the row of novels and short stories on her shelf, with the name Grace Loy in bold letters. She pulled one out; there above the title was a sticker, 'Winner of the Man Booker Prize for Fiction'.

Three episodes, three faces of education. In the first we see the dilemma of indigenous communities caught between, on the one hand, an increasingly unviable isolation, prey to exploitation at the hands of corporations and the destruction of the local environment, and, on the other hand, a school system that might equip them to defend their interests but at the expense of their knowledge systems, language and cultural integrity. In the second, we see the fragility of educational access for the poor, vulnerable to competing responsibilities of paid work, household chores and care of siblings, as well as direct discrimination and precarious quality in the school. In the third, the extraordinary potential of education to transform lives (as long as it is based on meaningful learning in relationships of care and inspiration) accompanied, as all transformations are, by loss as well as gain.

These vignettes point us at the same time to the great possibilities of education, the current realities of educational injustice, but also the need to think about *which* education we might want. The episodes are all located in low- and middle-income countries (LMICs), sometimes (problematically) described as 'developing countries', or the Global South. The book as a whole, in fact, will concentrate mainly on these regions of Asia, Africa and Latin America. The reason for this focus is not that infringements of the right to education cannot be found in the high-income countries of Europe, North America, Australasia and East Asia – there are many of course, though they may manifest themselves in more subtle ways. The focus on LMICs stems from the book's engagement with the right to education in relation to international development, and specifically to the Education for All (EFA) initiative. Debates around the right to education in the very diverse countries considered to be 'developing' are particularly critical on account of the severe lack of resources evident in many systems, leading to limited coverage and issues of quality, as well as complexities regarding the relevance, cultural sensitivity and political orientation of curricula in postcolonial contexts.

The EFA initiative launched in Jomtien, Thailand in 1990, has given significant impetus to the undertaking of ensuring global educational justice. In part, it is a fundraising movement, but the challenge of getting all children into school is far more than a question of money. Obstacles to access to school and meaningful learning are multiple and complex. Yet in the urgency of the task, the question of what school is for has become largely forgotten. As emphasized by Yates (2012), EFA is too much about *techne* (the methods or activities) and not enough about *telos* (the purposes or ends). This book represents a pause in the bustle of activity, a standing back to observe the shape of a wall being constructed, a moment of reflection. But this is far from an indulgence, an intellectual curiosity. Ultimately, it is not *any* education that will do.

The majority of literature on EFA addresses difficulties in implementation – the task of establishing universal education systems of high quality. This book instead focuses to a large extent on the vision rather than the strategy of EFA: that is to say, the principles underpinning the goal. The assumption that all actors are aiming for a similar end-point is a dangerous one, and greater clarity on the normative basis of EFA is needed before coordinating efforts to achieve it.

The emergence of Education for All

The World Conference on EFA aimed to reignite the faltering progress of educational development, which had suffered from the 1970s onwards through changing priorities, economic decline and structural adjustment programmes. In the decades following the Second World War, education systems in many countries had expanded rapidly, spurred on by the new-found belief that their economies would benefit as a result. The large number of countries that gained their independence in this period looked to education systems as a means to nation-building, as European countries had in the previous century. However, after the initial expansion had satisfied the educational needs of the elites, and the promise of mass education in delivering rapid economic growth in many cases had not borne fruit, the initial advances could not be sustained.

At Jomtien, there gathered together representatives of 155 governments, 33 intergovernmental organizations and 125 non-governmental organizations (NGOs), convened by the four main agencies of United Nations Children's Fund (UNICEF), United Nations Development Programme (UNDP), the World Bank and United Nations Educational, Scientific and Cultural Organization (UNESCO). According to Little (2008: 53), regardless of any initiatives that followed, the conference was highly significant simply through bringing all these groups together: 'it heralded the beginnings of a global compact/coalition of ideas about and finance for education that would far outweigh anything that had gone before'. The *World Declaration on Education for All* and *Framework for Action to Meet Basic Learning Needs* (or Jomtien Declaration), which emerged from the conference, has served as a founding document for EFA.

The Jomtien Declaration puts forward a statement of the importance of education, a vision of what education should involve and a strategy of international cooperation to achieve it. In essence, the Declaration asserts the necessity for all people around the world to have their 'basic learning needs' met, focusing on universal access to primary school, but also youth and adult education, attention to quality and to inequities in relation to gender and ability. It also outlines the political conditions necessary for achieving EFA, the need to mobilize resources and have broad cooperation intra-nationally and internationally. The emphasis on universal primary education – along with World Bank research (e.g. Psacharopoulos 1985) that showed greater economic returns to primary in comparison to secondary and higher – led to increasing prioritization of this level (Heyneman 2003). The consensus of the Jomtien Declaration and subsequent EFA initiative contrasted with the smorgasbord that had characterized educational aid previously, according to Mundy (2006: 27):

> From high-level manpower planning to vocational education, non-formal education, adult literacy, higher education and back again, a vague and expansive menu of what was 'needed' was reported or endorsed in a succession of international conferences and publications.

Certainly, some momentum was gained from the Jomtien conference, yet the progress fell far short of the optimistic targets set. A follow-up event, the World Education Forum in Dakar, Senegal, took place ten years later in 2000, on the date on which the goals of Jomtien were supposed to have been met (but had not). The Dakar Framework for Action reaffirmed much of the previous vision, but outlined more concrete targets and mechanisms of implementation. The six proposed goals were as follows:

1. expanding and improving comprehensive early childhood care and education, especially for the most vulnerable and disadvantaged children;
2. ensuring that by 2015 all children, particularly girls, children in difficult circumstances and those belonging to ethnic minorities, have access to and complete, free and compulsory primary education of good quality;
3. ensuring that the learning needs of all young people and adults are met through equitable access to appropriate learning and life-skills programmes;
4. achieving a 50 per cent improvement in levels of adult literacy by 2015, especially for women, and equitable access to basic and continuing education for all adults;
5. eliminating gender disparities in primary and secondary education by 2005, and achieving gender equality in education by 2015, with a focus on ensuring girls' full and equal access to and achievement in basic education of good quality;
6. improving all aspects of the quality of education and ensuring excellence of all so that recognized and measurable learning outcomes are achieved by all, especially in literacy, numeracy and essential life skills.

In contrast to these six, a narrower vision of just two goals was put forward in the other influential goal-setting task of the year 2000, the Millennium Development Goals (MDGs). These were: universal primary education (although importantly stipulating completion rather than just initial enrolment); and eliminating gender disparities in both primary and secondary levels. It is perhaps understandable that with only eight goals relating to all aspects of human existence, a vision of education of satisfactory breadth could not be ensured. Yet the focus on primary education here reaffirmed the existing tendency to the detriment of other levels and forms of education.

According to Mundy (2006), even more than the 1990s, it is the period since 2000 in which the most significant shift in international support for education can be observed, moving from the fragmented and incoherent array of bilateral programmes that had existed since the Second World War, to a much more coordinated effort – involving a rapprochement between the market-friendly Bretton Woods organizations with the basic needs and poverty focused UN agencies and INGOs – along with significantly increased resources. Packer (2007) also emphasizes the change since 2000 in the emergence of the EFA architecture and increase in initiatives and activities, accompanied by systems of targets and monitoring.

A significant new mechanism emerging was the Fast Track Initiative (now the Global Partnership for Education), launched in 2002 by the World Bank and partners, a multilateral scheme that provides extra resources for low income countries to fund universal primary education and technical support for planning. The establishment, also in 2002, of the annual Global Monitoring Report produced by UNESCO has also provided educationists and policy-makers with comprehensive statistics and analysis on which to base initiatives. UNESCO is nominally the lead agency for EFA, but with its limited budget is overshadowed in influence by the World Bank. Other major donors are bilaterals including Department for International Development (DFID), United Nations Agency for International Development (USAID) and Swedish International Development Agency (SIDA), while there are international non-governmental organizations (INGOs) such as Save the Children, Oxfam and ActionAid with significant education programmes, and advocacy groups such as the Global Campaign for Education.

The flurry of activity around international education is perhaps more surprising given the backdrop of downward pressure on aid budgets. A key reason why education has begun to take on a more central role in this context is that it has increasingly been seen as a motor for (economic) development. This instrumental framing of education – a far cry from the intellectual and cultural value and the role in mutual understanding that characterized the founding of UNESCO – will be a key point for discussion in the subsequent chapters.

EFA has a high profile in LMICs – particularly in Africa and Asia (much less so in Latin America), and has brought tangible changes in policies and practice. While the emphasis on education as a whole, and particularly on access for marginalized populations, has been welcomed by many, there have also been concerns. The support from the World Bank and major powers such as the United States and United Kingdom has inevitably raised suspicions that there is more to the initiative than selfless concern for the disadvantaged. Some have seen EFA as a concerted attempt to prime the global poor for the bottom rung of the globalized capitalist system, and prepare their hearts and minds for consumption. Even among those who do not adhere to Marxist positions, there are concerns about the top–down nature of the initiative, through which countries are rewarded with funding only if they have presented a plan consonant with donor visions of appropriate policy and planning.

The state of education worldwide

So how have two decades of EFA left the global scenario of education? At latest estimates, there are some 61 million children out of school around the world (UNESCO 2012). In many ways, this figure is only the tip of the iceberg. Carr-Hill (2012) estimates that the real number is likely to be twice this, given the undercounting of populations in particular circumstances – refugees, internally displaced peoples, nomads, those living in slums etc. – and the increased likelihood of these populations having out-of-school children. Furthermore, this figure only includes those completely out of school, and not those who have irregular attendance, who are significantly over age or who drop out soon after the start of the school year.

Access is not only a problem of lack of schools or places within schools, but also a question of demand, given economic pressures on families, responsibilities of children for household work and care of family members, and lack of value attached to formal education (sometimes with good reason). The challenge of universal primary education then is more than a financial one, although sufficient funding is a necessary precondition: the annual shortfall of funds for basic education is estimated at £11 billion for the 46 low-income countries covered (UNESCO 2010). This is a significant sum, but less than one-fifth of annual spending on arms of either the United Kingdom or France, and just 1.5 per cent of that of United States (*Guardian* 2012).

As might be expected, out-of-school children are not evenly distributed around the world or between different social groups. Over half of the out-of-school children are in sub-Saharan Africa – some 23 per cent of children in the region do not complete primary education – with a further 13 million in South and West Asia, representing 8 per cent of the age group (UNESCO 2012). Nigeria alone has over ten million children out of school, with Pakistan over five million, and India and Ethiopia over two million. Over 40 per cent of these out-of-school children across the world live in countries affected by conflict.

Certain groups within countries also have a higher propensity to be out of school. Girls have significantly lower rates of enrolment than boys at primary and secondary levels in many LMICs, and two- thirds of illiterate adults are women. The wealth of a family, unsurprisingly, is strongly linked to educational prospects. According to UNESCO (2011), 28 per cent of the wealthiest quintile in Cambodia have completed secondary school, while this figure falls to 0.2 per cent for the poorest quintile (based on the 23–7 age group). A number of other factors are also influential in reducing a child's chances of access to education: belonging to a minority ethnic or linguistic group, being a nomad, having a disability, being affected directly or indirectly by HIV/AIDS, living in rural areas, among others. Furthermore, there are intersectional dynamics, for example with socio-economic background, and rural/urban magnifying gender disparities.

The latest UNESCO Global Monitoring Report (2011) indicates faltering progress towards the six EFA goals established at Dakar. Early years education is broadly recognized as fundamental for subsequent educational success, as well as developing social skills, ensuring adequate nutrition and health care (e.g. World Bank 2011). While access to this level has increased rapidly, there is still only a gross enrolment rate of 44 per cent across the world. In achievement of universal primary education, again there have been significant rises over the past decade, especially in the two regions with the lowest enrolment – sub-Saharan Africa and South and West Asia – but progress is slowing. By 2015 the number of out-of-school children according to current projections might actually go up to 72 million. The picture is similar with gender parity. There have been steady gains in expanding access for girls, but they still make up 53 per cent of the children out of school, with disparities most notable in South and West Asia. And this is only considering parity of enrolment, and not the broader and more demanding goal of gender equality in education. There are also 74 million adolescents out of school (UNESCO 2011): many countries enrol only half of the age group in secondary schooling, and only half of these manage to complete a full cycle (CREATE 2011). Tertiary access is as low as 6 per cent for sub-Saharan Africa.

The news is even worse for the remaining two targets. Around 17 per cent of the world's adult population (some 796 million) still lacks basic literacy. With some notable exceptions (such as China and Vietnam) progress towards the goal of halving illiteracy rates has been poor, and the lack of concerted action in this area betrays the lower value attached to it in relation to universal primary education (UPE) (Robinson 2005). Quality of education also poses a serious challenge. Not only is there a significant lack of teachers, but often they have insufficient training, have high rates of absenteeism, and face other significant difficulties in exercising their profession – not least of which, low salary and public esteem (Tao 2012). Class sizes of 100 are common in many low-income countries, and rarely are there sufficient text books, let alone other teaching aide. Schools in remote areas are typically multigrade, but without appropriate pedagogy to ensure progress for students of different ages.

This passage sums up poor levels of learning in schools in many low- and middle-income countries:

> In India, one survey in 2009 found that just 38% of rural grade 4 students could read a text designed for grade 2. Even after eight years of school, 18% of students were unable to read the grade 2 text. In 2007, the Southern and Eastern Africa Consortium for Monitoring Educational Quality (SACMEQ) assessments highlighted acute deficits in learning achievement in low income countries. In Malawi and Zambia over a third of grade 6 students were unable to read with any fluency. (UNESCO 2011: 15)

Quality can, of course, be gauged in different ways (as will be explored in chapter 4), but as can be seen, serious challenges can be observed whether we focus on basic inputs (qualified teachers, facilities etc.), processes (pedagogy, relationships, management) or outcomes (test scores).

It is clear by now that the goals set for 2015 will not be met, and discussions are already underway to develop a new suite of targets. Despite the real progress in some respects, this is still a bleak picture all in all. Yet the type of account outlined above – one rehearsed frequently in updates on progress towards the EFA goals – makes a large assumption: that we are agreed on what we are doing and why we are doing it. While enshrined in the Jomtien and Dakar statements, this consensus is both more fragile in practice and more problematic in principle than is acknowledged.

Competing drivers for EFA

If we can all agree that education is a good thing, does it matter why we agree? Should we not just be thankful that we can gather diverse supranational agencies, national governments and NGOs together in a conference and unite in a campaign for universal primary education? It certainly would not matter (or at least not matter so much) if we were dealing with supply of clean water. Whatever the ideological differences around aid and diverse motivations for development work, ultimately water is water. But not so with education. There is no standard, neutral education that we can happily pipe into every village in the world. Often the basic skills of numeracy and literacy, or the subjects of national language, maths and science, are taken to be standard and universal in this way, but even these apparently neutral areas raise a multiplicity of problems. What proportion of the curriculum should these fundamental subjects take up, and what should populate the rest of the curriculum? What place should religion and citizenship have in the curriculum? Through which teaching methods should they be taught, and in which language of instruction? How should students be grouped together and assessed, and should all have the right to progress to the subsequent levels? Educational provision then at any level requires a vast range of decisions, ones that are underpinned by moral and political values, and cannot simply be answered through appropriate application of research evidence. As Paulo Freire argued, education is never neutral.

EFA, like government education policy in almost every country in the world, is strongly influenced by a theory that is so etched into our minds that it has become common sense, a truth so apparently obvious that it is hardly worth stating: that education makes people into better workers and will enhance economic growth. When Adam Smith first put forward this claim in *The Wealth of Nations* in 1776, it was far from an obvious point, and it was only with the testing of the idea by US economists in the mid-twentieth century that human capital theory became firmly established (Becker 1964; Schultz 1961). The theory proposed that education was a worthwhile investment both for states and for individuals, and in many instances gave greater returns than other kinds of investment.

Going hand-in-hand with human capital theory in the early expansion of education systems in newly independent states was modernization theory – with its economic, sociological and psychological variants (Inkeles and Smith 1974; McClelland 1961; Rostow 1960). Some countries were struggling to develop economically, so the theory held, because they lacked modern institutions and modern attitudes among the population – and schools were central to this task. In response to these theories that were linked to the project of Western capitalism, *dependency theory* (e.g. Frank 1967; Santos 1970) provided a critique of the idea that blame could be laid at the doorstep of impoverished states themselves, instead asserting that underdevelopment was caused by their dependent relationship with the wealthy nations. The educational implication of this theory was that countries needed to *delink*, to divest their systems and curricula of the vestiges of the colonial past and continuing neo-colonial interests.

Alongside these emerging drivers was a rather older one, that of nation-building. School systems, teaching in a national language (serving possibly to displace a former colonial language, or to suppress local languages), the propagation of national myths and so forth have been used to foster a sense of nation as well as forming functionaries to serve it (Green 1990). The nation-building rationale led to the establishment of many national universities, for example, even when there may not have been justification from a purely economic perspective.

These theories have developed along a historical trajectory, but remain to this day, jostling for space (McMillan 2010). According to Little (1999), the landscape of development became even more diverse from the early 1990s, with the ends of material wealth being challenged by alternative conceptions of human development and greater cultural awareness. Post-structural thought and post-colonialism have challenged the grand narratives of both free-market liberalism and Marxism, and in the last decade Amartya Sen's capability approach has been increasingly influential. In more recent times the big theories that have motivated educational development have been joined by concerns over security. Some attention to education can be attributed to the post-9/11 agenda, and the belief on the part of certain powers that formal education systems will help alleviate the poverty that fuels extremism, as well as undercutting other forms of education – such as madrassas – alleged to foster fanatical views (McClure 2009).

Of course, the above drivers for government policy are not necessarily what motivates teachers, students, teacher educators, advisers and all the other 'stakeholders' in the system. These may be driven by a quest for social justice, to raise consciousness, to empower girls, to improve conditions for students with disabilities. Or as teachers they may simply see the job of education as a job, as a means to salary and survival. As Dewey (1966 [1916]: 107) stated, '[I]t is well to remind ourselves that education as such has no aims. Only persons, parents, and teachers etc., have aims, not an abstract idea like education.' We are, therefore, reckoning with a highly diverse topography of understandings of education, of incentives and commitment.

One driver not mentioned as yet is the rights-based approach, that is to say, the idea that people should have education not because it will bring benefits to the economy or the nation, but because it is a fundamental entitlement of all humanity. This last driver will form the subject of the next section – and indeed the book as a whole.

The human rights-based approach

A right, most simply put, is a justified claim on others. A human right is a right that pertains to all human beings and only to human beings, and so is distinct from the rights that might be held by virtue of citizenship of a particular territory. (I will here take 'human rights' and 'universal rights' to be synonymous.) Human rights are seen to be justified because they protect those aspects most fundamental to our humanity – our survival, wellbeing and dignity as people. They are 'high-priority claim[s] or authoritative entitlement[s], justified by sufficient reasons, to a set of objects that are owed to each human person as a matter of minimally decent treatment' (Orend 2002: 34).

The meaning, significance and historical development of human rights will be outlined more fully in Chapter 2. Yet it is important to highlight at this stage one fundamental aspect of a rights-based approach that distinguishes it from the dominant driver of EFA, human capital theory – that is, its non-conditional nature. Education is not seen to be justified by a particular return, economic or otherwise. It is seen to be an entitlement for all human beings, whether or not they subsequently go on to contribute to gross domestic product (GDP) or make some other contribution to society. (The reasons *why* it may be considered an entitlement for all human beings will be explored in Chapter 3.) Of course, it still may be seen to be *desirable* that they make this kind of contribution, but education is not rationed on this basis. This distinction is significant since it undercuts the cost-benefit logic. For some populations, there will be occasions on which the cost of education will outweigh the subsequent benefit: for example, if there is a very remote location in which there may be few children of school-going age, or people with severe disabilities for which schools are ill-equipped to deal, or a number of other situations in which extra costs might be involved. Without a notion of entitlement, these people simply would not receive education.

The first, and most significant, reason for adhering to a rights-based approach, therefore, is because of the importance of unconditionality of access to education. Human capital theory is problematic, both in its susceptibility to the utilitarian tendency of allowing minority interests to be steamrollered by the majority, but also in its predominantly economic focus. A second characteristic is the rights-based approach's positioning of people as agents rather than beneficiaries. Possessing, claiming and exercising a right is an active stance of holding one's government and others to account; it is a question of justice. Without a notion of right, inhabitants of impoverished countries become beneficiaries, objects of a charity that is as uncertain as it is disempowering. Third, rights-based approaches are attentive to processes as well as outcomes, with concern for whether, for example, principles of participation were upheld in the course of achieving a desired result. Fourth, framing education as a right highlights the importance and urgency of the task: universal access is not an aspiration that we can fit in where possible if time and resources permit. It is an absolute requirement of justice, an immediate obligation, and one that implicates all human beings, directly or indirectly.

For a significant period after the Second World War, 'development' and 'human rights' work in the international context continued in a fair degree of isolation from one another. The emergence of rights-based approaches to development from the 1990s represented a coming together of the two – spurred by the controversial endorsement of the the 'right to development' by the United Nations in 1986 (Cornwall and Nyamu-Musembi 2004; Gready and Ensor 2005). A range of development agencies incorporated human rights into their programming, and the UN published a statement of principles for rights-based approaches, the 'Common Understanding' (United Nations 2003). Despite the advantages of rights-based programming in the framing of the inhabitants of impoverished countries as agents of justified entitlements, there have been reservations that these approaches are merely 'new wine in old bottles', dressing up the same old development practice in a more fashionable clothing.

In fact, human rights as a whole have been the subject of sustained critique over the years. To start with, there are doubts over the very possibility of the notion of human rights – Bentham's famous 'nonsense upon stilts'. There are those who consider that rights can only exist within a bounded polity, and others that the whole concept is baseless, and that all that exists are needs and interests.[1] Sen (2004) groups these critiques into three types: *legitimacy* – the position that only legal rights exist; *coherence* – that it is hard to specify a duty-bearer; and *cultural* – that Asian values, for example, are inimical to rights.

Interestingly, contemporary concerns over rights have come from the political right and left. The former critiques claim that rights go too far in pursuing equality and restricting liberty (in the non-interference sense) and the latter that they do not go far enough. So rights are objected to by conservatives and libertarians in providing excessive protection for individuals (i.e. freedom from detention without trial) and making excessive demands on others (i.e. taxation for universal healthcare). This form of critique is common in the popular press today. Socialists, on the other hand, have critiqued rights for providing only minimal guarantees – appeasing worker demands but stopping short of full equality – and for reinforcing bourgeois capitalist values. Rights have also been seen as strongly bound to patriarchy, and to have hidden beneath their universality the ongoing marginalization of and discrimination against women.

Other positions critique the *nature* of the moral guarantees provided by rights. The 'ethics of care' (Noddings and Slote 1996), for example, sees the contractarian nature of rights as rather cold and impersonal, instead looking to the feelings of affection for those close to us as the basis of morality. In a similar vein, others point to the individualism of rights (though in fact rights pertain to groups as well as individuals). Importantly, the universalism of rights is also the object of concern (e.g. Pollis and Schwab 1980). Sen (2004) and Spring (2000) argue that human rights are not an exclusively Western idea, even though the recent history of institutionalization of rights is predominantly European. There are many moral and political traditions worldwide that corresponds closely to the notion of human rights. Yet is it possible to determine human rights that apply to all of humanity, across all different contexts? And who is deciding what those rights are? As Ife (2009: 126) states, human rights 'are inevitably, drafted and agreed to by small groups of people in positions of privilege. They are politicians, diplomats, academics, opinion leaders and a few prominent human rights activists'. They therefore 'remain largely *a discourse of the powerful about the powerless*, and this is itself a human rights abuse: a denial of the right to define one's rights' (original emphasis). At the same time, the universalism of rights is essential so as to include all people in the protections that now only some enjoy – to avoid the cases so frequently seen in history of certain populations being viewed as dispensable and unworthy of the treatment given to other human beings.

For those who broadly agree with the principles of rights, there are also concerns that the rhetoric does not translate into reality. The cruel irony is that the groups whose human rights are most infringed are frequently those who are in the least favourable position to do anything about it. As stated by Cornwall and Molyneux (2008: 9)

> [The dilemma] is the gulf that exists between elegant laws and the indignities of women's everyday realities, and between being accorded a right and being in any position at all to make use of it.

Only some of the critiques of rights reviewed above are based on misunderstanding (e.g. that rights encourage self-seeking attitudes), or on illegitimate moral and political preferences (e.g. desire to maintain elite privilege); many represent real and significant difficulties as regards the grounds, legitimacy, process of establishment and implementation of rights and must be continually engaged with and responded to.

Grassroots rights

The conception of rights underpinning this book goes some way towards addressing concerns about their decontextualized, distant and universal nature. First, it is a *deliberative* conception of rights (Sen 2004), or in Ife's (2009) terms, *bottom-up*. The existence and validity of rights are not seen to be derived from their enshrining in law – rights are primarily moral, and only secondary legal. The moral validity of rights in turn is determined through deliberation in this conception, through open public discussion. Their plausibility is 'dependent on their ability to survive and flourish when they encounter unobstructed discussion and scrutiny' (Sen 2005: 160). Clearly, the conditions for horizontal and open debate in practice are rarely present, but this empirical fact does not undermine the principle.

Another way of framing this distinction is to see rights not as *discursive* (i.e. contained in formal documents) but *reflexive*, occurring:

> when people address the ideas themselves and, rather than accept the dominant discursive construction uncritically, think about and define what human rights mean in their own context. (Ife 2009: 135)

A further variant of this approach is that rights are formed through *struggle*, through the concerted actions of oppressed groups to obtain justice (e.g. Bowring 2012).

A grassroots approach certainly responds to concerns over the unresponsively universal nature of rights and their Western bias. But will a bottom-up process not lead to an unwieldy multiplicity of different versions and sets of rights? Do not human rights require by definition a universal set? This paradox is addressed (if not completely resolved) through the process of deliberation: individuals and groups will have different sets of values and priorities, but through open debate, forms of consensus can be reached that attend to our common concerns.

The importance of legal frameworks, in contrast, is asserted by Tomaševski (2001a: 8):

> A well-established adage posits that no right can exist without a remedy. This truism is sometimes forgotten for economic and social rights, including the right to education, thereby divorcing them from their grounding in law and transforming them into a secular religion. Such experiments are not likely to take root, nor are they likely to be beneficial for the human rights cause, unless the core of human rights is preserved and strengthened – rights entail

corresponding obligations and ought to be accompanied by access to remedy for alleged denials and violations.

The points made here are valid in terms of the upholding of rights in practice, and certainly in current circumstances we are dependent on an effective legal framework and mechanisms for recourse, in addition to a culture of human rights. Yet this question of implementation is distinct from the underpinning notion of the right itself – its emergence, recognition and validity. As always, we need to ensure law is in accordance with justice, and we cannot simply derive notions of justice from existing law. As Ife (2009: 145–6) states, documents and treaties:

> have important symbolic significance and can be used as powerful tools for pursuing human rights goals . . . They can still thus contain wisdom – indeed inspiration – and be useful to people thinking through the ideas of rights and duties in their particular location, but they will be by no means a final authority and should be open to question and to scrutiny like any other construction of human rights.

The intention here is in no way to play down the importance of law in protecting the right to education: on the contrary, it is absolutely essential, in conjunction with other forms of action. Nevertheless, law does not contain the answer to the question of whether there is a valid claim that all people have a right to education, and what that right corresponds to. The book, therefore, will focus on the philosophical foundations of rights and their incorporation into moral and political commitments in individuals and collectives. Normative debate on the subject of rights – without being constrained by current legal formulations – is not only possible but essential to the establishment and legitimization of rights.

In accordance with this view, the book addresses primarily the challenge of building a human rights culture:

> If indeed human rights are about the achievement of our humanity, this occurs in relationships rather than in courtrooms, and the focus of human rights work needs to be on culture and relationships. This of course includes relationships within community as well as within families, households, workplaces and public spaces. (Ife 2009: 139)

One advantage then of the 'constructed rights' tradition (as opposed to the 'states obligations' or the 'natural rights' ones [Ife 2009: 73]) is that they entail a much broader participation: human rights work in education becomes, then, not just a task for lawyers and administrators, but for teachers, communities and students themselves. Furthermore, this kind of approach can balance the necessary universality of human rights – protections of that which is common to all humanity – with acknowledgement of difference and the structural injustice that can be hidden by universalism.

Another point of relevance here is that human rights do not claim to be a total theory of justice (Griffin 2008). It is true that the framework of rights stops short of demanding full economic and social equality in society, but this is because it is an approach focused on protecting the most basic and immediate requirements for a dignified human life. There may certainly be considerations of equality that we would like to apply beyond the requirements of rights, and that we may consider as essential for social justice. Human rights in this sense are minimum requirements.

These issues of the nature and validity of human rights generally speaking will not be the main focus of the book, however. There is already extensive literature on human rights from legal and philosophical perspectives, and this book does not intend to break new ground in this respect. The focus instead will be on the educational implications of human rights, and the right to education specifically. While there is a moderate body of literature applying and interpreting existing human rights law, few works have explored from first principles what kinds of education we should all have a right to. The book is unashamedly normative – it aims to put forward a particular political and pedagogical position, rather than to conduct a dispassionate analysis of the current situation – although, being one that is based on criteria in the form of ground rules, is inclusive of a wide diversity of educational and societal visions.

As stated at the start, there are two principal questions addressed by this book. Do all people have a right to education? And if so, what is it a right to exactly? There is something of a paradox in this duad of questions. If we start by determining whether we are justified in claiming a right to education, then we are forced to examine what exactly we mean by education. And yet, if we start by stipulating a definition of education, we may be excluding from the definition forms of education that there may in fact be a right to, or conversely including forms to which there may not be a right. So we are necessarily left in the position of feeling our way between the two questions, moving slowly as if climbing up a narrow crevice with one foot on each side.

Distinctive challenges are presented in assessing the right to education: it is not like the rights to clothing and housing, for example, in the case of which it is relatively easy to say whether the rights are or are not being fulfilled. There are three aspects of education that create particular complexities. First, education exists in a variety of different forms, some of which may in fact be undesirable (though we may choose to restrict the use of the term 'education' to the desirable ones). Second, education points beyond itself, being a preparation for other activities as well as a potentially valuable experience in itself, and so attention is needed to both the ends and means and the relationship between them. Third, students do not necessarily leave the classroom with what has been presented to them (and it is very difficult to predict exactly what they will take away with them). All of these complexities and uncertainties – and the rich spontaneity of education – will need then to be taken into account.

There are certain important questions relating to educational rights that cannot be covered in this book. One highly controversial issue that will not be addressed in full is the rights of parents in relation to the rights of children. Parental prerogative to choose the form of education of their children is established in international law and some parental discretion is both inevitable and desirable, but raises potential conflicts with the interests of their children if forms opted for are restrictive of their future opportunities. Another complex question concerns the compulsory nature of primary education. This obligation has been the cause of well-known litigation on the national level, such as the successful appeal of the Amish community against the minimum school leaving age of 16, which they claimed undermined their children's faith (in this case, the state of Wisconsin in 1972 made an exception and allowed them to remove their children after eighth grade – approximately age 14). Another area that will not be covered in full is educational *responsibilities*. The question of who the duty-bearer is for the right to education is complex (as it is with all welfare rights), involving parents, communities, different levels of government and the international community. While the arguments presented here have some ramifications for duty bearers, the question would require a separate treatment to be covered in full.

This book draws on a range of influences. While the account presented here does not adhere to all aspects of Paulo Freire's thought, I am strongly indebted to his notions of *conscientization* and *dialogue*, his insistence that education can never be neutral, and the linking of the pedagogical and the political. John Dewey's insights into the relationship between means and ends, and between democracy and education have also been fundamental. It would be impossible to write about the right to education without acknowledging the work of Katarina Tomaševski, a pioneer both in advocating adherence to the right among nation-states, and in expanding our theoretical understanding of the scope of the right. In terms of understandings of human rights, I have already mentioned the influences of Amartya Sen and Jim Ife – the latter's work I came across only after most of the book had been written, but I found there a very strong resonance with the ideas I was tentatively outlining. I have also been influenced by a range of contemporary scholars applying the ideas of capabilities, deliberative democracy and broader theories of social justice to education, such as Elaine Unterhalter, Melanie Walker, Michael Fielding and many others.

Some of the theoretical underpinnings of discussions of the curriculum stem from my previous book *Rethinking Citizenship Education*, particularly the notion of *proximity* employed in Chapters 4 and 8. Many of the ideas presented in this book also draw on my own experience as a teacher, most recently in university classrooms, but also in secondary schools in London and Tanzania, non-formal education with street children in Rio de Janeiro, and in rural Brazilian landless communities, language teaching for adults and many other experiences – not least of which bringing up two children of my own.

Structure of book

The chapters of this book – with the possible exception of the first two and the last – are freestanding in the sense that they engage with distinct aspects of the question, and have to some degree a self-contained argument. Yet there is also a progression through the book from the question of what we have a legal right to, to that of why we might have that right, what kinds of education the right corresponds to (in terms of forms of institution, curriculum and pedagogy, and age range) and finally implications for policy and practice.

Chapter 2 provides an overview of international law on education, from the seminal statement in the Universal Declaration of Human Rights (UDHR), through the subsequent legally binding instruments. It also assesses some of the mechanisms for implementation of the right, and the conceptual frameworks that have emerged to interpret it and fill out its substance. Chapter 3 puts the legal apparatus to one side, and returns to the more fundamental question of why we might be justified in claiming a right to education in the first place. After having assessed prominent general justifications for human rights, there is consideration of existing treatments of the right to education in the literature, and their focus on the two elements of socialization and autonomy. An alternative conception based on understanding and agency is put forward – though it is acknowledged that a universal right can include diverse conceptions of education, as long as it conforms to fundamental criteria.

Chapter 4 draws on these justifications to re-engage with the problematic identification of the right to education with schooling evident in international rights instruments. An alternative emphasis on learning outcomes is considered, but found also to be flawed. Instead, a conception of educational processes is put forward as the basis for the right. These discussions are continued in Chapter 5 with a consideration of the potential of schools – in their curriculum, management, relationships and ethos – both to infringe and uphold human rights, and the necessity of consonance between rights *to* and rights *within* education. Another of the problematic elements of the legal right is taken up in Chapter 6, addressing the restriction of the right to the level of basic education. Is it possible to uphold a right to higher education, or even education throughout the life course?

Following that, Chapter 7 presents an alternative conceptualization of the issues from the perspective of *capabilities* of Amartya Sen and Martha Nussbaum. The chapter considers critiques of rights-based approaches from this viewpoint, providing a defence of rights while incorporating some of the key insights of capabilities. Chapter 8 presents the main thesis of the book in the coming together of the ideas of the right to education and human rights education. Fulfilment of the right to education in all its aspects will necessarily entail the learning and practising of human rights within educational spaces. Conversely, the building of a human rights culture and society will enhance spaces for learning. Does this vision of the dissolution of the barriers between preparation and expression, between learning and performance lead to the redundancy of school? Ultimately yes, but not in an imperfect world. Schools are needed to provide a jolt in the system, to break the vicious cycle; for all their faults they can provide this space for rupture. These and other implications of this vision for EFA and educational practice in all contexts are drawn out in the final chapter.

Note

1   Gregory (1973) puts forward an argument of this type in relation to education.

2

The Right to Education in International Law

Origins of rights

The Cyrus cylinder is a beautiful stone object, gently tapering at each end and marked with delicate inscriptions in cuneiform. I came across it one day in the British Museum, where it was displayed in a special exhibition on Babylon and described as the world's first human rights charter.[1] The proclamation was issued by the Persian King Cyrus in the sixth century BCE, who on conquering Babylon guaranteed protection of the local population's right to worship their own gods, restored their temples and allowed captured peoples to return home. The Cyrus cylinder may not represent a comprehensive covenant of human rights perhaps, but for the age it was a significant recognition of fundamental entitlements.

It is frequently heard that human rights are a 'Western' idea. This kind of assertion is dubious not only because the very concept of 'Western' tends to ignore the substantial influence of North Africa, the Middle East and South and East Asia on the foundations of European thought. Also, as discussed extensively by Amartya Sen (e.g. 2004), the theory and practice of human rights and democracy can be seen in many traditions around the world – appearing in a variety of guises, from the Buddhist councils of Emperor Ashoka's India to the local meetings of Nelson Mandela's childhood in Mqhekezweni, South Africa. Having said that, there is no doubt that the *institutional* representation of rights in the contemporary age can trace its lineage to the European tradition. Human rights particularly – as opposed to rights of national citizenship – are linked to the ideas of 'natural law' and 'natural rights': that human beings have God-given freedoms that are more fundamental than the human regimes under which they happen to live. This idea was notable in its questioning of the absolute power of the monarchy in Europe and providing (as John Locke did) a justification for overthrowing oppressive regimes. The English Magna Carta of 1215, like the Cyrus cylinder, was far from being a universal or comprehensive rights instrument, but it did dare to limit the power of the ruler in accordance with the interests of the ruled, and for that was highly significant.

The widespread recognition of rights, however, can be traced to what have been called the two 'rights revolutions'. The first of these revolutions came in the eighteenth century with the overthrowing of absolutist aristocratic and colonial regimes in Europe and North America. The United States Declaration of Independence, adopted on 4 July 1776, stated:

> We hold these truths to be self-evident, that all men are created equal, that they are endowed by their Creator with certain unalienable Rights, that among these are Life, Liberty and the pursuit of Happiness.

The religious origins of the human rights tradition can be clearly seen here – as well as a majestic confidence in the existence of rights, seen as they are to require no external justification. This historical period, however, represents the start of the secularization of human rights. Some similarities with the US Declaration of Independence – along with differences of emphasis in the specific rights accorded – can be seen in the French Revolution which followed soon after. The first two articles of the Declaration of the Rights of Man and of the Citizen, approved by the National Assembly of France, 26 August 1789, state:

1. Men are born and remain free and equal in rights. Social distinctions may be founded only upon the general good.
2. The aim of all political association is the preservation of the natural and imprescriptible rights of man. These rights are liberty, property, security, and resistance to oppression.

What characterizes rights declarations at this stage is their emphasis on civil and political rights, and protection against abuses such as arbitrary imprisonment and confiscation of property. In fact, the French Constitution of 1793 did include education and welfare rights: '22. Education is needed by all. Society ought to favour with all its power the advancement of the public reason and to put education at the door of every citizen.' However, these were left out of the revised version which eventually gained sway. Furthermore, the notion of men being 'equal' referred to in both of these declarations is far from the full economic and social equality advocated by the socialists of the following century. So there are limitations as regards the range of rights protected, but also obvious restrictions on the persons included in the category of citizen, most notably the exclusion of women (though later challenged by thinkers such as Mary Wollstonecraft and John Stuart Mill).

The second 'rights revolution' of the years following the Second World War went a long way towards addressing both of these concerns. All human beings were now to be included among the rights holders, and the range of rights would be extended to include social, economic and cultural rights (including those to work, food, housing and taking part in cultural life). To a large extent, these rights were championed by the communist countries after the Second World War, while the civil and political rights were seen as the preserve of the USA and her Allies. The seminal expression of human rights – which brought together both of these groups – is the UDHR, adopted by the newly formed United Nations on 10 December 1948.

Along with the first 'generation' or 'wave' of rights (civil and political) and the second (economic, social and cultural), reference is also made a *third* group of rights emerging in recent decades. This third generation has been referred to as solidarity or collective rights, relating to the self-determination of colonized territories, the environment, indigenous peoples, and national development, among other issues. (The term 'generation' is commonly used in terms of these phases, although it is problematic, given the lack of a neat chronology, and the internal incoherence of the three groups.) Each successive generation of rights has raised new scepticism as to its validity, as will be discussed in the following chapter. Later rights instrument such as the Convention on the Rights of the Child (CRC) bring the different generations of rights together into the same document. In fact, this coming together of forms of right was given strong affirmation in the Vienna World Conference on Human Rights in 1993, in which the principles of indivisibility, interrelatedness and interdependence were emphasized, and subsequently reaffirmed in the UN (2003) framework for rights-based approaches to development.

This chapter provides an outline of the right to education as expressed in the law. For the most part, it addresses the international rights instruments emerging from the United Nations, but there is also a discussion of national law in relation to the Indian Right to Education Act of 2009. There is also a discussion of the monitoring role provided by UNESCO, the UN Special Rapporteur for education and the Right to Education (RTE) Project set up by Katarina Tomaševski. For the most part, this chapter is descriptive, providing an overview of official expressions of the right, the legal interpretations and mechanisms for implementation and monitoring. A more critical discussion of the problems associated with justifying the right and identifying its scope and applicability will be provided in Chapters 3 and 4. The chapter is necessarily a brief overview of human rights law relating to education, and does not aim to be a detailed or comprehensive account: some such accounts already exist (e.g. Beiter 2006; Hodgson 1998). The aim here is to assess the ways in which education is understood in human rights law so as to inform the later discussions on conceptualizations of the universal entitlement underpinning EFA.

International rights instruments

One of the significant entrants to the second generation of rights that had for the most part been absent before was education. Compulsory state-funded education (at the elementary level) had in fact become part of national law in a number of countries (e.g. Prussia, France) by the nineteenth century, but now began to appear at the international level. The expression of the international right to education was strongly influenced by the Soviet Union, which provided the earliest commitment to universal, free of charge and state-provided education (Beiter 2006).

While implied by the Declaration of the Rights of the Child of 1924, the first explicit statement of the international right to education is in the UDHR of 1948.

UDHR, 1948

Article 26

1. Everyone has the right to education. Education shall be free, at least in the elementary and fundamental stages. Elementary education shall be compulsory. Technical and professional education shall be made generally available and higher education shall be equally accessible to all on the basis of merit.
2. Education shall be directed to the full development of the human personality and to the strengthening of respect for human rights and fundamental freedoms. It shall promote understanding, tolerance and friendship among all nations, racial or religious groups, and shall further the activities of the United Nations for the maintenance of peace.
3. Parents have a prior right to choose the kind of education that shall be given to their children.

As can be seen, there are three elements to this initial expression of the right. The first concerns the levels of education, with a strong guarantee for free elementary education – along with fundamental education, which is understood to be basic literacy, numeracy and other essential skills for those adults who may have missed out when of school-going age. There is some ambiguity as to whether 'free' refers just to the direct costs of schooling, or also to incidental costs such as books and uniforms – the latter being significant barriers to access in many low-income countries.

For elementary education, there is also the stipulation for its being compulsory. The compulsory nature of the human right to elementary education has raised concerns, as it has in national law: an example outlined in the previous chapter being the Amish religious community in the United States, who in the 1970s successfully challenged the obligation to send their children to public schools until the age of 16 (Brighouse 2006). In fact, it seems counter-intuitive for any human right to be compulsory, given that rights are ultimately freedoms. The contradiction has been explained by the fact that it is not binding on the rights-holders themselves (children), but on their parents or guardians, ensuring that the children's rights are not compromised by their time being used for other purposes, such as salaried employment or household duties (Hodgson 1998). There is also the argument that a child when young and immature 'needs to be protected against itself', given that she may not be aware of the importance of education for her future life (Beiter 2006: 31). As Tomaševski (2004: 6) states:

> Children cannot wait to grow, hence their prioritized right to education in international HR law. The damage of denied education while they are growing up cannot be retroactively remedied.

Nevertheless, the compulsory nature of formal education remains problematic – both in terms of principle and in its practical consequences of shaping attitudes towards that experience. According to Halvorsen (1990), there was also substantial disagreement between countries on this point in the drafting of the Declaration.

Section 2 of Article 26 relates to the aims of education, and links in strongly with the overall aims of the United Nations in the post-war period. Finally, there is the brief and enigmatic statement about parental prerogative. As with the compulsory nature of primary education, there were also contrasting positions on this point taken by the different nations (Halvorsen 1990), with the proviso proposed on account of concerns over possible state indoctrination enabled by section 1. There are, therefore, two aspects of the right to education, the *social* aspect and the *freedom* aspect (Beiter 2006). The former obliges states to provide education, while the latter obliges them to refrain from imposing or restricting choices of forms of education (though they are charged with regulating quality and ensuring minimum standards). The potential clashes between the second and third sections (in cases in which parents wish their children to study in schools that do not promote 'understanding, tolerance and friendship among all nations, racial or religious groups') are plain to see.

As a 'declaration', the UDHR is a statement of ideals and not binding on states-parties. Subsequently, the aspirations of the UDHR were made concrete in the legally binding documents of the International Covenant on Civil and Political Rights (ICCPR, 1966) and International Covenant on Economic, Social and Cultural Rights (ICESCR, 1966). Together these three form the International Bill of Human Rights. Subsequently there have been a range of further rights instruments, amongst these are the International Convention on the Elimination of All Forms of Racial Discrimination (1965), Convention on the Elimination of All Forms of Discrimination against Women (CEDAW, 1979), and Convention on the Rights of Persons with Disabilities (2006), as well as numerous other declarations and recommendations.

While the UDHR is fundamentally important in terms of its pioneering vision, the most significant expressions of the right to education in terms of their legal force are the ICESCR and CRC.

ICESCR, 1966

Article 13

1. The States Parties to the present Covenant recognize the right of everyone to education. They agree that education shall be directed to the full development of the human personality and the sense of its dignity, and shall strengthen the respect for HR and fundamental freedoms. They further agree that education shall enable all persons to participate effectively in a free society, promote understanding, tolerance and friendship among all nations and all racial, ethnic or religious groups, and further the activities of the United Nations for the maintenance of peace.
2. The States Parties to the present Covenant recognize that, with a view to achieving the full realization of this right:
   a. Primary education shall be compulsory and available free to all;
   b. Secondary education in its different forms, including technical and vocational secondary education, shall be made generally available and accessible to all by every appropriate means, and in particular by the progressive introduction of free education;

    c. Higher education shall be made equally accessible to all, on the basis of capacity, by every appropriate means, and in particular by the progressive introduction of free education;

    d. Fundamental education shall be encouraged or intensified as far as possible for those persons who have not received or completed the whole period of their primary education;

    e. The development of a system of schools at all levels shall be actively pursued, an adequate fellowship system shall be established, and the material conditions of teaching staff shall be continuously improved.

3. The States-Parties to the present Covenant undertake to have respect for the liberty of parents and, when applicable, legal guardians to choose for their children schools, other than those established by the public authorities, which conform to such minimum educational standards as may be laid down or approved by the State and to ensure the religious and moral education of their children in conformity with their own convictions.

4. No part of this article shall be construed so as to interfere with the liberty of individuals and bodies to establish and direct educational institutions, subject always to the observance of the principles set forth in paragraph I of this article and to the requirement that the education given in such institutions shall conform to such minimum standards as may be laid down by the State.

As can be seen, the expression of the right to education in the ICESCR follows the UDHR to a large extent, while providing some greater detail and in some cases more extensive demands on States. An important development is 2(d) which acknowledges more explicitly a right to education for those who have missed out in the conventional age range. There is also reference for the first time to teachers and their well-being, although with a rather loose requirement for 'continuously improving' their material conditions. The 'fellowship system' mentioned here refers to forms of grant or scholarship for students at the levels of education at which free provision is not available (Beiter 2006). The requirement for free of charge education previously applied to elementary education is here extended to secondary and higher education, although on a basis of progressive realization. This form of expression effectively acknowledges two 'tiers' of rights obligations, with some rights not required to have immediate implementation. This less urgent obligation is certainly realist in terms of the capacities of LMICs in the 1960s (and even today) to provide universal access to state-funded education, yet unfortunately it also provides 'wriggle room' for states to postpone indefinitely this important commitment. As Grover (2004) laments, there is no international obligation to free of charge and compulsory secondary education (let alone higher education), and national level law largely reflects this, with only a handful of countries ensuring such an obligation.

Notable for its absence in section 2 is a requirement for the provision of pre-school education: in fact this level is largely absent from all international rights instruments. Given the wide consensus on the importance of this level (e.g. UNESCO 2006), this is a significant omission in the ICESCR (Article 18 of the UNCRC, however, does provide a limited endorsement of a right to early childhood care and education). According to Hodgson (1998), the exclusion of the pre-school level, and higher education, were due to states' reluctance to fund this level universally, rather than any principled justification.

As regards the parental prerogative, these articles provide a clear expression of the interlocking of the civil and political rights on the one hand (of freedom from state interference) and of economic, social and cultural rights on the other hand (of provision of educational opportunity). Here it is specified more clearly that the right of parents to choose the form of education of their children is qualified by minimum standards established by the state. Section 4 serves to reconcile the apparent contradictions between the entitlements of parents and children, or between the obligations of parents and states, though by no means resolves them completely.

Furthermore, there is an additional article, quoted below, which assesses state action, and can be seen as a forerunner to the provisions made in the later EFA initiative.

Article 14

> Each State Party to the present Covenant which, at the time of becoming a Party, has not been able to secure in its metropolitan territory or other territories under its jurisdiction compulsory primary education, free of charge, undertakes, within two years, to work out and adopt a detailed plan of action for the progressive implementation, within a reasonable number of years, to be fixed in the plan, of the principle of compulsory education free of charge for all.

The ICESRC is considered by theorists to be the most authoritative expression of the right to education (Beiter 2006; Hodgson 1998), given its legally binding nature and its wide ratification (160 states-parties). However, the later CRC of 1989, which also contains provisions relating to education, has perhaps become the most influential of all international rights instruments.

The CRC is well known as being the most ratified of all of the United Nations rights treaties (only two countries at time of writing have not signed up, the United States and Somalia). It is also groundbreaking in its framing of children for the first time as rights-holders rather than recipients of protection. It is, therefore, significant to a discussion of the right to education not only in as regards the modifications made in the articles relating to education specifically, but also in its broader application to children, who are the group most fully covered by the right to education. The requirements made in the Convention have been categorized into three 'Ps': protection, provision and participation. The first two of these, but not the third, had been present in the pioneering Geneva Declaration of the Rights of the Child endorsed by the League of Nations in 1924, and drafted by the founder of Save the Children, Eglantyne Jebb. The Declaration of the Rights of the Child of 1959 that preceded the Convention, also emphasized protection and provision, but not participation.

So in the CRC there are articles relating to traditional understandings of protection of children from harm (e.g. abuse, neglect or economic exploitation); to provide services and opportunities (e.g. nutrition, clothing and participation in cultural life), and most innovatively and controversially to allow children participation in decisions that affect them, although with the proviso that this participation should be in accordance with age and maturity.

The first article relating to education is as follows.

Convention on the Rights of the Child, 1989

Article 28

1. States Parties recognize the right of the child to education, and with a view to achieving this right progressively and on the basis of equal opportunity, they shall, in particular:
   a. Make primary education compulsory and available free to all;
   b. Encourage the development of different forms of secondary education, including general and vocational education, make them available and accessible to every child, and take appropriate measures such as the introduction of free education and offering financial assistance in case of need;
   c. Make higher education accessible to all on the basis of capacity by every appropriate means;
   d. Make educational and vocational information and guidance available and accessible to all children;

   e. Take measures to encourage regular attendance at schools and the
      reduction of drop-out rates.
2. States Parties shall take all appropriate measures to ensure that school
   discipline is administered in a manner consistent with the child's human
   dignity and in conformity with the present Convention.
3. States Parties shall promote and encourage international cooperation in
   matters relating to education, in particular with a view to contributing to the
   elimination of ignorance and illiteracy throughout the world and facilitating
   access to scientific and technical knowledge and modern teaching methods.
   In this regard, particular account shall be taken of the needs of developing
   countries.

The mention of 'equal opportunity' here is potentially very significant in terms
of the stratification of schools in relation to quality and prestige, although not
precise enough in this expression to be effective (this aspect will be discussed
below in relation to the Convention Against Discrimination in Education).
One significant addition here is attention to attendance and dropout, given
the problems with identifying the fulfilment of the right to education with
initial enrolment in first grade, without ensuring successful progression and
completion. The requirement for providing educational and vocational guidance
is also new. Another highly important development in this article is the
requirement for discipline in schools to respect children's dignity, addressing the
problems of corporal punishment around the world. This addition is a welcome
acknowledgement of the indivisibility of rights (as discussed in Chapter 5), and
the importance of viewing the right to education together with other human
rights. There is one step backwards, however, in the removal of mentions of free
of charge secondary and higher education that had been seen in the ICESCR.

The reference to international cooperation again links in strongly with the
Education for All initiative launched the following year in 1990. It is followed,
however, by the rather jarring reference to 'the elimination of ignorance', which
seems to suggest that those without formal schooling (and the legal right to
education is primarily about *institutional* education) are necessarily ignorant.
'Modern teaching methods' also catches the eye – presumably referring to
the need for leaner-centred pedagogy rather than traditional teacher-centred
approaches and rote learning – although raising the rather alarming spectre
from the post-war period of 'modernization' as the answer to the problems facing
LMICs.

The below is a further article in the CRC relating specifically to the aims of
education.

Article 29

1. States Parties agree that the education of the child shall be directed to:
   a. The development of the child's personality, talents and mental and physical abilities to their fullest potential;
   b. The development of respect for human rights and fundamental freedoms, and for the principles enshrined in the Charter of the United Nations;
   c. The development of respect for the child's parents, his or her own cultural identity, language and values, for the national values of the country in which the child is living, the country from which he or she may originate, and for civilizations different from his or her own;
   d. The preparation of the child for responsible life in a free society, in the spirit of understanding, peace, tolerance, equality of sexes, and friendship among all peoples, ethnic, national and religious groups and persons of indigenous origin;
   e. The development of respect for the natural environment.
2. No part of the present article or article 28 shall be construed so as to interfere with the liberty of individuals and bodies to establish and direct educational institutions, subject always to the observance of the principle set forth in paragraph 1 of the present article and to the requirements that the education given in such institutions shall conform to such minimum standards as may be laid down by the State.

Discussion of the aims of education in section 4, therefore, constitutes an expansion of the original expression in the UDHR, along with the addition of the natural environment, and a more detailed account of the importance of grounding in one's own culture and respect for others.

The above are the three most important general expressions of the right to education. A further rights instrument proposed by UNESCO also plays an important role: the Convention against Discrimination in Education of 1960. This convention is highly significant as it predated the ICESCR and influenced its expression of the right to education in Article 13, as well as presenting demanding obligations on states in relation to equality of opportunity.

Article 1

1. For the purposes of this Convention, the term 'discrimination' includes any distinction, exclusion, limitation or preference which, being based on race, colour, sex, language, religion, political or other opinion, national or social

origin, economic condition or birth, has the purpose or effect of nullifying
or impairing equality of treatment in education and in particular:

(a) Of depriving any person or group of persons of access to education of
    any type or at any level;

(b) Of limiting any person or group of persons to education of an inferior
    standard;

(c) Subject to the provisions of Article 2 of this Convention, of establishing
    or maintaining separate educational systems or institutions for persons
    or groups of persons; or

(d) Of inflicting on any person or group of persons conditions which are
    incompatible with the dignity of man.

2. For the purposes of this Convention, the term 'education' refers to all types
   and levels of education, and includes access to education, the standard and
   quality of education, and the conditions under which it is given.

Article 2

When permitted in a State, the following situations shall not be deemed to
constitute discrimination, within the meaning of Article 1 of this Convention:

(a) The establishment or maintenance of separate educational systems or
    institutions for pupils of the two sexes, if these systems or institutions offer
    equivalent access to education, provide a teaching staff with qualifications
    of the same standard as well as school premises and equipment of the same
    quality, and afford the opportunity to take the same or equivalent courses of
    study;

(b) The establishment or maintenance, for religious or linguistic reasons, of
    separate educational systems or institutions offering an education which
    is in keeping with the wishes of the pupil's parents or legal guardians, if
    participation in such systems or attendance at such institutions is optional
    and if the education provided conforms to such standards as may be laid
    down or approved by the competent authorities, in particular for education
    of the same level;

(c) The establishment or maintenance of private educational institutions, if the
    object of the institutions is not to secure the exclusion of any group but to
    provide educational facilities in addition to those provided by the public
    authorities, if the institutions are conducted in accordance with that object,
    and if the education provided conforms with such standards as may be laid

down or approved by the competent authorities, in particular for education of the same level.

Article 1 here outlines the requirements for non-discrimination, while Article 2 acknowledges the circumstances in which differentiated provision might be acceptable. This Convention is significant in guarding against a superficial fulfilment of a universal right to education, while simultaneously confining certain proportions of the population to inadequate provision. It applies most readily to minority ethnic, religious and linguistic groups, which in the post-war period had suffered explicit discrimination. It is much harder to apply this requirement to the subtle forms of discrimination – on the basis of social class, race/ethnicity, gender, etc. – that take place even in an integrated system.

The stipulation here that public schools must have an even quality[2] goes beyond the previous emphasis on minimum quality (given that the latter can lead to serious inequalities). This aspect of the right is rarely upheld in practice. Indeed, it would surely be impossible to find a single education system in the world that to some extent at least did not infringe the requirements not to: 'limit [...] any person or group of persons to education of an inferior standard'. The key concern is that these inequalities in educational provision translate (in a persistent if not deterministic way) into broader social inequalities.

The above represent the key legal expressions of the right to education. From these rights instruments, Coomans (2007) has attempted to establish a 'core content' of the right to education, that is:

> a tool for identifying those elements of the normative content of HR that contain minimum entitlements ... with a view to assessing the conduct of states in this field in general, and to identify violations in particular. (p. 1)

This core content consists of the following elements: access to education on a non-discriminatory basis; the right to enjoy free and compulsory primary education; quality of education; free choice of education; and the right to education in the language of one's own choice. This final point, however, is acknowledged to be controversial, with states having obligations not to prevent members of linguistic minorities being taught in their mother tongue outside the mainstream system, but with no state obligation to fund these institutions.

There are also a number of more specific rights instruments that have mentions of education. Among these, the CEDAW is of central importance, given the very widespread historic and current marginalization of girls and women in the education system.

CEDAW, 1979

Article 10

States Parties shall take all appropriate measures to eliminate discrimination against women in order to ensure to them equal rights with men in the field of education and in particular to ensure, on a basis of equality of men and women:

(a) The same conditions for career and vocational guidance, for access to studies and for the achievement of diplomas in educational establishments of all categories in rural as well as in urban areas; this equality shall be ensured in pre-school, general, technical, professional and higher technical education, as well as in all types of vocational training;

(b) Access to the same curricula, the same examinations, teaching staff with qualifications of the same standard and school premises and equipment of the same quality;

(c) The elimination of any stereotyped concept of the roles of men and women at all levels and in all forms of education by encouraging co-education and other types of education which will help to achieve this aim and, in particular, by the revision of textbooks and school programmes and the adaptation of teaching methods;

(d) The same opportunities to benefit from scholarships and other study grants;

(e) The same opportunities for access to programmes of continuing education, including adult and functional literacy programmes, particularly those aimed at reducing, at the earliest possible time, any gap in education existing between men and women;

(f) The reduction of female student drop-out rates and the organization of programmes for girls and women who have left school prematurely;

(g) The same opportunities to participate actively in sports and physical education;

(h) Access to specific educational information to help to ensure the health and well-being of families, including information and advice on family planning.

Of interest here are the specific references to the curriculum and representations in textbooks. Questions of curriculum are largely absent from international rights instruments – aside from very broad statements of aims. While understandable on account of the difficulties of obtaining agreement from all states parties on an overly specific vision of taught content, this silence brings with it its own problems, as discussed in Chapter 4. CEDAW is one of a number of treaties and declarations relating to specific groups – for example, the Convention Relating to the Status of Refugees (1951) and the International Convention on the Elimination of All Forms of Racial Discrimination (1965) – with educational requirements relating mainly to discrimination.

This section has provided an overview of the key international rights instruments relating to education. In addition to these, further detail is provided by the 'General Comments', for example No. 1 on the aims of education in the CRC and No. 13 on Article 13 of the ICESCR, as well as secondary literature. Furthermore, there are a number of regional rights instruments that contain mention of education, such as the Charter of the Organization of American States (1948), the African Charter on Human and Peoples' Rights (1981) and the EU Charter of Fundamental Rights (2000). Needless to say, national constitutions also incorporate various rights relating to education – one of these, that of India, will be discussed below. There have been some significant instances of legislation in recent years, such as the decision of the Economic Community of West African States (ECOWAS) in 2010 that education is an enforceable right in Nigeria, and the Colombian Constitutional Court decision, also in 2010, that public primary schools cannot charge fees.

It is important to point out that while the declaration and framework emerging from Jomtien and Dakar (discussed in Chapter 1) do hold to a notion of a universal entitlement to education, they are not rights instruments as such. As can be seen, there are some significant differences between rights and EFA frameworks. First, the rights instruments are skeletal in their conceptualization of education, providing for the most part only some overarching aims in accordance with the principles of the UN (although the CRC is more comprehensive in this respect, referring to school discipline and teaching methods). Importantly, the EFA declarations bring the emphasis to *quality* in a much more substantial way. The Convention on Discrimination in Education, as seen above, did make important guarantees about *equality* in educational quality, although this is most readily applied to blatant discrimination against visible groups. The EFA movement as a whole has brought out the important message that there is only a point in a right to education if that education is of a certain quality.

The second major difference is that education in the rights instruments is an immediate obligation, rather than a target for a future point in time. Distinctions are made in human rights between those provisions that are immediately enforceable (e.g. prohibition of discrimination in education) and those that allow for progressive realization (e.g. free and universally available secondary schooling). Even so, there is a significant difference in that the EFA goals are aspirations for something the international community would like to achieve in the future, rather than moral or legal obligations in the present moment. In this way, Beiter (2006) sees the main problem of the EFA declarations being to frame education as a 'human need' rather than a 'human right'. Rights instruments also place the primary responsibility for provision on nation-states (with freedom for private ventures). However, the clauses in the CRC on international cooperation brings it closer to the vision of joint responsibility of governments, NGOs and donors put forward in EFA.

The EFA frameworks, therefore, at the same time represent both a step forward and a step back from the UN rights instruments: they fill in the conception of education considerably and broaden the picture, but at the same time weaken the obligations and depart from a fuller sense of a human right.

Upholding human rights in practice

Yet what is the use of all these grand pronouncements? Does it not add insult to injury that international organizations proclaim the existence of universal rights while those same rights are routinely abused and neglected in practice? Certainly, advocates of human rights are constantly confronted with the critique that these declarations are no more than rhetoric (Wellman 1998).

There is a range of ways in which attempts are made to ensure the full implementation of the rights contained in the declarations. Sen (2004) makes a useful distinction between the three elements of *recognition*, *agitation* and *legislation* as approaches to promoting rights. Mostly we associate the upholding of human rights with legislation, and while Sen acknowledges its importance, he points out cases in which punitive legislation would not be appropriate, and the need to acknowledge the other routes to promoting human rights, such as recognition. As seen in the endorsement of the UDHR, declarations and charters that are not legally binding can nevertheless have a strong influence on the behaviour of governments and individuals. Lastly, agitation – through advocacy, protest, monitoring violations and promoting public discussion by civil society groups – can be central both to the recognition of new rights, and the enforcement of existing rights. The rest of this section will address the work primarily of the United Nations to promote rights through legislation and recognition, while the next section will look at the case of agitation in the RTE

Project – one of a number of organizations playing important roles in advocating for the right to education.

States that ratify international treaties are obliged to incorporate them into national law, with obligations to respect, protect and fulfil the rights in question (UNESCO 2008). The problem, of course, is that in the absence of a global government, aside from moral pressure, there are few ways of *forcing* states to comply even when they have a legal commitment through conventions. There are, nevertheless, a range of mechanisms through which implementation in practice is promoted. The international body entrusted with the promotion of these rights and making recommendations on human rights violations is the UN Human Rights Council, established in 2006 and replacing the previous UN Commission on Human Rights. Another key body is the Office of the United Nations High Commissioner for Human Rights (OHCHR) – currently Navanethem Pillay of South Africa – which works with individual member states to ensure the upholding of human rights on the ground, engaging in public information activities as well as monitoring member states' compliance with treaties. Specific treaties have their own monitoring bodies such as the Committee on Economic, Social and Cultural Rights that monitors the ICESCR, and the Committee on the Rights of the Child for the CRC.

UNESCO, the key UN agency on the right to education (although UNICEF has a significant role relating to children's education in practice), has a range of standard-setting instruments, including conventions (adopted by a two-thirds majority) and recommendations (needing a majority vote). UNESCO conventions relating to education are the Convention against Discrimination in Education (1960) already discussed and the Convention on Technical and Vocational Education (1989). The Recommendations are as follows:

- Recommendation against Discrimination in Education (1960)
- Recommendation concerning the Status of Teachers (1966)
- Recommendation concerning Education for International Understanding, Cooperation and Peace, and Education relating to Human Rights and Fundamental Freedoms (1974)
- Recommendation on the Development of Adult Education (1976)
- Recommendation on the Recognition of Studies and Qualifications in Higher Education (1993)
- Recommendation concerning the Status of Higher Education Teaching Personnel (1997)
- Revised Recommendation concerning Technical and Vocational Education (2001)

These are monitored by UNESCO's Committee on Conventions and Recommendations, although with some difficulty: to exacerbate the low level of ratification of education conventions by member states, there is also a low level of response in submitting reports on these conventions (Gamarnikow 2011; UNESCO 2008). UNESCO's capacity for ensuring compliance is fairly weak generally speaking given its limited political clout, and the organization can do little in terms of funding educational projects itself due to its small budget – a little more than US$300 million per year at time of writing. (This financial weakness has been exacerbated by the withholding of US dues following the full recognition of Palestine as a member in 2011.)

Katarina Tomaševski and the RTE Project

In 1998, the post of Special Rapporteur on the right to education was created by the UN Commission on Human Rights as part of a broader attempt to address the neglect of economic, social and cultural rights. The Special Rapporteur produces annual reports of the state of the right to education, as well as responding to allegations of rights infringements and conducting ongoing dialogue with governments. The first holder of the post, Katarina Tomaševski, became a key figure in both the active defence of educational rights and in their conceptualization. In 2004, she was succeeded by Vernor Muñoz Villalobos of Costa Rica, and in 2010, by Kishore Singh of India.

Tomaševski was a human rights lawyer, who was born and grew up in the former Yugoslavia and studied at the University of Zagreb, but in later years was based in Sweden. In particular, Tomaševski's work fills in the rather sparse conceptualization of the right to education in the international rights instruments: addressing the dangers of identifying the right with mere enrolment in school and acknowledging possible rights abuses *within* schools. The best-known expression of this conceptualization is the '4 As' scheme. Tomaševski (2001a, 2003, 2006a) proposed that for the right to education to be fulfilled, the four elements of availability, accessibility, acceptability and adaptability all had to be in place.

Availability refers to the fundamental question of provision of educational institutions and opportunities. In its most basic form it depends on the existence of schools, but also includes presence of teachers, school facilities and infrastructure. As well as government provision of education, this requirement also includes the right for non-state actors to establish and run educational institutions.

The second 'A' relates to the key human rights principle of non-discrimination. The requirement for *accessibility* acknowledges that the existence of educational spaces is no guarantee that all individuals and groups will have access, or at least not on the same terms. This requirement addresses the obstacles that there may be to accessing educational provision, whether financial or other, and may require different forms of affirmative action to ensure all groups have effective access.

Acceptability relates primarily to the curriculum, and the second part of Article 26 of the UDHR on the aims of education. The key point here is that it is not access to *any* kind of education that counts: the right to education has only been fulfilled if certain conditions are in place, such as it being offered in an appropriate language of instruction, avoiding indoctrination, and respecting the cultural background of learners. Beyond this, there is also a broader concern with the quality of education, including the preparation of teachers. Following the CRC, this provision also monitors corporal punishment and other forms of abuse.

Finally there is *adaptability*, which assesses how far education institutions are inclusive of different groups in society and adapt to their particular needs. These groups would include working children, nomadic peoples, and religious minorities, among others who may have particular needs relating to access and learning. There is also an element in this requirement relating to the changing needs of society through time.

The 4 As scheme incorporates the elements of the basic right in international law (such as the state's obligation to provide education but also allow parental freedom), includes some new elements (e.g. adaptation of schools to include diverse groups) and incorporates requirements of other human rights (e.g. the right for teachers to form unions).

In her writings, Tomaševski (e.g. 2006b) presented a series of hard-hitting critiques of the World Bank and of the spinelessness of governments, focusing particularly on the damaging effects of school fees. After her death in 2006, her work was continued through the RTE Project, a mainly web-based initiative with an advocacy role, monitoring the upholding of the right around the world and disseminating research. A partnership between ActionAid, Amnesty International and the Global Campaign for Education, it functions with a small core team with the support of international advisers. Despite its limited resources, it has a significant role in monitoring national legislation in accordance with international law, but also in awareness raising. Significant reports include Angela Melchiorre's international study on the relationship between the duration of compulsory schooling in different countries and the minimum ages for employment, marriage and criminal responsibility (Melchiorre 2004; Melchiorre and Atkins 2011). The project also makes available a case law database.

A recent contribution of RTE has been the development of a set of indicators. This work stems from a critique of conventional education indicators – such as the Education Development Index – which are seen to be insufficiently attentive to states' obligations, and only assess initial enrolment. The alternative indicators have the following characteristics: they evaluate the extent to which states respect, protect and fulfil human rights; they focus on discrimination by disaggregating by certain vulnerable groups (on the basis of gender, geographical region, rural/ urban, minority and income, among others); they gauge whether participatory approaches have been used when implementing human rights; and lastly they assess whether accountability mechanisms are in place. The proposed scheme is based on the 4 As, along with an additional branch of 'Governance Framework', comprising the components of: normative framework; educational policy, plan of action, monitoring, recourses, budget, international assistance and cooperation. Around 200 indicators have been identified to monitor the components of each of these five branches (De Beco et al. 2009; Right to Education Project 2009). As a whole, therefore, the work of Tomaševski and the RTE has made a significant contribution to the development of a more complete framework for the right to education.

Other schemes for understanding the right to education

There are obvious problems with identifying the right to education with initial access to schools, or even continued enrolment in school. The first of these is that schools may be places in which other kinds of human rights abuse may take place – such as physical punishment, humiliation and sexual violence (these questions will be discussed further in Chapter 5). Part 2 of Article 26 in the UDHR affirms the need for mutual respect and peace as aims for education, but in addition, schools need to be acknowledged as spaces in which non-educational activities also take place. This concern has led to an emphasis on rights within education, as in the requirement for the full set of human rights to be upheld during the educational process.

A further question is that there is little point in a child being in school if little or nothing of use is being gained from it. As discussed above, this has led to an emphasis on *quality* of education, often associated with learning outcomes.

More broadly, we can see this as a requirement for rights *through* education. In this way, learning allows us to exercise and defend the full set of human rights. This three-way scheme of rights *to, within* and *through* education has been used by a number of theorists (e.g. Subrahmanian 2005; Tomaševski 2001b). Verhellen (1993) and Verheyde (2006), express this idea in a slightly different way, focusing specifically on the obligations of States Parties in relation to the CRC. For the authors, the right *to* education refers to the direct implementation of Articles 28 and 29 (corresponding to access to education and educational aims respectively); rights *through* education refers to the indirect promotion of the convention through making children and adults aware of the rights contained within it; and rights *in* education, the upholding of the full set of rights expressed in the Convention, including the right to self-determination, 'in that it goes without saying that education itself has to respect all children's rights delineated in the Convention' (p. 203).

How does this three-way scheme relate to the 4 As? Tomaševski (2001a) presents the relationship in the following way. The right *to* education incorporates both *availability* (fiscal allocations matching human rights obligations; schools matching school-aged children [number, diversity]; teachers [education and training, recruitment, labour rights, trade union freedoms]), and *accessibility* (elimination of legal and administrative barriers, financial obstacles, discriminatory denials of access and obstacles to compulsory schooling [fees, distance, schedule]). Rights *in* education incorporates *acceptability* (parental choice of education for their children [with human rights correctives]; enforcement of minimal standards [quality, safety, environmental health]; language of instruction; freedom from censorship; recognition of children as subjects of rights), and some of the aspects of *adaptability* (minority children, indigenous children, working children, children with disabilities, child migrants and travellers). The remaining aspects of adaptability (concordance of age-determined rights; elimination of child marriage; elimination of child labour; and prevention of child soldiering) are incorporated within rights through education.

However, the above is not the only possible way to link the frameworks: for example, acceptability is also strongly linked to rights through education, as in the significance of the curriculum for meaningful learning. The element that the 4 As framework says least about, in fact, is quality of education in the sense of opportunities for and achievement of learning. It is important, therefore, to look at the 4 As framework in conjunction with the other schemes which treat quality more fully. As will be discussed further in chapters that follow, the current approach of the World Bank and other agencies is to emphasize learning outcomes to the exclusion of many other factors, leading to a neglect of the process aspects of education, including possible human rights infringements within schools. The 4 As framework is admirably attentive to these aspects, but says little about the kinds of learning taking place. We need to hold these two visions together.

Due attention to learning and quality is provided in the 2007 UNESCO/UNICEF report, entitled *A Human Rights-Based Approach to Education for All*. The report (drafted by Gerison Lansdown) puts forward a distinct scheme for understanding the relationship between rights and education, again with three components:

> **The right of access to education** – the right of every child to education on the basis of equality of opportunity and without discrimination on any grounds. To achieve this goal, education must be available for, accessible to and inclusive of all children.
>
> **The right to quality education** – the right of every child to a quality education that enables him or her to fulfil his or her potential, realize opportunities for employment and develop life skills. To achieve this goal, education needs to be child-centred, relevant and embrace a broad curriculum, and be appropriately resourced and monitored.
>
> **The right to respect within the learning environment** – the right of every child to respect for her or his inherent dignity and to have her or his universal human rights respected within the education system. To achieve this goal, education must be provided in a way that is consistent with human rights, including equal respect for every child, opportunities for meaningful participation, freedom from all forms of violence, and respect for language, culture and religion. (UNESCO/UNICEF 2007: 4)

How, then, do these schemes fit together? Clearly the third of these – right to respect within the learning environment – has much in common with rights within education. And the first – right of access to education – can be identified with the right to education. The second – right to quality education – is closest to rights through education (cognitive and emotional outcomes) although it also has some elements of rights within education too (a healthy and safe environment), and the right to education, given that we can only consider the right to education has been fulfilled if it is of an acceptable quality.

The two schemes can be visualized thus:

3 dimensions of educational rights	UNICEF/UNESCO (2007) scheme
Right to education	Right of access to education
Rights through education	Right to quality education
Rights within education	
	Right to respect within the learning environment

Of the two schemes, that of rights to, within and through education is rather neater conceptually. However, the advantage of the UNESCO/UNICEF scheme is that it uses language that is familiar, and that is already embedded within EFA discourse. 'Access' and 'quality' are at the heart of most international educational work, and respect for learners – while rarely practised – is at least readily understandable. So strategically, this is a useful scheme. The other side of the coin is the danger that expressions that are used regularly outside a rights context (e.g. 'quality') may struggle to free themselves of those associations and assert the fuller and more demanding conception required in a rights-based approach.

There are, therefore, an array of conceptual tools serving to fill in the rather sparse initial casting of the right to education in international law. These frames are widely utilized by human rights advocates, though arguably have had little impact on broader EFA work and at the national level. Finally, we turn to this national level itself, and the case of India – a significant example of the passing into national law of some of the demanding requirements of the international instruments reviewed above.

India, the Right to Education Act

In August 2009, the Government of India passed a groundbreaking bill, guaranteeing educational rights for the whole population aged 6–14. The Right of Children to Free and Compulsory Education Act provides a strong legal guarantee of non-discriminatory universal provision – mainly through the public system, but also with some requirements for private schools. The main elements are as follows:

(1) Every child of the age of six to fourteen years shall have a right to free and compulsory education in a neighbourhood school till completion of elementary education.

(2) For the purpose of sub-section (1), no child shall be liable to pay any kind
    of fee or charges or expenses which may prevent him or her from pursuing
    and completing the elementary education.

There follow explicit guarantees of inclusion for children with disabilities, and of
special provision for out-of-age children, and an extension on the age range so
that they may complete elementary education. Provisions for non-discrimination
include a ban on screening procedures and on denial of admission for lack of
proof of age.

There are a number of practical requirements included in the Act:

- The government must construct new schools within three years in those
  neighbourhoods that are not already served.
- Teachers will acquire the requisite training and qualifications in five years.
- Private schools must allocate a quarter of their places to disadvantaged
  groups (scheduled tribes, scheduled castes and impoverished families).
  These schools will be reimbursed by the government for this provision.
- Constitution of School Management Committees with broad representation
  of different groups, and responsible for creating the school development
  plan.
- A ban on teachers engaging in private tutoring.

Attention is also paid to attendance and ensuring completion as well as admission,
to infrastructure (e.g. a library for every school) and quality of education. The
specifications for curriculum and pedagogy follow a broadly child-centred line,
emphasizing 'activities, discovery and exploration' and 'helping the child to
express views freely'. In terms of the UNICEF/UNESCO (2007) three elements,
there is also some mention of 'respect for learners', with a requirement that 'No
child shall be subjected to physical punishment or mental harassment'. The Act
also incorporates broader requirements for children's rights.

As can be seen, the provisions above are highly significant in terms of
incorporating international law into national legislation. Particularly noteworthy
are provisions to ensure teachers are adequately qualified, to combat teacher
absenteeism, the attention to hidden as well as direct costs, and the placing of
(albeit tentative) equity requirements on private schools. Yet inevitably, the Act
has been followed by criticism. Concerns have been raised about what has been
left out as much as what has been put in the Bill, the lack of a viable plan to
implement it, as well as simply the distance between the rhetoric and the reality.
Dubey (2010), for example, critiques the Act for: failing to calculate and provide
for the financial requirements before passing the law; not stipulating norms such

as distance of school from pupils' homes, space and infrastructure within the school etc; not including a strong emphasis on common local schooling; failing to challenge the restrictive emphasis on basic literacy and numeracy in favour of broader human development; not including preschool education within the right; including only weak recommendations on mother tongue instruction; and having an insufficiently powerful overseeing commission.

Of course, nobody is under the illusion that proclaiming the right to education in India will automatically ensure that the right to education is upheld – even if there is a viable and well funded plan. So the question is, what is the function of a law of this kind? Proclamations of this type attract so much criticism that the impression is given that it would have been better for the law not to have existed at all – as if it were only rubbing salt into the wounds.

There are, however, reasons why even law that is not fully upheld is better than no law at all. First, even in a flawed and corrupt legal system, there is the possibility of litigation to ensure educational access. (For an example of how marginalized groups can use constitutional law to gain access to essential services even in a faulty legal system, see the work of the Landless Movement in Brazil – Brandford and Rocha 2002.) Second, this form of proclamation can instil in the population a sense that quality education for all is a justified claim and not an unreasonable or utopian dream. Last, in common with non-legally binding declarations, it can have an aspirational role, providing a vision to work towards.

Legislation, and the existence of international and national rights instruments, are therefore key pieces of the puzzle of ensuring universal access to education quality – even though, as argued above, human rights should not be seen as gaining legitimacy solely through their being enshrined in law, and that we should acknowledge other significant means of promoting and upholding them. Nevertheless, there remains the question of why we might take so much trouble to promote and defend education at all. Are we really justified in claiming a universal right to education?

Notes

1 There are other candidates for this accolade.
2 'To ensure that the standards of education are equivalent in all public educational institutions of the same level, and that the conditions relating to the quality of the education provided are also equivalent' (Article 4(b)).

3

Justifications for the Right to Education

The idea of human rights is known throughout the world, and most states have signed up to international treaties that bind them into incorporating these rights in national law. Yet the matter of what exactly human rights are is far from being resolved. It is not just a question of the exact list of rights that we should subscribe to, but the more fundamental question of their nature and our grounds for upholding them. As Griffin (2008) points out, it is not only that there exist different *conceptions* of human rights based on diverse moral positions, but that there is uncertainty as to the very *concept*. As he states: 'When during the seventeenth and eighteenth centuries the theological content of the idea was abandoned, nothing was put in its place' (p. 2). Of the many critiques of human rights, perhaps the most simple, and devastating, is the one that says that they simply do not exist (or in Bentham's phrase, that they are 'nonsense upon stilts').

This chapter addresses fundamental questions of the nature and scope of human rights. The aim here is not to provide a comprehensive review of the general literature on rights – a task that has been amply undertaken elsewhere – but simply to set the backdrop of prominent arguments before assessing how these apply to the specific right to education. Once a general justification for human rights has been established, would it be possible to simply read off a justification for the right to education? To be sure, some pointers will emerge, but the task may not be so straightforward. First, if there is any kind of plurality in the general justification, the right to education may veer towards one or other factor. Second, there may be elements that are specific to education, such as a kind of 'meta-justification' if it is seen to underpin other rights or the processes of formation of our very conception of rights.

This chapter will put forward a specific conception of the underpinnings of the right to education, based on the two elements of agency and understanding. While there will be some discussion of the different forms of education that might correspond to this right, this aspect will be more fully unpacked in the chapters that follow. For the purposes of the current discussion, education is understood both in the formal institutional sense and in terms of purposeful learning outside institutions.

Human rights: Initial thoughts

Kymlicka's (2002) discussion of 'illegitimate preferences' in relation to utilitarianism provides a useful starting point for the notion of rights. Imagine a wealthy community faced with a local government proposal to construct social housing for unemployed families in their neighbourhood. This proposal will of course provide tremendous benefit for the small number of impoverished families, but will reduce the value of the properties of the majority. According to a utilitarian calculation, the proposal would be rejected since the sum of the preferences of the large majority will outnumber even the more intense preferences of the small minority. And yet, this result appears morally repugnant. To take an educational example, there are populations for whom it is both challenging and expensive to provide access to schooling. According to a cost-benefit analysis along the lines of conventional human capital theory, there may not be a justification for providing basic education for those with severe disabilities, or access to secondary level for teenagers in very remote rural communities, where it may not be viable to construct a school. Again, these examples are striking in their unfairness. One way of understanding a right, then, is as a form of threshold that it is not acceptable to cross even in the event of maximizing overall utility. Housing must be available for all, and those with disabilities and in rural areas must have access to education, even if denying these things would provide benefit to society in an aggregated sense. (This idea can be qualified by the requirement that the good or service in question is an important or essential one: we may not consider such a threshold to exist in relation to, for example, possession of sports cars or access to self-tanning salons.) Similar ideas are expressed in the description of rights as 'trumps' (Ronald Dworkin) and 'side-constraints' (Robert Nozick) on the pursuit of general welfare. However, while the above characterizations appear to place rights in opposition to utilitarian calculations, there are in fact utilitarian versions of rights, as will be discussed below. Furthermore, there is an even more basic role for rights – one that characterized their emergence historically – in protecting individuals not from utility maximization, but from the self-seeking actions of the few, in oppressing others so as to gain personal advantage.

Rights can relate both to welfare and agency. The example of housing above relates to the former, and other examples would be freedom from physical aggression and murder, adequate nutrition and so forth. Yet much of the area covered by rights relates not to our interests in this sense, but to our ability to make decisions (even in cases in which our decisions might work against our interests). A clear example of this kind of threshold is the right of an individual to refuse to participate in a medical trial, even if that trial will bring tremendous benefits. Justifications relating to agency have a long history, underpinning in particular the right not to be enslaved: Griffin (2008) refers to the debates in the sixteenth century over the Spanish enslavement of New World natives, and the link between human dignity, autonomy and liberty. This aspect of rights has led to assertions that only those with rational autonomy can be rights-holders – that is, excluding those who are human but either through illness, impairment or age are unable to exercise their decision-making capacities fully. As will be discussed below, there are concerns over this kind of restriction, leading Pogge (2002: 58) to expand the category to 'human persons with a past or potential future ability to engage in moral conversation and practice'. However, the extent to which those without full consciousness and agency (e.g. adults in a coma, or very young children) can exercise rights is the subject of ongoing debate.

Rights can also apply to different forms of social organization. Unlike the legal rights of citizenship, *human* rights are those that apply not just to those in a particular nation-state or polity, but to all human beings. The idea of human rights is suggestive in two important ways: first, that these rights need to be upheld for people who do not live in states that are providing these guarantees, and hence entail some global obligations; second, that the justification for these rights have something to do with the nature of humanity, an idea that will be expanded on below.

Pogge (2002: 58) states that: 'A commitment to human rights involves one in recognizing that human persons … have certain basic needs, and that these needs give rise to weighty moral demands.' To claim that an interest or a need is a right is to say that it is so fundamental for the human being that no one should stand in the way of a person realizing it, and society should be organized so that all have access to it. (Of course there may be exceptional cases in which rights can be overridden, but only in the case of coming into conflict with another fundamental right.) In response to Gregory's (1973) argument that education can be justified on the basis of interests and needs, but not rights, Wringe (1986: 23) states:

> In debating whether there is a right to education, therefore, we are concerned to know whether failure to provide education for some members of the world's population *hic et nunc* constitutes grounds for moral indignation, or whether the universal provision of education is simply a desirable policy objective which may, without injustice, be postponed until such time as it reaches the head of

someone's list of priorities. To assert that there is a right to education is to assert that this latter characterization of the moral situation is inadequate.

Human rights therefore imply moral concern that requires immediate rectification, and responsibility that goes beyond those with a direct involvement. The nature of international responsibility will not be the main focus of this book, but the discussion will follow Pogge's position in acknowledging that endorsement of human rights entails some responsibility for opposing infringements around the world, wherever they might be.

> Recognizing these basic needs as giving rise to human rights involves a commitment to oppose official disrespect of these needs on the part of one's own society (and other comparable social systems in which one is a participant). (Pogge 2002: 58)

The participation referred to here is possible even beyond national borders – through international organizations, popular movements, campaigns, etc. – with the globalized nature of the contemporary world enhancing the potential and avenues for influencing other countries and communities.

So rights and human rights are protections for individuals (and groups) against illegitimate attempts either to maximize overall utility at the expense of a few, or simply to pursue selfish ends. Yet why is it that we consider it important or essential to provide these guarantees to individuals?

Status-based and instrumental justifications

Justifications for rights can be broadly divided into two types: status-based and instrumental (Wenar 2005, 2010).[1] Status-based justifications are founded on deontological positions that view certain moral duties as being essential, independently of consequences. These justifications claim that people have rights on the basis of certain attributes they possess as human beings. For example, on the basis of the ability for rational thought, all people should have the right to make choices about their lives, or on the basis of the inherent dignity of each person, no one should be subjugated to another's will. This approach is associated with Kant's emphasis on treating people as ends in themselves, rather than means to other ends. As Wenar (2005: 179) states:

> The rational nature of each person determines her moral status as a sovereign and inviolable being, and the dimensions of her sovereignty and inviolability

are marked out by the fundamental rights that entitle her to protection against oppression and abuse.

Despite the difficulties of identifying the essential characteristics of human beings, and deriving moral obligations from them (Peters 2002), many theorists have provided this form of grounding for human rights. The tradition of 'natural rights' is status-based in this way, on the grounds that human beings are the creations of God, and as such have certain entitlements to enable them to pursue godly lives. While adhering to the idea of natural rights, John Locke also put forward an argument on the basis of 'self-ownership': human beings 'own' their own bodies, and therefore have a range of entitlements, such as to the fruits of their own labour, to be free from enslavement and so forth. The idea of self-ownership has been influential since Locke's time, but is rarely used today as a justification for rights. Instead, international law is based primarily on the notion of human 'dignity' – an idea that has wide acceptance, being a universal characteristic, and not dependent on specific cultures – although having an indeterminate meaning.

Many contemporary philosophers in this way have grounded human rights in universal human values such as autonomy, self-government and freedom from subjugation to others. Unique among animals, we are born as individuals with a capacity for rational decision-making and a life project, and this characteristic is seen to be so fundamentally important to human beings as to warrant the highest degree of protection. Griffin (2008), for example, has put forward an argument for understanding human rights as the protections of our human standing or *personhood*, which in turn rests on 'normative agency'. (For Griffin, the term 'agency' is not enough, since there is a sense in which higher animals are agents: he prefers the term 'normative agency', to indicate that form of agency 'involved in living a worthwhile life' [p. 45].) Agency involves a defence of the individual against subordination to others' interests, but there is nothing necessarily *individualist* about it – agency can be collective as long as it involves a willing association.

An objection to agency or autonomy as a justification for all rights, as pointed out by Knowles (2001), is that it seems counter-intuitive to claim that a person has a right not to be killed only in so far as it would violate their ability to live an *autonomous* life. Certainly the simple fact of human beings' experience of pain seems to give strong support for protections against torture and aggression, for example. The notion of right does imply freedom, and the possibility of deciding to waive the exercising of that right at a particular point in time – in this way, rights are linked to the capacity for decision-making (while recalling Pogge's point that we need to include those with a past or potential future ability for rational autonomy). Nevertheless, we cannot exclude from the category of rights those relating simply to the protection of welfare.

While there are a range of variants of the status-based approach, they involve predominantly deontological obligations to protect capacities and interests seen to be fundamental to human life. Instrumental approaches, on the other hand, which are often linked to utilitarianism, view rights as being justified on the basis of the positive consequences that will accrue to individuals and society. In this perspective:

> [I]ndividual rights are simply tools for increasing weal and decreasing woe. If ascribing a right will maximize utility, a utilitarian will ascribe it; if not, not. Interests, not dignity, have justificatory priority for the utilitarian, and the value of rights derives entirely from the goodness of the states of affairs in which the agglomeration of interests is largest. (Wenar 2005: 179)

At first sight it appears counterintuitive to claim that rights are justified on the basis of their effects. Surely, the fact that a person has a *right* to something (such as the right to choose whether or not to participate in a medical trial) means precisely that she has that right regardless of individual or social consequences (such as benefits to the people who will take the drug in question). Nevertheless, there are persuasive arguments in favour of acknowledging consequences to some degree. Scanlon (2003), while rejecting a 'pure' utilitarianism – rights being 'more concerned with the avoidance of particular bad consequences than with promoting maximum benefit' (p. 35) – asserts that rights are justified on the basis that their assignment will prevent what would otherwise be unacceptable results (i.e. people's mental and physical suffering and enslavement). Certainly, the fact that rights are dependent on their historical and geographical context (Bobbio 1996) means that some attention to the conditions of society and implications of the existence of the right in that society are necessary.

There are, therefore, strengths and weaknesses to both approaches. The status position appears too rigid, given that consequences can never be ignored completely. On the other hand, the instrumental approach appears too flimsy – given its difficulty in answering questions such as, 'Why should it not be a rule ... that one should frame an innocent man if this will prevent a major riot?' (Wenar 2010), and its dependence on uncertain empirical predictions. Sen (1982), for example, acknowledging the inadequacies of both deontological and consequentialist approaches, proposes ways of incorporating both within a new concept of 'goal rights', 'in which fulfilment and non-realization of rights are included among the goals, incorporated in the evaluation of states of affairs' (p. 15). Griffin (2008) describes his own position as *teleological* rather than *consequentialist* in acknowledging a role for considering effects. Human rights in this sense have a special importance, but are not entirely immune to other considerations, they are 'resistant to trade-offs, but not too resistant' (p. 37).

It is possible, therefore, to retain elements of both of these approaches. Nevertheless, only some consequences can justifiably be taken into account: namely, those which relate to more effective ways of addressing the concern that gave rise to the right in the first place (Scanlon 2003). The position adopted in this book, therefore, is that rights are justified primarily by the fact that human beings are ends in themselves rather than means (status-based), but that consequences are important when they relate to the areas of concern that give rise to rights (instrumental).

Nevertheless, whether status-based or instrumental, obtaining any kind of clear grounding for human rights is highly difficult – other than largely rhetorical notions such as 'human dignity'. This difficulty has led some theorists to appeal to the *practice* of human rights. In fact, people can endorse the same rights on different grounds: Griffin (2008: 25) recounts the response of the drafting committee of the UDHR (who came from different philosophical viewpoints), 'We agree about the rights but on the condition that no one asks us why.' The difficulties of forging agreement on the fundamental justifications for rights, coupled with the widespread acceptance of specific human rights has led to many to believe (e.g. Bobbio 1996), that the quest for a unifying theory is unnecessary. Knowles (2001) calls this the 'no theory theory'. What counts here is that rights that are claimed are accepted by others and respected, regardless of any underlying principle. Rawls's 'overlapping consensus' appeals to this kind of approach in calling on people with different underlying belief schemes to agree on common principles including human rights.

Beitz (2009), in this way, takes issue with grounding human rights in nature or the characteristics of the human being as such, and the philosophical quest for their 'existence in the moral order that can be grasped independently of their embodiment in international doctrine and practice' (p. 7). Instead, he sets out to examine the practice of human rights, one that is 'both discursive and political' in the interactions between states. He qualifies his position, however, by stating that practice should govern our understanding of the concept of human rights, but not necessarily the reasoning over what actions they entail and by which agents.

Taking as a starting point only the practice of human rights is problematic in the sense that – while they command widespread recognition – we are of course far from a situation in which the actions of individuals and states do uphold human rights. Current practice infringes and ignores human rights as much as it endorses them. An approach from practice would seem satisfactory in a deliberative and just community, but would force us to accept a narrow range of rights in oppressive regimes. Yet while it seems clear that the grounds for human rights should have some moral basis outside of current custom, the process of deciding on a list of rights for the contemporary age should not be an exercise in lone philosophical abstraction: as argued in the introduction, this process should be one based on public deliberation – and it can certainly be a process consistent with the overlapping consensus approach of finding common ground between those with otherwise divergent philosophical and religious positions.

While it is not the purpose of this book to present a new perspective on human rights per se, a few words are necessary about how the notion will be understood in the chapters that follow. I will follow authors cited above in considering that human rights are protections of fundamental aspect of human life, creating weighty moral demands on others. These rights revolve largely around human agency, but include protection of the interests of those currently unable to exercise agency. As stated above, there is a deontological side to rights in the sense that they must be protected even if infringing them would maximize overall utility. And yet it would be foolish to be blind to consequences: ultimately if our aim is to protect personhood, then some trade-offs may be necessary.

Finally, as discussed in Chapter 1, it is important to note that human rights are not the whole of morality: they provide certain fundamental protections, but we have other kinds of moral obligations (such as to family and others close to us), as well as other political obligations (say to equality) that go beyond human rights.

Welfare rights

There are, however, those who accept the idea of rights – and even human rights – generally, but do not accept that those rights extend to provision of services such as education. This brings into play the distinction between non-interference and welfare rights. As seen in the previous chapter, the first generation of rights consisted of protections in the civil and political spheres, and it was not until well into the twentieth century that social, economic and cultural rights came to the fore. While the latter are now firmly entrenched in international law, philosophical concerns about their validity have not been resolved.

The first and most important objection relates to the duty-bearer for these rights. In the case of a non-interference right, it is for the most part immediately apparent who the duty-bearer is: for example, the person who would directly prevent me from expressing my opinion, or would try to kill me. However, in the case of welfare rights it is less clear. There is no one person or even a group of people who have responsibility for ensuring I am healthy, this duty is diffuse. The second objection, simply, is that these claims – however important they may be – cannot be fulfilled in practice for all people in the world, particularly in the so-called developing countries.

Neither of these objections is insurmountable. To start with the easiest, resource constraints cannot function as a veto for a right considered to be morally valid – unless of course it were *impossible* rather than simply *difficult* to uphold (the latter being the case with welfare rights). Sen (2004: 348) terms this the *feasibility* critique, stating in his rebuttal:

> The understanding that some rights are not fully realized, and may not even be fully *realizable* under present circumstances, does not, in itself, entail anything like the conclusion that these are, therefore, not rights at all. Rather, that understanding suggests the need to work towards changing the prevailing circumstances to make the unrealized rights realizable, and ultimately, realized.

Furthermore, in a complex society, the institutional arrangements for protecting civil and political rights are both expensive and dispersed among a large range of people and institutions. Many of the considerations, therefore, are the same as with welfare rights.

The question of the duty-bearers – which Sen (2004) refers to as the *institutionalization* critique – is a highly complex one that I will not be able to address in full here. Yet it should be possible to understand responsibilities for upholding welfare rights in a diversified way, with particular people having initial responsibility (e.g. parents, those working in established education institutions) and yet all of humanity having residual responsibility (in the case of moral obligations of wealthy countries to assist the development of educational systems in poor countries). In addition, as argued in the previous paragraph, the upholding of civil and political rights also involves diffuse obligations of this sort.

Recent theorists – such as Amartya Sen and Martha Nussbaum – have in fact shown the strong relationship between non-interference and welfare rights. Griffin (2008) too proposes that being an agent requires not only autonomy and liberty, but also minimum provision, consisting of education and information, the resources and capabilities necessary to act. In addition, it is possible to see the right to education itself as involving both provision and non-interference, as will be discussed below. As outlined in the previous chapter, since the CRC, international law has also brought welfare and non-interference rights firmly together, and asserted their essential indivisibility.

The right to education: On shaky ground

I will start by setting to one side two common justifications for the right that do not provide a firm basis. Both of these are strong reasons for providing education, but are not reasons for there being a *right* to education.

In his review of international law on the right to education, Hodgson (1998) outlines four justifications for the right: *the social utilitarian or public interest perspective* – based on education's role in supporting democracy, world peace and preservation of community culture; *a prerequisite to individual dignity* – through the imparting of essential skills and of abilities for reasoned analysis allowing for a dignified life in society; *a prerequisite to individual development* – providing the opportunity for individuals to realize their potential; and finally, *the individual welfare perspective*, given that in current societies individuals without education struggle to ensure their basic needs.

The first of these is distinct from the others because it is oriented around benefits to society generally rather than the rights holder. This kind of argument commonly underpins provision of universal education and compulsory attendance, and represents a key purpose of education. However, this kind of appeal to societal benefits cannot be the basis of a *right* to education (Snook and Lankshear 1979). As discussed above, aggregation of maximum benefit for society is out of step with the basic notion of a right – in that the latter is, among other things, a protection of the individual against precisely that kind of benefit maximization. Of course, the features mentioned by Hodgson such as peace and democracy will also bring benefits to the rights-holder, so in this case it is not a question of the individual being sacrificed for the collective. Nevertheless, while peace and democracy in society may be the motivations for providing education generally speaking, they are not a basis for the right as such.

This principle holds true whether we consider the right to pertain only to individuals, or also to groups. For example, a proposed right for an indigenous community to have access to schooling in their own language and engaging with their cultural heritage will be justified on the basis of either benefits to or characteristics inherent in the indigenous group, and not on the positive outcomes that it would bring to others in society (though it may well bring these outcomes too).

A second invalid basis for the right to education is its instrumental value (as in Hodgson's fourth justification above, 'individual welfare'). The right to education is commonly seen in this way as fundamental to the exercising of the whole set of human rights. Most commonly of all, it is seen as justified through its role in ensuring economic opportunities and reducing poverty (e.g. Grover 2004) – a role that is seen to be particularly crucial in the context of the knowledge economy/society (Peters 2002). Yet however justified these arguments are for providing education, purely instrumental views of this sort cannot provide an adequate justification for a right. In part, this relates to the contingency of the role of education. As Snook and Lankshear (1979: 36) point out:

> [I]f education is justified instrumentally any claim to a right to education rests on the correctness of the means-end model. The link remains an empirical one and may be broken by changes in the world.

Allowing contingent conditions to be seen as rights in themselves would lead to absurd conclusions: access to school is only allowed in many countries if a child is wearing a school uniform, but we wouldn't consider there to be a right to the uniform itself. In the United Kingdom, very often one's postcode unfairly determines the quality (or at least the prestige) of one's child's school – yet the right in question here is not to have a house in a particular location, but to quality schooling. There are a vast number of conditions which may all need to be in place in order for there to be access to school: we could even assert a right to paper clips, as these may be needed to collate the school application form that in turn is required for a child to be admitted into a school.

If education is *only* seen as an effective means to achieving other valued functionings such as employment or nutrition, then it is not a right in itself; the rights are to work or nutrition, with education merely a conduit. For it to be considered a right in itself, education must have some intrinsic value (although it can simultaneously have instrumental value). Health is also essential in order to be able to work: but we do not justify the right to health on this basis alone. In this way, education cannot just be a 'service right', it must have some kind of worth in itself. Again, as with the above point, the instrumental value of education may be a strong justification for making it generally available in society, but it is not a basis for its constituting a right in itself. The General Comment on Article 13 of the ICESCR does in fact acknowledge the intrinsic value of education underpinning the right as well as its instrumental value, stating: 'a well-educated, enlightened and active mind, able to wander freely and widely, is one of the joys and rewards of human existence'.

In discussing instrumentality of education, it is useful to draw on the distinction made by Peters (1967) (following Ryle) between education as a 'task' and an 'achievement' word. The task sense of education by definition has some instrumentality, in that it must have some aim or aspiration that guides it. If it is also intrinsically valuable, it is the process or experience of education that is valuable – for example, there may be something of value in the *experience* of a classroom dialogue independently of any positive outcomes. In the achievement sense, education has intrinsic value if being educated is a good in itself, regardless of any other benefits accrued. The value rests on the worth of the skills, dispositions and knowledge acquired: for example, it might be seen to be a good thing in itself to be conversant with mediaeval Italian poetry, even if that knowledge does not lead to enhanced work opportunities (although intrinsically valuable education will in addition often have instrumental value).

However, some apparently instrumental roles played by education do provide compelling grounds for a right. The informed reflection on one's own beliefs and on the purpose of one's life that is central to normative agency is enabled by the knowledge, skills and dispositions developed through education: to reflect critically, a person needs herself to have been educated, nobody can do it for her. The necessary role of education here then gives it a value that would constitute grounds for a right. A distinction, therefore, is needed in the instrumental role of education between cases in which a range of factors might promote the extrinsic benefit, and those in which only education or necessarily education must be involved. For example, schools have a fundamental role in many countries in providing meals to children; education systems as a whole also play the role of sorting and classifying young people for the benefit of employers: yet neither of these roles necessarily needs to be carried out by educational institutions. The 'welfare perspective' proposed by Hodgson is instrumental in this sense, while in contemporary societies education is often necessary in order to ensure basic provisions (i.e. to gain employment, or to negotiate the benefits system), it is quite conceivable that a society can be organized in which food, housing, health etc. were provided to people in the absence of education. (And in fact, many populist governments in history have aimed to provide basic necessities for the population in the absence of education and informed rights claims – in Latin America termed *asistencialismo*.)

However, in a 'necessary instrumental role' sense, the line between intrinsic and instrumental becomes somewhat blurred – education is instrumentally valuable for critical citizenship, but we can see criticality as simply an expression of the intrinsic value of education. It is not so much that education is instrumental in forming citizens, but it is *constitutive* of it, in that citizenship contains within itself an ongoing process of learning, exploration and dialogue.

Justifications: Socialization and autonomy

A range of justifications are provided for the right to education that avoid the two traps outlined in the previous section, for the most part fitting into two broad areas: first, the process of socialization into the basic codes for functioning in society; and second, the development of a capacity for autonomous living and choice of the life to be led. These can be seen to relate respectively to the welfare and agency aspects of rights in general. The two appear to go in opposite directions: the first inducting an individual (often uncritically) into a form of living, and the second allowing the individual to reflect on it and choose to leave or remain within it. Socialization draws the individual closer to others, while autonomy ensures that individual is not subsumed by, subordinated or subjugated to them. (The latter, however, is dependent on the former, since we cannot freely choose whether or not to follow a particular life course unless we have some knowledge and understanding of it.)

Haydon (1977), in fact, distinguishes between three possible bases for the right. The first of these is the *socialization* referred to above, the acquisition of the basic capacities for functioning in a society, including language and other abilities necessary to live together with others. This is considered to be a right as it is needed in order to have a genuinely human life. The second – termed *optional education* – refers to the development of intellectual capacities associated with liberal education, and with the idea of the 'educated person' put forward by Richard Peters and Paul Hirst. While Haydon considers that there might be a non-interference right possible here (i.e. that people should be 'left alone' to pursue their own intellectual development), people do not have the right to call on the time and resources of others for this purpose, as it is a luxury and not 'necessary' for functioning in society. Of relevance to the later discussions in Chapter 6, he considers this form of education particularly unnecessary 'at the higher levels' (though not undesirable). The third form – *autonomy* – is located between the first and second, in that it is more extensive than socialization, but does not move into the terrain of luxury. According to this view, we have a right to be autonomous beings, but need the assistance of others in achieving it. Basic education is a right, therefore, as it is essential to autonomy:

> Some degree of diversity of cognitive development is a condition of rational choice: there must be at least some awareness of alternatives between which one might choose, and some notion of criteria by which alternatives can be assessed. (p. 241)

For Haydon, therefore, the right is justified through the importance of socialization and autonomy for living a fully human life.

Snook and Lankshear (1979) also propose a basis for the right in what appears to be a division into two of the process of 'socialization': first, the basic requirements of survival provided to the child in the first few years of its life; and second, the knowledge, skills and dispositions needed for living in particular societies (this second type ensures not survival but 'happiness'). An alternative basis for the authors is initiation into 'lifestyles' (linked to Peters's conception of education as initiation), not apparently in the contemporary rather frivolous and commercial use of the term 'lifestyles', but more as in a 'way a life', involving some kind of moral sense. Importantly, this third form must have intrinsic value (even if it also has instrumental value). While the first two are seen to be welfare rights, the third is a non-interference right, since it relates to the kinds of lives that individuals deem appropriate for themselves, and for this reason others are neither able nor entitled to determine the content of the education. There are some links between this idea and the autonomy proposed by Haydon, as the latter requires familiarization with different alternatives from which the individual can choose.

While the elements of socialization and autonomy characterize accounts of the right to education, there are some other justifications put forward in the literature. A rather particular account is provided by Olafson (1973). His main argument is that education is not a *general* right as normally conceived (i.e. one applicable to all people) but a *special* right (i.e. something like a promise, stemming from a specific relationship), one derived from the responsibilities of parents towards their own children and more broadly of one generation to the next. Children having been brought into the world have a right to attain various competencies, and parents/ the older generation having brought them into the world have a duty to provide those things. (The possibility is kept open for the community or polity providing education in the absence of parents.) Olafson's proposal that education should be considered a special right has, however, been met with scepticism by subsequent commentators (e.g. Snook and Lankshear

1979; Wringe 1986). In terms of why education is needed, Olafson provides two principal reasons. First of these is again socialization, with a conception similar to that of Haydon above, developing competencies that will enable the child 'to care for itself and generally to lead a life of its own' (p. 185). Skills and knowledge for caring for oneself go from the very basic – language capacity for communicating, basic conceptual schemes and appropriate behaviours – to the very complex in large and diverse contemporary societies. The second justification is citizenship and political participation: following a broadly accepted line of argument, democratic society is seen to depend on citizens having the minimum level of education that will allow them to exercise their rights (voting, standing for political office, etc.) and fulfil their duties (jury service etc.), thereby bringing benefits both to the individual rights-holder and the rest of society.

This latter point appears to be an instrumental justification, but as discussed in the previous section there is a significant difference here. Education is essential to civic participation, as there is no meaningful way of participating in politics (at least not in the active sense employed here) without knowledge and skills, the ability to engage in deliberation, reflect on one's views and understand the views of others. Education is constitutive of critical citizenship, so in this sense it does constitute a valid basis for the right.

An appeal to civic participation as the grounds for the right is also evident in Curren (2009). The author, like Snook and Lankshear (1979), bases his notion of education in initiation, in this case into 'practices that express human flourishing' (p. 52), a conception broader than the emphasis on the forms of knowledge of Peters and Hirst. This conception has a bearing on the content of education (discussed in the following chapter), but also provides a justification in that these practices are seen to be intrinsically valuable. Curren's primary concern is with the challenges of diverse contemporary societies, and education's essential role in making possible Rawls's vision of an 'overlapping consensus' between people with divergent religious and political views.

> Since we are social beings who must often act collectively through our governments to protect and advance our well-being, civic education that enables us to be capable and informed participants in democratic processes is surely one aspect of a well-rounded preparation to responsibly secure the satisfaction of our needs. (Curren 2009: 50)

This right to civic education and participation relates to the global as well as to the national and community levels. In addition to the above role of civic education in the collective protection of interests, Curren also puts forward an argument based on establishing a legitimate rule of law, in that respect for persons as rational beings will entail a right to education, in order to allow citizens to understand laws they are expected to follow and be able to meaningfully influence and endorse them.

A similar position – one based on autonomous membership of a political community – is seen in Wringe (1986). He asserts two justifications for the right to education. The first is a justification of education as a welfare right, which, based on the idea of the social contract, asserts that people would have no reason for endorsing the society they live in if they were not granted certain benefits.

> To this extent the justification of the right to education, in the sense of right to a very basic initiation into the forms of human understanding, is in line with that offered for welfare rights in general. The deprivation involved in its denial is such as to invalidate the claim that someone may be denied this benefit and still reasonably be expected to keep the law and observe the rules of the moral community. (Wringe 1986: 31)

The education referred to here is of the 'socialization' type as seen above in Haydon and others. The second justification, however, goes beyond this to more extensive forms of knowledge and understanding. Education in this sense is seen to underpin other human rights, along the lines of the notions of indivisibility, interrelatedness and interdependence discussed in the previous chapter. Yet in the sense employed by Wringe, education is not purely a service to other rights, but has again a *constitutive* presence, being central to enhancing agency and autonomy, and in the contemporary world essential for avoiding subjugation and exploitation by others. A similar position is put forward by Spring (2000), who sees education as a key tool for minority groups such as indigenous peoples in successfully negotiating the challenges of globalization.

Does the civic participation justification represent a third type distinct from socialization and autonomy? One way of viewing it is as a sphere of application of both these qualities: at once a learning to interact and communicate with others, understand political codes, customs and concepts; and at the same time a political autonomy, entailing the ability to form independent views and resist indoctrination, oppression and subjugation.

Towards an underpinning conception

The dual elements of socialization and autonomy proposed by the authors reviewed – and associated capacities such as civic participation – do provide a sound basis for the right. These are both fundamental to human life and require education for their realization. Yet surprisingly absent in the discussions of the right to education is another element – *understanding*. Human beings pursue learning not just so they can acquire practical abilities, but to turn unknowns into knowns, to find out about themselves and the world, to explore the mysteries of the universe. Attention is needed in the right to the human capacity for understanding, to curiosity about and interest in the world, making possible the pursuit of an ever deeper grasp of the nature of things. Reflexive consciousness and the capacity to understand is a fundamental human characteristic (it is immaterial whether exclusively human) and the ability to pursue enhanced understanding must be cherished for all people. Understanding is both intrinsically valuable – constitutive of a rewarding life – as well as having instrumental value in underpinning of the capacities of being, feeling and acting. Of course, direct instruction is not always needed for developing understanding, but some external assistance, whether formal education or informal guidance, is needed for human beings during their lives, in conjunction with their own efforts, in pursuing knowledge of the world.

This book will orient itself around two fundamental justifications for the right to education: first, the notion of *understanding* discussed above, and second, *agency*. A full mapping of these concepts and justification for them will not be possible here, but some brief points will be of use. The importance of agency (or 'normative agency' in Griffin's terms) has been outlined above. I prefer the term 'agency' to 'autonomy' not because of significant conceptual differences, but because of the associations of the terms. 'Autonomy' for many is suggestive of a rather cold distancing of the individual from others, and has been interpreted as implying ontological individualism, and as being a Western value incompatible with other cultures. While none of these features is inherent in the concept of autonomy, to avoid red herrings the term 'agency' is preferred. Agency involves the freedom of individuals to pursue their life goals (freedom in a non-interference sense, but also involving positive provision in society), but can be a collective as well as an individual notion. A further point is that autonomy does not express well the kind of 'agency' involved in political participation and civic life.

The ability to act in the world in accordance with one's purposes is strongly linked to the possession of knowledge, skills and reflective capacity. Griffin (2008), for example, sees education as fundamentally linked to the basic rationale for human rights in personhood. In his view, an essential part of agency is that 'one's choice must be real; one must have at least a certain minimum education and information' (p. 33), so that we move from having the potential for agency to actually exercising agency. This view is echoed in much writing in philosophy of education which emphasizes the pre-eminent role of education in autonomy (e.g. Callan 1997; Levinson 1999; White 1990). Agency and choices depend on information and information requires literacy; pursuing aims also requires further skills and knowledge, and the ability to deliberate and scrutinize. Connected to this, Curren (2009) also asserts that children have the right to be able 'to revise one's conception of how to live a good life', and reflect critically on one's family and local belief systems, (of course this is the *ability* to scrutinize one's belief, and not an obligation to reject one's beliefs). As discussed above, this element also includes the political agency needed to be an active and critical citizen, able to subject authority to scrutiny and to influence decision-making.

Placing agency and understanding at the forefront is not to deny the fundamental importance of socialization. A good deal of directed learning is necessary in order to engage in any kind of interaction with others, involving language and communication, basic skills and knowledge. Socialization on its own is a poor basis for the right as it restricts education to early childhood, and does not allow for an expansive conception of emancipatory learning through life. Nevertheless, it is a necessary first stage of all education and a necessary condition of a fully human life. However, this capacity is in fact entailed by the dual components of understanding and agency, it is the initial stage of autonomous reflective living to understand the social group of which we are a part and to be equipped to function within it.

It is not just a question then of being able to function in the world and make informed choices, but to understand and be able to transform it. These two elements are linked to characteristics that for all intents and purposes are universal: the existence of purposes, intentions and values, moral and otherwise, and held individually and collectively; and the capacity for learning and understanding. Emerging from this descriptive observation, is the normative claim that these are particularly important capacities that must be enabled and protected at all costs for all people: at least, the freedom to exercise these capacities must be available to all people, even if they decide not to exercise them (for example, a person is free to choose to live entirely isolated from the world, with no communication with others, but in order to make that choice, it is essential first to possess the ability to communicate and have had some interaction with others). So, all people should have the capacity for reflecting on and pursuing their goals; and they should have the opportunity to develop their understanding, as well as their talents and interests. While human beings have some innate capacities in these areas, all of them require education in order that they may be fully exercised. Education, however, is not just a pathway that leads to these capacities as if a separate entity; both understanding and agency are internal to education and have education as an inherent component. The effects of such an education are not *external* to it, they are *expressions* of it.

Hodgson's (1998) third element of 'individual development' comes into play here. The human capacity for development is not always sufficiently emphasized in discussions of the right to education. It is not just that human beings need to know particular things, and that the right to education enables them to do so, leading them from a state of lack to a fixed state of adequacy. Instead, human beings are in a constant state of change, so education becomes a way of fostering positive rather than negative movement. The malleable nature of the human being and the possibility of change make essential the opportunity for people to develop positive aspects of their selves. The element of 'development' would indicate an emphasis on childhood, and given the rapid pace of development in this phase of life and the heightened capacity for certain forms of learning (e.g. language), would justify extensive educational provision at this phase. However, development and learning (cognitive, aesthetic, moral etc.) continue throughout life, and this aspect of the right is not one restricted to childhood. Understanding and agency are both qualities that are developed progressively, rather than being acquired once and for all at a particular point.

In this way, the position put forward in this book departs from that of Griffin and Haydon in that the principle of personhood is seen as requiring not just a very limited amount of education so as to make choices, but continuous development. As will be explored further in Chapter 6, this means a right to a lifelong education. Following Griffin's idea of abstract principles which are then translated into increasing degrees of concreteness, this principle does not automatically imply a right to high resource full-time education throughout the whole of our lives. Of course, there are resource constraints, but in addition to this not all forms of meaningful learning require considerable resources, nor will there always be uptake. The right to lifelong learning requires both non-interference (e.g. free flow of ideas, no censorship, no child labour, no excessive forced labour for adults, etc.) as well as provision. Furthermore, this is an all-encompassing vision of learning, including not only formal education, but also non-formal provision, and personal and spiritual development. The kinds of intentional learning involved in the training of Buddhist monks also adhere to these principles of understanding and agency, although they may employ different methods from those of formal education and engage with distinct epistemological traditions.

As stated above, there are many other reasons why we should engage in education and have education systems beyond the fact that it is an individual right – many specific to particular societies, and others more universal. Some of the reasons for having education are as much for the benefit of others as for the learners themselves: take for example the argument for early childhood education for impoverished groups on the basis of the evidence to show a lower propensity to become a criminal in later life (Currie 2001). Olafson (1973) cites another example of nations developing education systems so as to train middle level technicians to fulfil certain human resource requirements (i.e. in the state's interest but not necessarily in the individual's).

Access to education for all people is often justified on the basis of equality of opportunity, particularly given the pre-eminent role qualifications play in determining an individual's employment, income and other life possibilities. Again, this is a highly important consideration, but not in itself the basis of a *right* to education, given that there are other ways in which the disparities in economic opportunities could be addressed (although equality of access to the intrinsic benefits of education does constitute grounds for the right). It is important to recall in relation to this point that human rights are not the totality of moral and political considerations, they are just a part of our moral reasoning and political organization, and questions of procedural and distributive justice will also impinge on the way we organize education systems.

This chapter has provided an outline of general justifications for human rights, justifications for the right to education specifically, and the principles underpinning the arguments presented in this book. However, there are three areas that are as yet uncertain: the first of these is the question of what the right to education is a right to exactly, concerning the forms, content or experiences of education involved. Second is the relationship between the right to education and other human rights, particularly when going to school may entail infringements of these other rights, or alternatively ensure that they can be effectively exercised. And third, there is the question of the scope of the right to education in terms of the human life course, whether the right applies only in childhood or in the same way throughout life. These questions will be dealt with in the three chapters that follow.

Note

1   A third approach – 'contractual' – is also to be found, referring to a conception of rights as those principles that would reasonably be agreed to by people in a collective.

4

A Right to What?
Inputs, Outcomes and Processes

Most agree that all people (or at least all children) should have education, and many defend education as a fundamental right. Yet what is meant by education here? Is it a right to school, and if so what kind of school? If it is a right to learning that could be obtained outside school, is it any kind of learning or only some? Is it a right to acquire particular forms of knowledge, to be able to undertake particular activities or to imbibe certain values? Are these attributes universal, or particular to each place, and if so who decides? These questions will form the subject of this chapter, which following the general discussion of justifications for the right to education above will address the question of 'a right to what'?

As discussed in previous chapters, existing studies (e.g. Beiter 2006; Friboulet et al. 2006; Hodgson 1998; Tomaševski 2003) have made extensive explorations of the legal frameworks of the right to education and its realization, but, with a few exceptions (e.g. Karmel 2009; Spring 2000; Vandenberg 1990) have devoted little space to discussing possible meanings of education. All too often, education is taken to be synonymous with schooling, and even then without an acknowledgement of the complexities of the school experience.

The chapter will start with an analysis of the right to education as expressed in the UDHR, identifying limitations in its focus on primary schooling. The chapter subsequently assesses other candidates for a basis for the right – in particular, learning outcomes – highlighting the advantages of these over an institutional focus, while at the same time identifying significant difficulties. Instead, a focus on engagement in educational processes is proposed. Finally, there are considerations of the notion of 'quality' and questions of formal/non-formal.

The conception of education in the UDHR

As seen in Chapter 2, the right to education is clearly established in a range of international agreements and incorporated into national law. Yet the legal right to education is a strange hotchpotch. It is in some aspects remarkably specific and prescriptive, and in others remarkably silent. Unusually, it is specific in relation to the forms of institution that must provide education, and to its duration, but (despite some broad recommendations concerning aims) not in relation to the types of process that are undertaken within them. In this chapter I will argue that the right to education should consist of the exact reverse.

The analysis here will focus on the relevant article of the UDHR. Some modifications can be seen in the later declarations and conventions, yet the subsequent instruments remain largely faithful to the principles established the original statement: because of this, and for reasons of economy, the current analysis will restrict itself to the initial declaration. Two highly controversial aspects of the right to education in the UDHR will not be covered in this chapter. The first is the third part of Article 26, namely, the prior right of parents to educate their children in accordance with their beliefs (as explored in Curren 2009). The second is the assertion that elementary education should be made compulsory. These are highly complex questions, and go beyond the remit of this particular discussion. I will here focus on the forms of education to which individuals may (or may not) have rights, rather than questions of public and private, and the balance of power and potential conflicts between state, parents and other stakeholders.

It is important to start by noting that the existence of a right to education of this sort at the international level is highly desirable and that those providing written expression to this and other rights have by and large done well in creating a form that is both demanding of states and inclusive of the conceptions of different cultures. However, as also highlighted in the analyses made by Karmel (2009) and Spring (2000), there are nonetheless problematic elements. Three of these will be outlined here: the identification of education with schooling; the restriction of the absolute right to the elementary level; and the lack of discussion of the forms taken by education.

Identification of education with schooling

Rights in international treaties are generally expressed in terms of principles – with the strategies for enforcing them left largely to individual states. In education, however, a particular approach is stipulated for the realization of the right: namely, the institution of school (and, to a lesser extent, university). The word 'school' does not appear in Article 26, but the categorization into elementary, technical, higher etc. makes its presence clear. In later documents, such as the Jomtien Declaration and the *General Comments* to Article 13 of the ICESCR, *primary* education is distinguished from *basic* education, with the latter being seen as the entitlement, and the former as the delivery system. Basic education is defined by Coomans (2007: 199) as including 'literacy, arithmetic skills relating to one's health, hygiene and personal care, and social skills such as oral expression and problem solving', as well as aspects relating to respect for human rights. Importantly, basic education can be acquired after a student has passed the normal age range of primary education. The General Comment on the Aims of Education of the Committee on the Rights of the Child (2001) specifically states that:

> 'Education' in this context goes far beyond formal schooling to embrace the broad range of life experiences and learning processes which enable children, individually and collectively, to develop their personalities, talents and abilities and to live a full and satisfying life within society. (p. 2)

Nevertheless, in practice education and schooling are often conflated, and interpretations of (e.g. Beiter 2006; Coomans 2007) and campaigns stemming from this right do on the whole interpret it as meaning school.

As a pragmatic strategy, a focus on schools may be sensible. They are a tried and tested method of delivery of instruction to large numbers of children, and while in their contemporary form having their origins in Europe, have been developed throughout the globe (either through conscious adoption or colonial obligation) and have near universal recognition. They also allow for ease of monitoring of access and achievement. However, there is an obvious limitation in equating education and schooling. If we imagine the two in a Venn diagram, there is a significant amount of each that lies outside the realm of the other. There is much that goes on in schools that is not education (e.g. child minding, provision of food, health care, and some less savoury aspects such as social control and indoctrination, not to mention Dore's (1976: xi) 'mere qualification earning'); and much education that does not occur in schools or universities (in families, community groups, religious institutions, libraries, political movements, etc.)

In the context of the quest for EFA, there are two strong reasons for not equating education and schooling. First, many schools around the world fail to provide an experience that can meaningfully be called education. To take one of a number of possible examples, Palme's (1999) ethnographic study of schools in Northern Mozambique provides a vivid if disheartening illustration of this fact. Pupils are seen to spend to the vast majority of their time listening without comprehension, copying without comprehension and simply waiting. Quantitative research on learning outcomes in many countries paints a similarly dismal picture of the effects of schooling (e.g. Watkins 2000; World Bank 2006). According to the World Bank (2011) only 47 per cent of fifth-grade Indian students surveyed could read a second-grade text. Yet in addition to being largely ineffective, school can be positively harmful. In Palme's study, the disjuncture between school and the local community is seen to lead to a radical devaluing and disowning of the latter among those few who survive through the grades. This long passage is worth quoting in full:

> Since actual teaching practices with few exceptions affirm student passivity, and since the use of Portuguese as the sole language of instruction imposes severe constraints on conceptual understanding and verbal exchange, virtually no negotiating ... takes place between pupils' previous conceptions and experiences on the one hand, and new experiences and information handed to them in the classroom or by the textbook on the other. It is no wonder, then, that the few students who manage to survive throughout the years are profoundly transformed by the education process and, because of the general amnesia produced by the nature of this transformation, normally conceive of the modern, educated world into which they had managed to enter being totally different from, and superior to, the backward world from which they came. (p. 267)

Serpell's (1999: 132–3) account of the role of schooling in Africa reaffirms this radical disjuncture:

> The consequence of this formalisation of education is that small numbers of individuals with great potential to contribute to the life of their local communities of origin are systematically extracted into a separate, and largely alien culture of bureaucratic power, while the majority of those enrolled in school leave it with a sense of frustration and personal inadequacy.

Furthermore, as will be outlined in greater detail in the chapter that follows, there are many activities and experiences undergone by children in schools that not only fall short of fulfilling the right to education, but actually represent abuses of their other human rights (Wilson 2004). These abuses have been well documented in empirical research, such as that seen in Unterhalter (2003) on

sexual violence against girls in South African schools, and the links with HIV/
AIDS infection:

> Going to school for young black South African women may well not provide
> openings for what they are able to do or be, but may be placing them at grave
> risk of severe trauma, infection and early death. (p. 16)

As indicated above, there may be infringements of cultural rights too, when
indigenous peoples and minority ethnic groups (and in some postcolonial
contexts majority groups too) are subjected to formal education systems that are
at best unresponsive to and at worst actively repressive of their cultures. Another
way in which schooling can infringe rights is in cases where – through high
stakes testing and other pressures – children are exposed to extreme stress and
very long hours of study (Spring 2000).

Of course, this is not to say that schooling is a meaningless or harmful
experience for all children in all LMICs. For a great many, even in very challenging
conditions, school is an inspiring and even liberating experience that opens
horizons and provides previously undreamt of opportunities. The point is that
it is not always so. The right to education, therefore, cannot just be equated with
a right to school, even if we add the epithet 'quality' to it (school *can* fulfil the
right to education, but it is neither a necessary nor sufficient condition for its
fulfilment).

On the other hand, while not all schooling is upholding rights, there may
be ways in which the right to education may be provided even in the absence
of a formal school system.[1] As outlined above, there are many arenas in which
education can occur, such as in apprenticeships, voluntary organizations and
local community settings. In order to assess whether the right to education is
actually being upheld in these initiatives, it is necessary to look more closely at
the notion of education, as will be discussed in the latter stages of this chapter.

Restriction of the absolute right

Article 26 does not only refer to primary education. It states that technical and
professional education must be made generally available, and higher education
too on the basis of merit. Yet it is only primary education that is seen as an
absolute right for all.[2] There seems, however, to be little justification for restricting
the right to this level. From the perspective of qualifications, a primary school
leaving certificate is of little use in a society in which an increasing proportion
of people complete secondary school and university. We could say that basic

literacy and numeracy – skills that can be mastered at the primary level – are the threshold of access to key functionings in society. Yet even here, there is no clear cut-off point: literacy is not something we either do or do not have, but a practice that is continually developed through our lives, often giving us greater opportunities and influence as it develops. Wherever the line is drawn, clear rationales are hard to come by. In terms of knowledge of the world, analytical skills, communication, aesthetic development and so forth it is difficult to declare a point at which education ceases to be a *right* and becomes just a *good*. The implication here is not that we reject the notion of a right to education, but that we recognize that the right has a much broader application than is commonly thought.

There are clear practical reasons for limiting the right to education to the primary level. It is a tangible goal, in that the institution is clearly recognizable, and the achievement of universal access can be relatively easily monitored. In some cases, primary education is established as a complete cycle in itself, rather than merely a preparation for further levels. Most importantly from a pragmatic perspective, it is not feasible for the poorest countries in the world to fund universal secondary education at the present moment, and it is beyond even most of the wealthiest countries to fund universal higher education. So there are many good reasons for conceiving primary education as the key universal entitlement. Yet, this pragmatic strategy must not be confused with a moral right. Someone who has completed primary schooling is likely to be severely disadvantaged in most spheres of life in a society in which the majority of people have had 12 or more years of schooling. There are also strong arguments for preschool education being considered a right, given its fundamental importance for subsequent child development (UNESCO 2006). Furthermore, if there is a human right to education, it seems appropriate to apply it not only across all levels of formal education, but in some way throughout life. This question will be discussed in greater detail in Chapter 6.

The nature of education

Lastly, an aspect closely related to the previous two points is that Article 26 says little about what education should involve. Some possible aims of education are mentioned, namely:

- The full development of the human personality
- Strengthening of respect for human rights and fundamental freedoms

- Promoting understanding, tolerance and friendship among all nations, racial or religious groups
- Furthering the activities of the United Nations for the maintenance of peace.

Interestingly enough, while rights should relate first and foremost to the interests of the rights-bearer, the aims here, with the exception of the first, relate principally to societal or global interests (although naturally they will bring benefits for individuals too). We could take issue with the choice of aims here, the omission of others, and the vagueness of the idea of 'development of the human personality'. The explicit mention of the United Nations in such a general statement of aims is also rather jarring to the twenty-first century ear – in an age in which faith in the organization is rather less starry-eyed (Spring 2000). Yet, most importantly, there is no mention of the characteristics of the educational process, nor of the ways it should and should not be carried out. The later *General Comments* do provide a fuller picture of the aims, emphasize the importance of child-friendly schools and highlight an important constraint on methods, namely that corporal punishment must not be employed (this is also emphasized in the UNCRC). The CEDAW (1979) also addresses aspects of educational processes, such as co-education, portrayals of gender in textbooks and teaching methods.

Yet, for the most part, mention of what education actually involves is conspicuously absent in these statements of rights. This silence is highlighted by Spring (2000), who recalls Isaac Kandel's critique of the conceptualization of the right to education as early as 1947. Kandel raised the key question, discussed above in relation to schooling, of how the right of access to education might result in the infringement of other rights, pointing particularly to nationalistic indoctrination, but also to racial segregation and reinforcement of social class inequalities. While the requirement in the UDHR for education to 'promote understanding, tolerance and friendship among all nations, racial or religious groups' would appear to address these concerns, attention is not paid to the ways in which teaching and learning are actually carried out. It is clear that there must be constraints on what can count as educational methods, both in terms of moral considerations and, as argued by Peters (1966), in terms of consistency with the concept of education. While respect for human rights and for the dignity of all human beings are certainly desirable outcomes of an educational process for young people, it is clearly not enough to state this as an aim and imagine that problems of the content of education have been resolved. It is not clear if this goal can be achieved through education at all, and if it is, how it can be achieved.

While the UDHR provides a historically significant endorsement of the right to education, and ensures important guarantees, it helps us little in terms of identifying the 'education' to which we may have a right. There are limitations in its restriction of the absolute right to the primary level – and in its focus on school. Schooling is a pragmatically convenient, but ultimately flawed, basis for the right to education. Yet, is it possible, in the absence of an institutional focus, to conceptualize the form of education underlying the universal right?

Three curriculum models

The next sections will explore the forms of education that might be seen to correspond to the universal right. In order to do this, there will first be a discussion of three prominent models of curriculum design: *content*, *product* and *process* (Stenhouse 1975). These three models are commonly referred to in the literature, and while they are sometimes subdivided, and further models sometimes added,[3] they represent a useful (if not entirely watertight) categorization of approaches to education. The models are significant since they (often unconsciously) characterize distinct approaches to the educational undertaking, and serve as possible candidates for determining the basis of the right to education.

Through history, education has often been based on *content*. Thus, the starting point for the curriculum is a body or bodies of knowledge (with associated skills and values), with educational success as the transmission of that knowledge and effective mastery of it by the students. Usually this content is divided into well-established academic disciplines (English, physics, geography, etc.) or cultural traditions, with delivery also following traditional methods. There are two main forms of justification of the content included. The first is that the preservation of cultural heritage is education's primary purpose and that the curriculum consists of a selection of the finest intellectual and artistic work of a given people. The second is that certain academic disciplines have intrinsic worth, and initiation into them is an essential part of a flourishing life (as represented by Hirst's [1974] seven forms of knowledge). External aims or objectives are not made explicit in the content approach since it is the transmission of culture and initiation into the disciplines themselves that are the overarching purpose.

It was largely as a reaction to the lack of clear aims in the above approach, and the lack of a clear justification beyond appeals to intrinsic worth, that the second paradigm emerged. The 'product' (or 'objectives') approach developed in the United States in the early twentieth century through the work of curriculum theorists such as John Franklin Bobbitt and later Ralph Tyler, drawing on Frederick Taylor's approach to the management of factory work. According to these thinkers, custom and tradition could not be at the helm of the school system, and instead it was necessary to orient the curriculum towards predefined objectives. Content and methods of delivery were to be chosen on the basis of their appropriateness for achieving these objectives, and could be modified or replaced if not effective. Clear objectives were seen to be the only way to provide a rational direction and organization to the school system, to make teachers accountable and provide justification for the tremendous expenditure on public education. The movement was particularly characterized by the use of behavioural learning outcomes – ones that could be easily defined, recognized and assessed.

The product model received strong criticism from those who saw its apparently rational and efficient approach to be detrimental to educational practice. Objectives (particularly behavioural ones) were seen to reduce teaching to a predictable and technical activity, making impossible unexpected moments of pedagogical creativity, and unduly restricting the possibilities of student response to the material. The emphasis on measurability was seen to lead to an impoverishment of educational aims along the lines of the saying attributed to Einstein: 'Not everything that counts can be counted, and not everything that can be counted counts.'

Increasing awareness of the flaws of the product model led to the emergence of a third approach, commonly called 'process'. Here, the curriculum was oriented neither around established bodies of knowledge, nor around clear objectives, but around valued processes to be engaged in by the students. Thinkers such as Lawrence Stenhouse and Jerome Bruner developed curricula from the 1960s in which the orienting principles were engagement of students and teachers in joint processes of enquiry and questioning of the bases of knowledge. The process model has links to the 'progressive' movement in education – but is not identical to it: process approaches can be applied to traditional academic disciplines too, when it is the procedures rather than the content of the subjects that are at the forefront, and when these procedures are questioned by teachers and learners (Stenhouse 1975).

All three of these models survive to this day, appearing in different forms and often jostling up against each other within a single curriculum. If we dislocate the models from their historical context for a moment, we can see their fundamental components. Each appears to highlight one of three aspects of the educational undertaking: aims, content and delivery (or teaching methods).

The product model focuses on aims, the content model on content, and the process model on delivery. However, the relationships are a little more complex than at first sight. In the case of the product approach, the aims are at the forefront, with the content and delivery subordinated to them. The content approach, however, does not specify its aims. Yet it is an inherent aspect of educational undertakings that some kind of purpose underlies them, whether explicit or not. In the case of the content approach, these aims are closely linked to the valued bodies of knowledge – the overarching aim being to create people who have fully internalized that knowledge. While modes of delivery are not specified, they are likely to follow traditional patterns, in the same way as the knowledge content. The process model again avoids specifying objectives, but this does not mean that there is no purpose to the undertaking. The purposes are here embodied within the processes. The content to be dealt with in this case emerges naturally from the modes of delivery, rather than being pre-specified.

At first glance it appears that each model subordinates two of the elements to the third, and is, therefore, in its own way one-sided. Yet, the process approach has a distinct advantage over the over two. This can best be seen through the notion of the *proximity* of ends and means (McCowan 2009). While all educational undertakings have some form of aim or purpose, the relationship between this purpose and the educational means varies greatly. The most common way of conceiving the relationship between ends and means in education is one of an empirical link of causality: the appropriate means are those which have the best chance of bringing about the ends. This can be called a relationship of *separation*. This way of viewing ends and means was critiqued by Dewey (e.g. 1964), who argued that conventional distinctions between the two were artificial. Contrary to the assumptions of a *separation* approach, there may in fact be concern about the nature of the means that is independent of the likelihood of actually causing the end to come about. In some cases, the ends will actually be embodied in the means. This, in contrast to the above, is a relationship of *harmony*. The third mode, *unification*, is a further extension of the harmony mode. Here ends and means join completely: the educational experience is in fact the end, or the end is an educational experience. The harmony (or unification) mode is preferable to the separation mode in any form of education that involves values (meaning, therefore, all except the most mechanical forms of training). If the values contained in the ends are not embodied in the means, it indicates that these values are being viewed as provisional and dispensable (McCowan 2009). Learners are also likely to perceive tensions between means and ends and this will inevitably affect the learning process.

In terms of the three models outlined here, the product approach is a clear example of separation, since objectives are established first, and then means are selected and modified in accordance with their success in achieving those objectives. The content approach has an appearance of unification, since it is the absorption of knowledge and culture that comprises the end. Yet the process of acquiring that knowledge may take a number of forms (and historically it has often taken morally suspect forms – such as rote learning underpinned by fear of punishment), since it is the acquisition, and not the process of acquiring, that is valued. The process approach, on the other hand, necessarily shows harmony, since the ends are not external to the educational experiences engaged in.

The right to education as process

There are, therefore, strong arguments in favour of the process model in education generally speaking. Yet should the right to education be conceived as a right to processes? As well as engagement in particular processes, could we not see the right to education as the right to exposure to particular content, access to particular inputs or the attainment of particular objectives?

Limitations of content

First, it might seem sensible to define the right to education in terms of bodies of knowledge to be acquired. We might for example, stipulate knowledge about chemistry, geometry, agricultural techniques, local religious traditions or basic economics. There are two main objections to this approach:

1. As discussed above, it is very difficult to justify the choice of particular content. In many cases (such as in the choice of subjects in the National Curriculum of England and Wales of 1988) content-led approaches are based on an adherence to tradition rather than any well thought-out justification (see Bramall and White 2000; White 2007). However, theorists such as Hirst (1974) and Peters (1966) have attempted to argue for the intrinsic value of certain forms of knowledge and initiation into them. Leaving aside the epistemological questions of whether there exist either objectively real bodies of knowledge, and of whether school knowledge is nothing more than the expression of a dominant social class (Young 2008), it is particularly difficult to justify the *universal* validity of established school

subjects (which have an uncertain relationship even to the seven forms of knowledge proposed by Hirst). It would be dogmatic to rule out altogether the possibility of intrinsically valuable knowledge, but academic traditions as we know them are firmly located within particular languages and cultures (as well as specific points in history), so it is problematic to establish them as the basis of a universally accepted right.

2. One way of avoiding the problems of universal content is to assert that the right to education involves initiation into the knowledge traditions of the particular community to which the individual belongs. It is clearly important that people have an intimate understanding of the cultural traditions around them. However, not all aspects of every culture can be said to enhance human flourishing and be compatible with human rights as they are currently expressed. Judgement is needed, therefore, to distinguish between those aspects of cultural heritage that are to be cherished, and those that are not. For this reason, initiation into culture per se cannot be the basis of the right to education, even though education will most often involve this form of initiation to a large degree. Other forms of justification are therefore needed, leading us into either the objectives or process approach.

Inputs

If we take a view broader than the content of the curriculum, it could be argued that the right to education is a right to certain inputs. In fact, policy and planning has largely followed this logic – determining that each child is entitled to a place in school, for a certain number of years, with particular facilities and a certain level of qualification of the teaching force.

Access to schooling, as the basis of the right to education, is an 'input' factor in this way. Given that schooling, as has been argued, is no guarantee in itself of meaningful education, perhaps by a more detailed stipulation of inputs (infrastructure, teacher qualifications, textbooks, etc.) we can define a more acceptable basis. However, as seen in Alexander (2008), the problem with focusing on input factors generally speaking is that they tell us little about how resources are used and what outcomes they lead to. To cite a phenomenon not uncommon in schools around the world, what use are the shiny new textbooks if they are kept locked in a cupboard for fear of spoiling them? What use are qualified teachers if they are absent, demotivated by poor working conditions or forced into a second job by low pay? What indeed is the point of a classroom if it is not a site for meaningful learning? The evident inadequacy of input gauges has in fact led to a shift in development agencies from a focus on school building and expanding access to an emphasis on quality and specifically on learning outcomes. It is to these gauges of learning that we now turn.

Learning outcomes

Given the problems of focusing exclusively on access to primary schools, *learning outcomes* appear at first sight a very promising candidate for the basis of the right to education. In place of a focus on inputs, many international agencies such as the World Bank are now using output indicators to gauge progress towards the EFA goals. This type of approach has also gained popularity in the form of 'outcomes-based education', introduced in a number of countries (e.g. Australia and South Africa).

The outcomes that have received most attention generally speaking have been performance of students on mathematics, science and language tests. While these indicators may facilitate international comparison, it is clear that a gauge of these specific skills based on written tests at a single point in time is an inadequate measure of educational outcomes broadly speaking. As Hahn (1987: 229) points out, in addition to achievement tests, we could take a number of different gauges of 'success' of education, including, 'The observation of children interacting in the playground with those from other cultural groups or of youth willing to educate others in their community about their rights ...' Nevertheless, the problems with learning outcomes are not restricted to questions of *which* outcomes are chosen. It is clear that some educational outcomes such as literacy, analytical skills and the ability to communicate are essential prerequisites to a full life. Nevertheless there are still problems with the identification of the right to education with a specification of these learning outcomes. Two of these difficulties will be outlined here.

Determining the level of outcome

It is hard to determine specific levels of outcome that would form part of a right. As discussed above in relation to the problematic nature of the restriction of the right to education to primary schooling, any stipulated level can be questioned. We could say, for example, that there is a right to the skills of basic literacy (leaving aside for the moment the question of whether such a thing can be defined). Yet, lacking *advanced* literacy in most societies will seriously restrict the individual's ability to gain access to valued forms of employment and further study, not to mention enjoyment of many forms of art and entertainment. It is hard to say confidently then that there is a right to basic literacy and not to advanced literacy. Outcomes, therefore, can only be put forward in very general terms.

A second challenge relates to the heterogeneity of the population. Differences in family background, inclination and ability ensure disparate educational outcomes even in countries in which there is universal coverage in the education system. These disparities could be addressed by targeted and effective allocation of resources, but in certain cases – such as for those with particular disabilities – successful learning outcomes may be distinct from those applying to the majority. Some proponents of learning outcomes – such as the 'millennium learning goal' discussed below – advocate tiered outcomes, but this would present an unwelcome challenge to the universality of the right.

Another problem is that when a particular objective is reached, by implication the right to education ends: that is, if a child were taught basic literacy at home at a very young age, there would be no further human right to literacy development. Or if we see outcomes in terms of particular cognitive skills, then the child who displayed these skills at a young age would have no further right to education at all. While very challenging in practice, the right to education should have some lifelong applicability at least. At a more profound level, it is misleading to see learning as leading to fixed outcomes of knowledge, skills and values – it being a more fluid experience, one of constant development. Education does not lead us to a particular point, it is an ever continuing process.

The constrictive effect of outcomes

There is a further problem with the use of aims and objectives in education (Jansen 1998; McCowan 2009). There is a tendency in contemporary societies to view education as a means of achieving a range of diverse aims, both national and individual. However, aims cannot easily be imposed on education in this way. In part this point relates to the inherently unpredictable nature of education. If we are dealing with education as opposed to training (in Peters's [1966] distinction) then there will always be an element of unpredictability in the process, with the learners able to reinterpret or discard the messages presented to them (McCowan 2008). Yet the subordination of education to particular aims can also have a constricting effect on educational processes. As seen above in Stenhouse's (1975) argument against the 'product' approach, education (as opposed to training, conditioning or indoctrination) is characterized by openness, and tying it down to particular results will constrain its potential. This is not to say, of course, that education should not have aims or purposes. On the contrary, it is impossible to conceive of education without purposes. Yet, as Dewey (1966 [1916]) argues, these aims must emerge from and be consonant with the nature of educational processes, and teachers and learners should have some involvement in shaping them.

It is absolutely right for there to be educational goals such as literacy, financial competence, awareness of the history of the community and of the world, and so forth. It is also valid to take effectiveness in achieving particular cognitive outcomes as one criterion of quality in education (among others). Yet while these are valid aims of education, the *achievement* of these aims cannot be the basis for a *right* to education.

Educational processes

Instead of learning outcomes, an alternative focus of attention is the educational processes that learners engage in. By way of illustration, processes might include enquiry, dialogue, development of reading comprehension, deliberation and exploration of difference. It is the value of the *activity*, rather than the educational 'material' or learning goal that matters here. The right to education, in this case, would be to engage in *processes* of, say, literacy development – rather than to achieve a specific level of literacy. For example, the focus could be on students engaging in research into a local environmental problem from which a range of knowledge, skills and values would emerge, rather than predefining the exact attributes to be acquired. Attention to processes means that the nature of the educational experience becomes of utmost importance, comprising teaching styles, relations between teacher and student, the learning environment, participation and so forth. This focus allows us to avoid the problematic task of determining specific outcomes, meaning both that educational experiences are not unduly restricted by predefined objectives and that we are not forced to stipulate an arbitrary level of achievement.

Beyond the educational advantages of avoiding an objectives-based approach – such as allowing for unplanned but nevertheless valuable pedagogical creativity and student responses (see Stenhouse 1975) – there is a further reason why processes should be at the centre of the right to education. Human rights must be a compatible set: while distinctions are made between *absolute* and *prima facie* rights, in a declaration such as the UDHR there are not supposed to be necessary trade-offs – the rights can, in theory at least, be upheld at the same time. (In practice, when countries are working towards upholding universal rights, there may well be decisions about whether one or another may be worked towards first.) This essential compatibility with the other rights makes the way in which education is conducted highly relevant. With the recent emphasis on rights-based approaches to development, international agencies are rightly paying more attention to the upholding of human rights *within* education (UNICEF/UNESCO 2007). Human rights-based approaches to development generally speaking are characterized by attention to processes – such as non-discrimination, participation – as well as outcomes. As discussed above, Wilson (2004) outlines a number of ways in which contemporary practices of schooling infringe human rights, including discrimination against minority and disadvantaged groups, degrading treatment of children, as well as lack of recognition of the rights of teachers. The literature on the '4 As' (e.g. Tomaševski 2003; 2006a) of the right to education also highlights principles to which educational practices must conform, particularly in relation to acceptability (issues of indoctrination, textbook censorship, medium of instruction, corporal punishment etc.) and adaptability (in relation to age, ability, gender, religion, etc.).

The above studies identify key *restrictions* on what can pass as educational practices within the right – in Wilson's (2004: 3) words, 'a lower limit on quality'.[4] However, there are also positive ways in which we may want to think about the manner in which education is undertaken. As outlined above in the discussion on the framework of *proximity*, in any form of education that involves values, the principles contained in the ends should be embodied in some form in the means (McCowan 2009). In this case, the implication is that the human rights, respect for them and active exercising of them should be incorporated within the educational process. The UDHR does call for education to promote respect for human rights, yet this is distinct as it is a proposed outcome, and not a principle intended to underlie the educational processes themselves. Instead, means should emerge from ends in the sense that the values (e.g. human dignity, active participation, freedom of expression, etc.) underpinning the human rights are upheld within the educational processes. This idea will be explored further in Chapter 8.

The argument presented in this chapter, therefore, is that the right to education is a right to engagement in educational processes. By casting out the content and objectives models, or a focus solely on inputs or outcomes, I am rejecting the types of justification that are normally given for the right to education (e.g. the acquisition of particular knowledge, skills and values that will help people in their lives). However, a process approach does not prevent people from achieving these valuable goals. The difference is that the goals are more open, and are shaped by those involved in the educational process. There are always (and should be) purposes to educational endeavours, so we could say that the right in this case would be to *purposeful* processes. A focus on processes is then desirable, but at a deeper level can also be seen as inevitable: there are no resting points in life that we can meaningfully describe as 'outcomes'; experience is constant movement, so processes in this sense lead not to results but to further processes. The purpose of educational processes, therefore, is to lead to ever enhanced future processes of learning.

The following section will assess how these elements of inputs, processes and outcomes manifest themselves in the approaches taken by development agencies influential in EFA and the debates on quality.

Quality in EFA

In 2003, Kenya introduced free primary education, following other Sub-Saharan African countries such as Malawi, Uganda and Zambia. In the year after implementation, grade one intake rose by a staggering 35 per cent, although enrolments declined slightly afterwards (Somerset 2009). The initiative has made significant gains in ensuring *availability* and *accessibility* of education (in the language of the '4 As' [Tomaševski 2006a]), removing direct fees, making the purchase of school uniform voluntary and limiting parental contributions (Somerset 2009). However, the aspect of *acceptability* has been less successful. While provision has been made for wider distribution of textbooks, the sudden expansion in enrolment has led to a shortage of teachers and a lack of adequate classrooms, leading to a general decline in quality (UNESCO 2005). Given the inevitable strain on quality provision, questions can legitimately be asked about whether the right to education has in fact been upheld.

The 'bums on seats' approach that characterized initial drives towards universal schooling in the post-war period, led to an inevitable concern along the lines of the above example that quality was being forgotten in the quest for quantity. The quality element was clearly present by Jomtien in 1990, and by now, most development agencies pay it substantial attention, at least in their rhetoric. However, there are inevitable disagreements on what constitutes quality. As discussed above, gauges of quality have frequently focused on 'inputs' such as teacher qualifications, teacher/student ratio, availability of textbooks, school facilities and so forth, yet recently, more complex notions of quality have emerged. The conceptualization in UNICEF (2000), for example, includes the elements of learners, environments, content, processes and outcomes:

- Learners who are healthy, well-nourished and ready to participate and learn, and supported in learning by their families and communities.
- Environments that are healthy, safe, protective and gender-sensitive, and provide adequate resources and facilities.
- Content that is reflected in relevant curricula and materials for the acquisition of basic skills, especially in the areas of literacy, numeracy and skills for life, and knowledge in such areas as gender, health, nutrition, HIV/AIDS prevention and peace.
- Processes through which trained teachers use child-centred teaching approaches in well-managed classrooms and schools and skilful assessment to facilitate learning and reduce disparities.
- Outcomes that encompass knowledge, skills and attitudes, and are linked to national goals for education and positive participation in society. (p. 4)

A similar scheme with three interlocking elements was put forward by the 2005 Global Monitoring Report focusing on quality (UNESCO 2005): learner characteristics (e.g. prior knowledge, school readiness), enabling inputs (e.g. teaching and learning materials, school governance), and outcomes (literacy, numeracy and life skills; creative and emotional skills), all influenced by a fourth element, context (e.g. labour market demands, parental support). The Edqual research consortium has also proposed diverse conceptualizations of educational quality in low-income countries, strongly rooted in social justice (e.g. Tikly and Barrett 2007, 2011). However, despite these and other rich and multifaceted conceptualizations of quality, for the most part development agencies are focusing predominantly on one aspect – learning outcomes. This focus corresponds to the belief that what really matters is achievement in learning, but is also pragmatically useful, given the ease with which quantitative data can be gathered, in contrast to the rather messier elements of process. This focus of attention has been stimulated by the interest of national governments in the Programme for International Student Assessment (PISA) results, and popularized by studies such as Barber and Mourshed (2007).

Leading the pack in this move is the World Bank, which has of late paid particular attention to learning outcomes (particularly in the form of cognitive skills), seeing them as being largely synonymous with quality of education (Hanushek and Woessmann 2007; Vegas and Petrow 2008; World Bank 2006). Moreover, Filmer, Hasan and Pritchett (2006) have proposed a 'Millennium

Learning Goal', following the MDGs. Focusing on countries such as Brazil and Mexico, which will fulfil the MDG for education in terms of enrolment but have worrying levels of achievement on standardized tests for large portions of the population, the authors propose this additional goal, drawing on the PISA assessment. Countries, according to this proposal, would establish 'upper' and 'lower' learning targets for their populations, with some room for national variation in terms of the level set.

The World Bank's *Education Strategy 2020* furthermore proposes replacing 'Education for All' with 'Learning for All', again following these quantitative learning outcomes.[5]

> The overarching goal is not just schooling, but learning. Getting millions more children into school has been a great achievement … The driver of development will, however, ultimately be what individuals *learn*, both in and out of school, from preschool through the labour market. (p. 1)

This change of emphasis follows changes in human capital theory research that shows that the cognitive skills of the population predict economic growth more effectively than schooling levels (e.g. Hanushek and Woessmann 2007). The learning outcomes valued are broader than the 3Rs, involving 'Social communication, teamwork, critical thinking, and problem-solving skills' (p. 26). Yet they remain skills tied closely to economic productivity, and lack an ethical dimension, or a sense of reflecting deeply on society and self, with a view to simply adapting to rather than transforming current realities.

The limitations of learning outcomes as a basis for a right have already been discussed above. The specific emphasis on learning outcomes by development agencies have also raied concerns (e.g. Barrett 2009). Barrett's (2011) close analysis of the Millennium Learning Goal commends it in some respects, viewing it as a significant improvement on gauges of enrolment, but finds it deficient in terms of the three elements of inclusion, relevance and democracy (educational principles derived from the ideas of Nancy Fraser). The form of assessment adopted fails to acknowledge the broad range of valuable learning that is possible, 'The measurement of learning outcomes is never just neutral measurement of learning but is always part of the learning experience' (p. 127). Despite efforts to make these tests culturally neutral, they also fail to acknowledge the practices and knowledge systems of diverse ethnicities and linguistic groups. The author proposes instead the establishment of a range of qualitative indicators of process, and that the goal itself should be formed through wide-ranging debate, a vision that resonates strongly with the position put forward in this book.

Nevertheless, despite these critiques of the emphasis on learning outcomes on the part of development agencies, there is very wide appeal to the apparent obviousness of the logic that

1. Education is about learning
2. To make sure learning has happened we need to assess it
3. Maths, science and national language are key learning areas, and can provide manageable test score data.

Therefore …

4. Educational quality should be gauged by test scores in maths, science and national language.

Propositions one, two and three are all true, but this does not, of course, lead inevitably to proposition four. There are clear gaps in the logic: first, there are ways to assess learning other than through test scores; second, there are other important subjects beyond these three; third, the manageability of these datasets should not be confused with their validity as a representation of all learning; fourth, educational quality encompasses more than learning outcomes.

In contrast, processes are largely ignored in current treatments in Education for All. The Jomtien Declaration too places emphasis primarily on learning outcomes:

> The focus of basic education must, therefore, be on actual learning acquisition and outcome, rather than exclusively upon enrolment, continued participation in organized programmes and completion of certification requirements. (Article IV)

In relation to the nature of the outcomes, the Declaration proposes that all should acquire particular skills and knowledge to prepare them for life – though it does not define these precisely. The Declaration does in places pay attention to processes, but subordinates them to the outcomes:

> Active and participatory approaches are particularly valuable in assuring learning acquisition and allowing learners to reach their fullest potential. It is, therefore, necessary to define acceptable levels of learning acquisition for educational programmes and to improve and apply systems of assessing learning achievement. (Article IV)

One recent report that does give due attention to processes within school is UNICEF/UNESCO (2007), with principles of human rights applied to curriculum, pedagogy and assessment, on the basis that, 'A rights-based approach to education calls for simultaneous attention to outcome and processes' (p. 15).

The processes in this case are judged on the basis of their being 'consistent with human rights principles and practices' (p. viii). Following general human rights-based programming for development, *participation* (of children and communities) is one of the key processes in question, as well as prohibition of physical punishment and generally respecting the 'identity, agency and integrity' (p. 28) of students within school. Attention is also paid to the utilization of assessment (to identify where extra support is needed rather than to punish), language of instruction and cultural sensitivity of the curriculum. Monitoring and evaluation in turn needs to address processes as well as outcomes. However, this kind of approach in practice is far from universal among development agencies, with the momentum clearly following the World Bank's attention to measurable learning outcomes, and national governments vying for success in international tests such as PISA.

In the EFA initiative, therefore, a general shift can be observed between an initial emphasis on access, towards greater attention to the quality of education. This shift is fundamental and must continue. It is clear that attendance in school does not in itself guarantee meaningful engagement in educational processes: the right to education is only upheld if the education provided is of a particular quality. However, very often quality is determined by inputs – such as school buildings, facilities, the availability of textbooks, teacher qualifications, etc. While an emphasis on these elements is certainly an improvement on paying no regard whatsoever to what happens in schools, they are imperfect proxies for the quality of the pedagogical experience: what matters is what is done with the inputs. The limitations of an input model have led to a focus on outcomes, and while in many ways these represent an improvement, there are significant drawbacks again as outlined above. Quality resides in the educational processes provided and the educational experiences had by the learners.

Having said this, in upholding the right to education, we need to bear in mind not only education itself, but also its prerequisites. As argued above, the right to education is a right to meaningful *processes* of learning, but this is not to deny the importance of the other elements of the quality schemes outlined above (e.g. UNESCO 2005; UNICEF 2000). In order for people to exercise fully the right, there need to be certain prerequisites in place (such as adequate nutrition, a place to study, etc.); and the existence of a supportive school and societal environment.

Formal versus non-formal education

From the above discussion of Article 26 of the UDHR, we have seen that school is neither a necessary nor a sufficient condition for the right being upheld. Yet despite its imperfections, is it perhaps still the best way of upholding the right? Or should it be abandoned altogether?

While there is extensive literature in the sociology of education on the role of schools in reproducing inequalities (e.g. Bourdieu and Passeron 1977; Bowles and Gintis 1976; Willis 1978), Ivan Illich in his well-known book *Deschooling Society* (1973) presented the most radical response. Together with colleagues such as Everett Reimer (1971), Illich argued not for reform of schools or even their transformation, but their complete removal.[6] Illich shared with other critics the view that the structure of the school system and hidden curriculum worked against low-income students and engineered their failure in comparison to the privileged. Yet in this critique he went further, highlighting the way the institution actually degrades learning:

> The pupil is thereby 'schooled' to confuse teaching with learning, grade advancement with education, a diploma with competence, and fluency with the ability to say something new. (p. 1)

The system of qualifications integral to education systems establishes a form of dependency (a critique shared with Dore's *Diploma Disease*) leading to a cycle of self-perpetuation for the institution:

> A successful school system schools parents and pupils to the supreme value of a larger school system, the cost of which increases disproportionately as higher grades are in demand and become scarce. (p. 10)

Furthermore, schooling for Illich restricts those seen as entitled to teach to the professional teachers, dividing 'any society into two realms: some time spans and processes and treatments and professions are "academic" or "pedagogic", and others are not' (p. 24).

In place of school, Illich proposed learning webs, in which peers support each other's learning in *convivial* relationships – the possibilities of which have been vastly expanded through the rise of the internet and other communication technologies. A contemporary application of his ideas has been in the *Unitierra* university in Mexico, an institution without buildings, programmes or diplomas (Barrón Pastor 2010). Whatever the viability and desirability of the alternatives proposed, Illich's critique remains a prick on the underbelly of the education beast, largely ignored but providing inspiration for those disillusioned with the system. It is a cogent account in principle, however unlikely it is that schools will be abandoned.

Something of a 'new wave' of deschooling has emerged in recent years. Rejection of formal institutions has been prominent in the United States in which homeschooling has increased in popularity for families concerned about the secular, liberal nature of school, and seeing the home as more conducive to religious inculcation. Theorists of contemporary change such as Charles Leadbetter have also proposed alternatives to school in the context of rapid urbanization in LMICs, the development of new technologies and the changing nature of the global economy (Leadbetter and Wong 2010). A well-known example of these new forms of learning is Sugata Mitra's 'hole-in-the-wall' experiment, through which slum-dweller children in India taught themselves how to use computers. Leadbetter's deschooling is clearly distinct from that of Illich in that the latter is based around values of equality, the intrinsic value of learning and the process of humanization, while the former sees education as a conduit for economic growth in a capitalist society.

In fact, a range of non-school forms of education have continued to exist alongside the mainstream system in high-, middle- and low-income countries. Targeted educational initiatives outside school (commonly termed 'non-formal education') encompass both compensatory school-like experiences for 'hard to reach' populations – 'second chance' or 'catch-up' programmes (World Bank 2011), and learning experiences of a very different nature and format (Hoppers 2007; Rogers 2004; Rose 2007). Non-formal education is sometimes provided for explicitly political ends, taking advantage of the greater freedom of the non-institutional space to develop empowering forms of pedagogy and curriculum, as in popular education in Latin America (Kane 2001; LaBelle 1987). In some places (though increasingly few), traditional educational forms in the community still exist, involving moral and spiritual development, trade apprenticeships, and the learning of community history, literature and arts. The most significant non-school providers, however, are religious institutions – either within monasteries, mosques and temples, or in specially created educational spaces, although in many cases this is a different form of schooling, rather than non-school education. Despite the overriding emphasis on school in rights instruments and EFA frameworks, there is some acknowledgement of the role of non-formal education here too. According to Verheyde (2006), the UNCRC is silent over the question of formal/non-formal education, although the Committee established to monitor the convention interprets the right as relating to both. The Jomtien Declaration also acknowledges a role for non-formal in addition to formal education (Article V).

Consideration of these different forms of non-formal education raises the question of means and ends. In some cases non-formal education appears just a more effective route to the same goals as formal schooling, and a replacement route for those who missed out. In others it provides a different form of education so as to achieve a different end, with aims distinct from those of the school system.

In many cases non-formal education is culturally sensitive, educationally relevant and politically engaged – providing a more meaningful experience than that available in formal institutions. Yet despite the availability and often the quality of non-formal education, school appears as strong as ever in the countries in which the institution was already established when Illich was writing in the 1970s, and has since made significant inroads into regions previously untouched by modern Western institutions. There are possible nefarious reasons for the expansion of school systems, so as to ensure the spread of global capitalism and the necessary attitudes to support it (although the latter could be supported through other mechanisms of media in the absence of school). Whatever the negative effects of schools, there are in fact a range of valid reasons for not abandoning them. First, from a pragmatic perspective, they enable instruction of large numbers of children, through a methodical curriculum and one that can be replicated for all and that lends itself to monitoring and regulation. Second, the more ad hoc learning that would take place in the absence of school is likely to benefit the privileged, given the extra difficulty that disadvantaged groups (through lack of resources and lower educational level themselves) would have in organizing learning opportunities for their children. So there is an argument for schools from the perspective of equality of opportunity. Third, schools allow for sustained interaction between an individual and diverse others in society, in a way that may not happen if children are only learning within the family and with acquaintances. (Of course, in practice schools are very often segregated according to social class, race/ethnicity or ability, but at least the potential is there for this kind of social mixing.)

Whatever the strength or weakness of the arguments on both sides, the undeniable fact is that families are choosing schooling for their children all over the world, even when alternatives exist. There are a range of possible explanations, from ill-informed choice (if families dismiss traditional education and endorse formal education purely out of prejudice or internalization of colonial norms), to a keen understanding that the school system, whatever its defects, unlocks the door to positional advantage and to essential life opportunities.

Some empirical illustrations will be of use here. King-Calneck (2006), for example, explores the educational work of the Brazilian percussion group Olodum. In addition to its musical work, Olodum since 1991 has run educational programmes as part of its broader mission to promote African Brazilian identity and culture, to campaign against discrimination and prevent the absorption of young black people into crime and drugs violence. These activities serve children from kindergarten to teenagers and young adults who have dropped out of school, and are free of charge. While Olodum for a time provided conventional primary school classes, for the most part educational activities have been run in parallel to the formal system. Students can study computing, English language or cultural activities such as painting, music and puppetry, all infused with aspects of African Brazilian culture and history. This focus allows the children to develop understanding of and positive attitudes towards their heritage – one which is systematically ignored and devalued in the mainstream school curriculum. It is clear that these activities are fulfilling the right to education, through enhancing children's knowledge and understanding of their culture, developing work skills and the ability to live fulfilling lives through cultural and artistic expression, via educational processes which respect their human rights.

Nevertheless, there is no question of these children and their families choosing this form of education in place of the formal system. In fact, there is abundant evidence from around the world that parents are reluctant to move to non-formal education in place of the formal system, even when it is more meaningful, relevant, enjoyable and effective than the available schools. In Dyer's (2000) study of Rabari pastoralists in Western India, the community rejected peripatetic non-formal education that appeared to fit well with their working patterns, in favour of sedentary formal education, even though the latter schools were perceived as being of poor quality. It is clear that the positional advantages gained through the formal system are considered indispensable in many cases, even in the absence of meaningful learning. As Dore (1976: 3) put it, 'Who would not want a visa into the bridge-head zone?' There is also a sense that initiation into the esoteric rituals of formal schooling enable understanding of other esoteric rituals in a modern bureaucratic society:

> Parents constantly reiterated that their children should 'improve' (*sudhare*) and become 'clever' (*hoshiar*), qualities that Rabaris associate with people who attend formal schools. Schools are also seen as places where people go to learn 'how to talk'. Knowing 'how to talk' seemed to represent for the Rabaris liberation from feeling disempowered and intimidated by modern institutions. (Dyer 2000: 246)

Valuable learning experiences can be gained in a variety of settings. However, informal and non-formal education rarely leads to the type of certification that grants positional advantage to individuals, with 'success' in the formal system in most societies being key to desirable employment and other valuable opportunities. However much one learns through non-formal education, and whatever the knowledge, skills and understanding one has, these opportunities are not available in most societies without this certification. This means that the right to education must acknowledge in some way the 'sorting' aspect of formal education.

There are, however, problems with conceiving the positional aspect of education as a right. For example, one of the key aspects of positionality is certification, with qualifications being essential for opportunities and influence in most contemporary societies. Yet, it is difficult to include them in the *right* to education since they normally function as a sorting mechanism for the employment market and higher levels of education, and to make them universally available would destroy their raison d'être. Yet while there cannot be a right to qualifications, it could be argued that there is a right not to be unfairly denied the opportunity to achieve them and access to the opportunities currently made available by them. People, in this way, would have a right not to suffer unfair positional disadvantage from schooling (or lack of it). These ideas will be taken up again in the final chapter.

Nevertheless, while we must pay attention to the role of contemporary school systems as sorting mechanisms for society, it is a contingent role and not one intrinsic to education. The right to education itself relates to engagement in meaningful learning processes – and it is these that we must use as our criteria for deciding whether to endorse the institution of school or abandon it. In this, the position presented in this book is similar to that put forward by the World Bank in its 2020 strategy, which argues for attention to learning in multiple spheres, whether inside or outside school. That is where the similarity ends, however, as the World Bank vision is one that prioritizes the economic over all other areas, lacks an ethical dimension and leaves little space for critical reflection.

But which processes?

The preceding sections have outlined an argument for attention to process in education. Yet is it any process that counts or only some? And how can we distinguish between them? R. S. Peters (1996) in his influential analysis of the concept of education proposed that while education can involve a very large range of different activities, these are constrained by moral considerations: the need to conform to the attributes of *wittingness* – the student has to be aware that she is being educated, and *voluntariness* – the student has to want to take part in the process (though this does not exclude coercion altogether). These two principles remove from our consideration processes of conditioning and indoctrination.

However, Peters's conceptual mapping above provides outer limits on what we can reasonably describe as education rather than presenting a specific normative proposal. Some writers addressing the right to education have instead proposed specific processes. Spring's (2000: 114) proposals for the universal right to education acknowledge process in addition to content:

> Because the right to education is justified by the need for people to weigh the advantages and disadvantages of the world's economy and culture, then access to the knowledge of that economy and culture and freedom to think about it are necessary for fulfilling this right. Liberty rights protect students from educational systems that are indoctrinating, propagandizing, nationalistic, and discriminatory.

While literacy and numeracy are central to Spring's vision, the emphasis here is not on achievement levels, but the educational experience itself: 'My intent is to provide the right to an education that maximizes the opportunity for all people to engage in this quest [for the good life]' (p. 156). Among the processes he proposes are the use of fantasy and imagination, with learners developing visions of alternative organization of society. Spring has a particular justification for the right to education (the predicament of indigenous groups in a globalized world) and proposes processes that link in with the need to be grounded in one's own culture and both to understand and be able to influence the global system.

Another theorist proposing a view of education as a human right based in part on process is Vandenberg (1990). This approach is an example of 'harmony' in the sense of establishing a consonance between the overarching ideals of the educational undertaking (in this case moral agency and human dignity), and its day-to-day workings. In addition to proposals concerning knowledge, the author argues that the 'hidden curriculum' must be imbued with human rights, through democratic values and a fair rule-set:

> The classroom as a community of scholars under law dedicated to maximising the learning of each student should be structured by the human rights to freedom, equal consideration, and brotherly and sisterly love to establish dialogical relations among students in an atmosphere of affection. (p. 93)

These schemes address the 'universal' right to education, but to what extent are they the same for everyone, and is there justification for any stipulation that is universal? Vandenberg (1990) explicitly frames his proposal for the right on the basis of its universality, recovering substantive human values in response to what he sees as the nihilism and moral relativism of the contemporary age. On the other hand, Karmel (2009) notes that the requirement for the 'full development of the human personality' in the legal right to education makes essential a degree of individualization of the curriculum, and guards against universal standardisation.

The universal nature of human rights generally speaking has been a source of critique from those fearing a smuggled-in Western bias or undermining of local cultures. Does the right to education as a right to educational processes deal more effectively with the problems of universality? Whatever process is selected, it is always possible to claim that it originates in a particular culture, or among a particular group within a culture and so dismiss its universal validity on that basis. Yet the inherently open nature of the processes in mind here means that they fare better than 'content' and 'objectives' in this respect. Dialogical and deliberative education can provide a space for difference in the context of universal entitlements. As Enslin and Tjiattas (2009) argue, we should not be faced with a choice between a crude universalism and restrictive particularism. Karmel (2009) actually bases his account of the right to education on the collected views of educators, demonstrating in practice this aspect of the construction of the right through interchange of views (although showing that in fact teachers were not generally engaged in such reflection and discussion). Process approaches also allow for incorporation of both indigenous (or local) knowledge systems, and standard academic modes within the curriculum.

There will inevitably be space for local diversity in the materialization of the right to education. To some extent education depends on what is meaningful for individuals and groups, and will vary in accordance with interests and needs. Education will also express itself in different ways within different cultures and languages. This diversity is acknowledged by the Jomtien Declaration: 'The scope of basic learning needs and how they should be met varies with individual countries and cultures, and inevitably, changes with the passage of time' (Article 1, Part 1). However, there are universal principles within which this diversity sits. Peters expresses these principles in a minimalist sense: education must be 'witting' and 'voluntary', that is to say, it cannot be mindless drill, nor indoctrination; the processes through which education is conducted must also be 'moral', in the sense of conforming the full set of human rights, as will be explored in the following chapter.

The purpose of this chapter is not to outline in detail my own vision of educational processes, but rather to establish the contours within which such visions can be drawn. In addition, as argued above, there are multiple possible valid visions, among which are those set forth by Spring, Vandenberg, etc. Nevertheless, some laying of my own cards on the table is necessary. In line with the justifications of *understanding* and *agency* put forward in the previous chapter, education at best involves an opening of the mind towards the world, as well as enhanced capacities for acting. The educator, therefore, provides learners with opportunities to reflect on themselves and the outside world, to act within it, and in turn to reflect on that action. Feelings, emotions and values imbue both understanding and agency. Following Freire (1972), the relationship of reflection and action has the characteristics of a dialectic, with the movement to and from each leading to ever higher realizations. Through acting within the world, experiencing life and interacting with others we gain vital understanding; and that understanding feeds into more purposeful, skilful and ethical action. These ideas will be drawn out more fully in the latter stages of the book.

There are, of course, difficulties with a process approach. It is much harder to monitor than a focus on, say, primary schooling or specific learning outcomes (although cogent pointers are put forward by Alexander [2008]). It also depends upon high levels of teacher motivation and initiative. If badly implemented, it can drift without direction. It is quite understandable, therefore, that those engaged in achieving EFA by 2015 discard it in favour of the familiar and tangible schooling. However, this pragmatic compromise should not be confused with a principled choice. The implications of this tension for policy and practice will be drawn out in Chapter 9, but next we turn to one of the key features of educational processes highlighted in this chapter: the infringement and upholding of the full set of human rights within educational institutions and experiences.

Notes

1   For the purposes of this study, formal education is taken to be synonymous with schooling, whether provided by the state or a private body, although following Rogers (2004) it is acknowledged that there are significant difficulties in providing a satisfactory definition of formal as opposed to non-formal education. A useful

definition is provided by the *Council of Europe Charter on Education for Democratic Citizenship* and Human Rights Education:

> […] 'Formal education' means the structured education and training system that runs from pre-primary and primary through secondary school and on to university. It takes place, as a rule, at general or vocational educational institutions and leads to certification.
>
> […] 'Non-formal education' means any planned programme of education designed to improve a range of skills and competences, outside the formal educational setting.
>
> […] 'Informal education' means the lifelong process whereby every individual acquires attitudes, values, skills and knowledge from the educational influences and resources in his or her own environment and from daily experience (family, peer group, neighbours, encounters, library, mass media, work, play, etc.).

2 Progressive realization of this right, even at primary level, is accepted in the case of states with insufficient resources.

3 Smith (2000), for example, adds in a fourth model termed 'praxis', referring to approaches with an explicit commitment to emancipation.

4 An exception to this is the discussion of pluralistic curricula within the 'acceptability' criterion, which might be considered a positive embodiment of underlying principles, as is reference to 'the acceptability of content from the perspective of promoting gender equality, the recognition of the religious identities of members of distinct communities' in Wilson (2004: 9).

5 The World Bank does acknowledge the importance of 'process' in converting inputs into learning outcomes: but understands these processes as occurring at a more distant level of provision – namely incentives for providers and vouchers, rather than something connected with the educational processes themselves.

6 According to Smith (2011), there are four aspects of Illich's critique of the institution of school: institutionalization itself, the notion of expertise, commodification and the counter-productivity argument whereby the institution actually works against the service it is supposed to promote.

5

Upholding Human Rights within Education

In many parts of the world, and for much of history, it has been considered quite normal for education to be underpinned by fear of physical punishment and humiliation. Even today, only 60 per cent of the world's children live in countries in which corporal punishment is prohibited in schools (Global Initiative to End All Corporal Punishment of Children 2010). Nevertheless, practices have changed significantly in recent years, and these changes have been given support by the CRC, and the adoption of rights-based approaches by a number of international agencies. Yet the conceptual basis of the upholding of the rights of learners (both children and adults) within educational institutions and experiences remains nebulous. As seen in Chapter 2, the UDHR proposes certain general *aims* for education – 'the strengthening of respect for human rights', 'promote understanding, tolerance and friendship', etc. – yet does not address the *processes* or *experiences* of school and other forms of education, and the ways these may infringe or uphold the full range of human rights. This chapter aims to address this omission by assessing the possible justifications for the upholding of human rights within education.

Most studies of rights in education focus on the specific rights that apply, and the ways of best implementing and enforcing them. This chapter addresses the prior question of why it is that we should uphold rights within education (beyond the right *to* education and rights *through* education). Facing up to this complex question head-on will enable both a rebuttal of critics of human rights in education, and a closer understanding of how best to work with rights in an educational context.

There are two potential objections to upholding rights within education. First, there is scepticism of human rights per se, questioning the basis of rights claims in any context. These general questions (summarized in Chapter 1) have been discussed extensively elsewhere (e.g. Beitz 2009; Bobbio 1996; Cornwall and Molyneux 2008; Sen 2004) with objections to rights including their lack of a 'natural' basis, doubts about their application to welfare as well as liberty, the patriarchal nature of rights schemes and their Western roots. The main focus in this chapter, however, will be on the specifically educational application of these debates, addressing the second question of whether (accepting the general validity of human rights) it is essential or desirable to uphold them within educational undertakings. The position might, for example, hold that the 'ends justify the means', with the future benefits of general learning or even learning about human rights justifying restriction of those rights during the process of education.

The discussion in this chapter relates mainly to the upholding of the whole range of rights within education, rather than the right to education itself (in the sense of *access*) or to 'human rights education' in the sense of developing knowledge and understanding of human rights declarations and conventions. There are, nevertheless, strong links between the three, as will be discussed below. Much of the analysis relates to schools – since they are the focal point of relevant literature and initiatives – although the arguments apply equally to other forms of education, and to adults as well as children.

The distinction between 'status-based' and 'instrumental' justifications for rights will be revisited, followed by an outline of how these approaches manifest themselves within education. A further distinction is made between instrumental approaches that might undermine the nature of rights, and those that can be complementary. Following assessment of justifications underpinning contemporary educational work, a normative argument is put forward based on the upholding and learning of rights as a conjoined realization. This conception allows us to work with rights in educational institutions in a way that attends to their dual nature as arenas of society in their own right, and sites of preparation for life in society.

General justifications for rights

In Chapter 3 we saw how human rights generally speaking can be justified in different ways. On the one hand, these rights can be seen to stem from essential characteristics of human beings, such as their rationality, or their dignity, or in religious traditions their creation by God. These characteristics provide a deontological basis for rights, meaning that we are bound to uphold them regardless of consequences.

Instrumental justifications, on the other hand, look precisely to these consequences as the basis for rights. It is justifiable in this sense to uphold human rights because they lead to desirable outcomes for individuals and society, to greater well-being and less suffering, or some other form of benefit. In this second approach, there does not need to be a natural basis for rights, nor universal characteristics of the human that would give rise to them. Both of these approaches have their merits, and extreme versions of either are largely untenable – some authors (e.g. Sen) have tried to bring the two together in a single conception. This book adopts a largely status-based position, but one that allows consideration of consequences, when those consequences relate to the areas of concern pertinent to human rights themselves – for example, enhancement of agency, protection from suffering and so forth.

An area of particular relevance for this chapter is that of children's rights. The specific rights of children had been recognised as early as the Declaration of the Rights of the Child of 1924, but only received comprehensive treatment in the CRC of 1989. Nevertheless, despite this legal recognition, and wide ratification, these rights remain controversial and patchily implemented in most countries. The first concern is over whether children need a different set of rights from adult human beings. In response to this concern, Brighouse (2002) identifies three justifications for a special set of rights for children: they are dependent on adults for their welfare, they are vulnerable to the decisions of others, and are in a phase of rapid development of their capacities. The possession of all three of these characteristics distinguishes children from adults and justifies a distinct set of rights.

The second concern is whether children can be rights-holders at all, given their limited agency (there being in the concept of 'right' an element of active exercising, rather than simply receiving a benefit). In the CRC, while children are not accorded the same self-determination rights as adults, they are entitled to express their opinions, and have those opinions heard and taken into account in matters affecting them in accordance with their age and maturity. A similar principle could apply to the exercising of rights generally speaking, with a process of transition through which children move from a more passive receipt of care to a more agentic role. A further point is that arguments are put forward for restricting people's rights during their childhood, so as to enhance their opportunities in later life. This view is particularly relevant to education. So the argument goes, it is so fundamental for children to acquire good habits, develop particular skills and other characteristics, that it is justifiable to restrict their freedom and coerce them in particular ways.

There is limited validity to this final point, but considerable care must be taken. It is certainly untenable to claim that no coercion can be exercised in relation to children: of course, a 2-year-old child must be prevented from running into a road with cars speeding past. Certainly, responsible adults should encourage children to spend time developing characteristics that will benefit them in the future, as well as the present. Yet these considerations do not open the door for a complete ignoring of the will and views of children. This last point is particularly relevant to education, since many abusive activities in schools – such as corporal punishment, humiliation, and extreme stress – are routinely justified on the basis of their future benefits. The discussions presented in this chapter, therefore, are particularly pertinent to the education of children, although the same principles also apply to adult education in its various forms.

Human rights infringements within education

Before assessing the implications of status and instrumental justifications for education, it is important to assess whether we are warranted in being concerned about the upholding of rights within educational experiences. While schooling and other forms of education are positive experiences for many, there is no doubt that considerable harm is inflicted in some cases, with a wide range of violations assessed in works such as Wilson (2004), Harber (2004) and Tomaševski (2001b). This section will provide a brief overview of these infringements.

Attention to rights violations in education frequently focus on the 'right *to* education'. Discrimination is strongly evident within both individual institutions and whole education systems. Well-known historical cases of discrimination include segregation of schools in the southern states of the United States, the separate and poorly funded Bantu education system in Apartheid South Africa. Furthermore, many if not most education systems display de facto if not de jure discrimination on the basis of socio-economic background, as well as ethnicity, religion, disability and gender. Exclusion from education also occurs commonly in the case of non-national migrants and refugees (Wilson 2004). In a number of African countries, becoming pregnant can result in temporary and often permanent exclusion from school for girls (Tomaševski 2001b). There are also controversies in European countries concerning the banning of forms of religious clothing in schools (Gereluk 2008).

However, there are also considerable violations of the 'rights *within* education' variety too. Perceptions of the darker side of schooling are captured memorably in Pink Floyd's song 'The Wall'. Educational institutions can be violent places, both in terms of institutionally sanctioned punishments, as well as other forms of violence between students, between teachers and students, and involving others from outside. Unterhalter's (2003) research on South Africa, for example, has shown the dangers to girls of subjection to sexual violence in schools, with the associated risks of contracting HIV/AIDS. These forms of gender-based violence have been extensively documented elsewhere (e.g. Bhana 2005; Leach and Mitchell 2006; Parkes and Heslop 2011). Children with disabilities suffer not only limited access, but also restrictions and indignities within the school (Rioux and Pinto 2010). Bullying, with its physical and psychological aspects, has been a prominent concern in high-income contexts such as the United Kingdom, United States and Japan.

Some human rights infringements relate specifically to educational processes. As stated above, corporal punishment is still endemic across the world (Global Initiative to End All Corporal Punishment of Children 2010; Wilson 2004). Even when not subjected to physical violence, pupils can endure humiliation by teachers and other pupils on account of difficulties in learning. Children and adults also suffer extreme stress in systems in which high stakes testing is common (Harber 2004; Spring 2000; Tomaševski 2001b). Indoctrination is a form of teaching that can be considered in itself a human rights infringement, given the negation of agency and self-determination. Education can never be politically or morally neutral (Freire 1972), yet there are differences in the extent to which worldviews are imposed on students, or alternatively they can form their own position in response to the views being presented. Conversely, instead of being imposed on students, information and diverse perspectives can be withheld through censorship, constituting an infringement of freedom of information. Controversies of this sort are most commonly seen in relation to interpretations of national history (Tomaševski 2001b).

The curricula of many education systems also serve systematically to undermine the cultures of minority (or in some cases majority) groups. Textbooks are particularly significant in this respect – as they are in relation to gender, sexuality and other bases on which discrimination takes place. In the Andean region, for example, education policy during the twentieth century was based on an explicit commitment to cultural and linguistic homogeneity in order to convert the large indigenous population into Spanish-speaking peasants (García 2004; Howard 2009). In postcolonial contexts, the undermining of culture can continue long after the colonizers have physically departed, with Mazrui (1975), for example, documenting the continuing presence in African universities of Latin, Ancient Greek and European mediaeval history but not African languages and philosophy.

Language is a central part of cultural marginalization. Lack of educational provision in the mother tongue of a local community not only serves to lessen students' chances of meaningful learning, but also to erode the viability of the language in the broader society. In Bolivian schools, for example, instruction has until recent reforms been predominantly in Spanish (Howard 2009), despite 36.5 per cent of the population having an indigenous language as their mother tongue – and two of these, Quechua and Aymara, with many millions of speakers across the Andean region. Numerous examples can be found of the suppression or lack of recognition of local languages in schools, such as Kurdish in Syria or Albanian in 1990s Kosovo, with over 200 million children across the world unable to study in their first language (Pinnock 2009). In addition to direct ways in which the curriculum can infringe rights, there are also many indirect ways such as promotion of racism and sexism, or incitement to genocide, extensively explored in Davies (2004).

Finally, while this chapter is focusing on learners, the human rights of teachers and others involved in education also need to be remembered. Teachers' rights can be infringed when they are excluded from organizing trade unions (Wilson 2004) – or targeted for persecution on account of their membership of a teachers' union, as is the case currently in Colombia – and when they suffer harsh working conditions and subjection to physical and verbal abuse.

Human rights violations in education are, therefore, a serious concern, particularly in impoverished countries with meagre resources, poor security and ineffective legislation, but in many instances also in high-income countries. As well as protecting from these abuses, it is important to remember the positive ways in which human rights can be promoted within education, for instance 'celebration and nurturing of learner creativity, use of local languages in schools, pupil participation in democratic structures and debate' (Tikly and Barrett 2009: 3), or in the pedagogical principles derived from the CRC put forward by Osler and Starkey (2005): dignity and security; participation; identity and inclusivity; freedom; access to information and privacy. These positive aspects are central to some of the current initiatives reviewed below.

Status-based approaches

What then are the implications of the status-based and instrumental justifications for human rights within education? When assessing status-based approaches, it is not always the case that the justifications are based on a clearly defined attribute of the human being warranting unconditional rights, but that these rights are considered necessary to uphold through their intrinsic merit, rather than any positive consequences.

There are two closely related aspects of the status-based approach when applying human rights to education:

1. The instantiation argument
2. The indivisibility argument.

Instantiation

The first aspect of the status-based approach is that it sees educational institutions and spaces as arenas of society in their own right. Schools, universities, and other educational undertakings are *instantiations* of society, and not just sites of preparation for it. This means that the rights that normally apply to individuals are applicable, and no special justification is needed. So, if people have the right to be free from physical aggression, rape, psychological abuse and other forms of degrading treatment, they have that right within educational institutions too.

Indivisibility, interrelatedness and interdependence

The second aspect involves the assertion that the full set of human rights is indivisible, and consequently the right to education must be compatible with other rights. The indivisibility of human rights is particularly emphasized in the CRC (Hart et al. 2001). The Convention is *comprehensive* in that it covers all forms of rights together, and as Verhellen (1993: 201) states, 'formulating all these rights in one instrument, it reflects the tendency to regard all rights as indivisible and mutually reinforcing in response to human needs'. This notion is sometimes expressed in terms of 'overlapping rights' (e.g. Coomans 2007: 3), with the right to education overlapping with others such as non-discrimination, freedom of religion, privacy, and cultural rights of minority and indigenous groups. However, there is potential overlap with every expressed right.

As discussed above, one particularly controversial area in education is the potential for formal education to undermine local and indigenous culture and languages. The notion of *indivisibility* ensures that we are not faced with a trade-off between, say, employment opportunities opened up by mainstream schools, and loss of cultural integrity: both of these interests need to be addressed. The provisions of the Convention against Discrimination in Education of 1960 states as follows.

Article 5

(c) It is essential to recognize the right of members of national minorities to carry on their own educational activities, including the maintenance of schools and, depending on the educational policy of each State, the use or the teaching of their own language, provided however:

  (i) That this right is not exercised in a manner which prevents the members of these minorities from understanding the culture and language of the community as a whole and from participating in its activities, or which prejudices national sovereignty;

  (ii) That the standard of education is not lower than the general standard laid down or approved by the competent authorities; and

  (iii) That attendance at such schools is optional.

The right of access to education must, in this way, remain 'undivided' from the right to cultural integrity. It is important to look not only at rights instruments pertaining to education, but also those with other foci, such as the UN Declaration on the Rights of Indigenous Peoples (2007), which states as follows.

Article 14

1. Indigenous peoples have the right to establish and control their educational systems and institutions providing education in their own languages, in a manner appropriate to their cultural methods of teaching and learning.

2. Indigenous individuals, particularly children, have the right to all levels and forms of education of the State without discrimination.

3. States shall, in conjunction with indigenous peoples, take effective measures, in order for indigenous individuals, particularly children, including those living outside their communities, to have access, when possible, to an education in their own culture and provided in their own language.

In both of these provisions we can observe attention both to difference and to universality, to the rights to maintain specific cultures, but also not to lose the universal entitlements that those from majority communities enjoy.

The approach of indivisibility, interrelatedness and interdependence is displayed in the work of the late UN Special Rapporteur for the right to education, Katarina Tomaševski. In Tomaševski (2001b: 8), for example, the assessment of the upholding of human rights within education stems from the question 'when is the right to education fully realized?': the conceptualization of the fulfilment of the right necessarily involves the fulfilment of the other rights (i.e. indivisibility). This approach is also found in the '4 As' scheme (Tomaševski 2006), in which the elements of availability, accessibility, acceptability and adaptability depend on the upholding of the full range of human rights.

There are particular ways in which education might be related to and dependent on other rights, and likewise other rights related to and dependent on it. There are certain prerequisites to education, such as adequate nutrition, health and so forth; it is unlikely that much meaningful learning will take place if a learner is cold, hungry and scared. Furthermore, understanding of rights is strongly dependent on the knowledge and skills gained through education, as is the effective exercising of those rights in society, and the upholding and defence of the rights of others.

This approach commands wide acceptance from those involved in human rights work, based as it is on established international agreements, and with a coherent conceptual basis. However, the challenges facing status-based approaches generally speaking is that they are easy to dismiss if there is not an acceptance of the basic premise that there are attributes of the human being that entail us having rights. In addition, they may not exercise strong influence on policymakers, with governments facing financial constraints potentially swayed more by arguments of effectiveness than those of principle, even when endorsing apparently entitlement-based policies such as EFA. As discussed below, this challenge has caused a number of proponents to couch their arguments in terms of positive results even if they have a status-based orientation themselves.

Instrumental approaches

The upholding of rights within education can also be justified in terms of the benefits brought. Some of these benefits are for the individual rights-holders themselves, and some are for a collective such as the school, the community or society as a whole. Again, some of these justifications see rights within education as a means of attaining general benefits, and some educational benefits specifically. However, the most important distinction that will be made here is between instrumental justifications that relate in some way to the upholding of rights, and those that are irrelevant to or even inimical to rights. I will argue that, while instrumental approaches are not necessarily flawed, the justifications in the latter case are the source of considerable concern.

Instrumental: Learning rights

human rights can be incorporated in the educational experience as a means of bringing about learning. (The proponents of learning via human rights may or may not also endorse the non-instrumental justifications for the upholding of these rights.) As will be discussed in the extended treatment of human rights education in Chapter 8, this approach is seen by some to be more effective than simply developing knowledge of human rights legislation and developing particular skills relating to their promotion. As Lansdown (2001: 35) states, 'Democracy cannot be taught in an undemocratic environment'. Students are seen to adopt values more deeply when they see them working in practice and engage in them themselves, and it is important that they see teachers and the institution as a whole 'practising what they preach'. As Howe and Covell (2005: 12) state in relation to democracy:

> Students are unlikely to learn democratic values and behaviours unless these are present throughout the school. The importance of democratic rights, values, and behaviours must be reflected in both the formal curricula, through explicit teaching, and throughout the hidden curriculum, as embodied in school structures, codes of conduct, mission statements, and classroom interactions that model democracy and respect for the rights of all.

One prominent aspect of the rights promoted by these instrumental approaches is children's (and adults') participation in decision-making. Participation is perhaps the most distinctive (and most controversial) aspect of the rights contained in the CRC. These participation rights have significant implications for the school setting, in which children's views have historically been ignored. In fact, there have been widespread calls for greater pupil participation in school (e.g. Cox et al. 2010; Flutter and Ruddock 2004; Macbeath and Moos 2004), although not all from the perspective of children's rights. A large part of the justification for this participation is in fact instrumental, the experience of involvement in decision-making being seen as an opportunity to develop knowledge, skills and values relating to subsequent democratic citizenship.

There are some contemporary examples of initiatives that aim to embody human rights – those of participation and others – so as to enhance pupils' learning (e.g. McEvoy and Lundy 2007). Much of this activity is focused on integrating the CRC into schools' activities, as promoted by UNICEF's Rights Respecting Schools Award scheme in the United Kingdom, and more broadly across the world its Child Friendly Schools, Amnesty International's Human Rights Friendly Schools and UNESCO's Associated Schools Project Network.

For example, the *Rights, Respect and Responsibility* initiative in the county of Hampshire in England, according to Covell (2010: 40):

> is exemplary not only in its incorporation of specific children's rights information across the formal curriculum, but also because of its integration of children's rights across the hidden curriculum – the modelling of respect for the child's rights in all aspects of the school social and regulatory function.

The CRC is seen in this initiative to be an effective code for behaviour in school, providing a basis in globally agreed values, and avoiding moral relativism. Importantly, this behaviour code is developed with input from pupils and there are a range of other opportunities for children's participation, as well as use of democratic forms of teaching.

While the initiative has a status-based underpinning in its emphasis on the unconditional nature of children's rights, it also appeals to the greater efficacy of rights-based approaches in bringing about student learning and other positive forms of attitude and behaviour. In particular, it is seen to be more efficacious than other approaches to Citizenship teaching in England, involving either fragmented content, teaching of skills that are not transferable into other areas, a perceived emphasis on negatives such as racism, or reading of 'virtue stories' that may be interpreted in unpredictable ways (Massey 2003). Covell and Howe (2001) make similar arguments in favour of human rights over other approaches to moral education and values teaching. Furthermore, the appeal to consequences in this case is a deliberate response to the popular perceptions of negative effects of upholding children's rights in schools (i.e. undermining of teacher authority, 'anarchic classrooms and unruly children' [Covell 2010: 48]).

Another important element is that, 'In learning about rights they learn that all children have the same rights, unconditionally' (Massey 2003: 3). This point can be seen as a particularly strong justification for the incorporation of rights within educational experiences. The actual experience of living within a rights respecting environment will mean that learners have to understand how their own actions must be modified in order to uphold the rights of others, in a way that would not be possible if they were simply taught *about* rights. According to Massey (2003), experiencing conflict between rights can also lead to the development of higher-order thinking skills. Covell and Howe (2001) argue that learning about rights enhances self-esteem, and that this positive view of the self enables greater respect for others and guards against victimization of minorities. The authors describe as a 'contagion effect' this movement from learning about one's own rights to increased support for the rights of others. Empirical research on this initiative confirms that it is effective in 'increasing children's enjoyment of school, self-esteem, academic motivation, respect for the rights of others, prosocial behaviours, and levels of participation' (Covell 2010: 41). Furthermore, the three-year evaluation of UNICEF's Rights Respecting Schools Award across the United Kingdom showed significant effects relating to: knowledge and understanding of the CRC; relationships and behaviour; empowerment to respect the environment and rights of others locally, nationally and globally; positive attitudes towards inclusivity and diversity in society; participation in decision-making in the school community; and improved learning and standards (Sebba and Robinson 2010). In contrast, the lack of these learning opportunities in non-inclusive schools are highlighted by Rioux and Pinto (2010: 635):

> Importantly too, exclusionary or disrespectful practices towards children with different levels of abilities in school are viewed as having consequences not just for the students but for all learners. Deprived from the early experience of respectfully dealing with and accepting disability as part of human diversity, non-disabled children will more probably become adults who will themselves reproduce, instead of combating, prejudicial and discriminatory practices towards persons with disabilities and their place in society.

While learning benefits are the most common in the literature, there may be other instrumental justifications for upholding rights within education. One of these is the potential positive effect on the rest of society of the very existence of these 'oases' of respect for rights. In this way, other schools and other forms of institution could be inspired by these examples and change their practice. This idea can be seen in the notion of 'prefigurative' spaces as exemplars, as discussed in McCowan (2010). One of the justifications for prefiguring a just, democratic society within political movements is that the latter can act as a beacon of hope of what is possible in the present and future.

Instrumental: Non-rights-based goals

The main problem with instrumental justifications for rights generally speaking is that since they depend on contingent relationships, the rights can be discarded if other means are observed to be more effective. The idea of rights being disposable in this way rather challenges our fundamental conception of their nature. Yet at least the forms of instrumental justification outlined above are strengthening the development of respect for human rights in society generally speaking. There are, however, instrumental approaches that could be either irrelevant to or even detrimental to the promotion of human rights.

As seen in the previous chapter, the Jomtien Declaration in this way appears to advocate participatory approaches as a means of achieving better cognitive outcomes. Learning acquisition, of course, is a good thing, but the danger is that participatory approaches are *only* valued insofar as they are successful in this respect. If learning is gauged primarily by scores on Mathematics and national language tests – as it often is – then there may be evidence that in some cases success is linked to traditional didactic pedagogy and harsh discipline. Furthermore, it is absolutely possible for one to develop a high level of basic skills and simultaneously develop intolerance for human rights. In relation to the types of learning valued, the requirement in the Dakar education goals underpinning current EFA initiatives that 'recognized and measurable learning outcomes are achieved by all' to a large extent militates against the affective aspects of human rights learning, given the difficulties in developing standardized quantitative measures.

Rights-based approaches to education more broadly are also justified instrumentally in terms of general international development goals. UNICEF/ UNESCO (2007) provides a range of justifications for a rights-based approach:

> Needs-based development approaches to education have, to date, failed to achieve the Education for All goals. Because it is inclusive and provides a common language for partnership, a rights-based approach – although certainly not without tensions and challenges – has the potential to contribute to the attainment of the goals of governments, parents and children. Girls' right to education, for example, can be achieved more effectively if measures are also implemented to address their rights to freedom from discrimination, protection from exploitative labour, physical violence and sexual abuse, and access to an adequate standard of living. (p. 11)

This passage shows evidence of the aspect of interdependence of rights discussed above. However, while the report provides a very welcome endorsement of rights-based approaches, there are questions concerning the ways the benefits are framed. Justifications are presented that focus on the development and efficiency concerns of governments – but without a clear link to rights at all. The document states:

> Treating children with dignity and respect – and building inclusive, participatory and accountable education systems that respond directly to the expressed concerns of all stakeholders – will serve to improve educational outcomes. In too

many schools, the failure to adapt to the needs of children, particularly working
children, results in high levels of dropout and repeated grades. (p. 12)

Reducing dropout and repetition are laudable aims, but are here justified not
in terms of the rights of learner but by being 'cost-effective and sustainable'.
In addition, a rights-based approach is seen to 'produces better outcomes for
economic development':

> Measures to promote universal access to education and overcome discrimination
> against girls, children with disabilities, working children, children in rural
> communities, and minority and indigenous children will serve to widen the
> economic base of society, thus strengthening a country's economic capability.
> (p. 13)

It is far from conclusive that rights-based approaches do actually produce better
economic outcomes: there have been many historical examples of rapid national
economic growth brought about in conjunction with (and possibly because of)
abuses of human rights. The point is that human rights must be upheld whether
or not they contribute to macro-economic growth, so justifying them in terms
of economic benefits is potentially dangerous.

A partially instrumental approach is also shown in Lansdown (2001). While
the author endorses the 'principled' argument for humans rights in education,
she also proposes 'pragmatic' ones, namely: enhancing the skills necessary
for the world of work and creating effective schools. It seems likely that these
instrumental justifications are provided to encourage governments that might
otherwise be sceptical of rights to adopt these approaches. However, this 'icing
on the cake' approach of dressing up principled arguments in pragmatic terms
is not without its dangers. The rights-based approaches may be abandoned if
others appear to be more efficacious.

While the documents reviewed above are based on a genuine commitment
to rights, there are a number of ways in which governments and schools might
promote rights-based approaches without a genuine concern for the rights
of individuals and groups involved. Participation, for example, can serve to
legitimize an authority's decision-making, while not allowing real influence of
the participants – corresponding to Hart's (1992) first three rungs of the ladder
of participation, from 'manipulation', through 'decoration' to 'tokenism': as he
states, 'Children are undoubtedly the most photographed and the least listened
to members of society' (p. 9).

Given that educational experiences are by definition a preparation for
something outside of themselves (in addition to being valid experiences in

themselves), it is unavoidable that instrumental concerns will come into play. The problem is that if we go too far down the road of instrumentalism, these arguments could be used very easily to *restrict* rights in schools. If we take as our measure of educational outcomes the results on basic skills tests, there could even be 'justification' for the reintroduction of corporal punishment in schools – although in practice the most common response is the establishment of a stressful environment of regular high-stakes assessment, with little room for broader aesthetic and emotional development. A purely instrumental approach of this sort is, therefore, clearly insufficient. It must always be seen in conjunction with the fundamental entitlements associated with persons as ends in themselves.

*

There have been two intentions in this chapter. First, the grounds for upholding human rights within education have been explored, in relation to status-based (deontological) and instrumental (consequentialist) approaches. Neither of these is seen to have a monopoly on justifications, and as argued by Sen (1982) both can be taken into consideration. Specifically in relation to education, human rights must be upheld in the learning environment just as they would be in any other environment (instantiation), and because educational rights cannot be separated from the full range of other rights (indivisibility, interrelatedness and interdependence). A rights-respecting environment can also provide an important learning experience. However, rights within an educational setting should not be promoted solely for non-rights ends: for example, to enhance the prestige of a school for the purpose of attracting prospective clients, or to promote work skills for national economic growth.

Yet does it really matter what the motivations for a rights-based approach are as long as rights are being promoted? In this age of restricted public funds and increasingly hard-nosed economic orientation of education, is it being excessively precious to demand not only support for rights but also the right kind of motivation for that support? I would argue that the motivation is fundamentally important for two reasons:

(a) *Deep rooting.* When rights-based approaches have been adopted strategically in order to achieve a non-rights goal, they are less likely to take root, will be incorporated only superficially into the curriculum and are at risk of being discarded.

(b) *Understandings of rights.* The motivations for rights-based approaches
    affect the ways those rights are framed and understood by all actors
    involved. If a rights respecting school is justified on the basis of the
    inherent dignity of human beings, it will positively influence the intensity
    and manner in which the rights are worked with.

Justifications, therefore, are important in relation to the sustainability of
rights-based approaches and the ways the rights are incorporated within
educational practice. In addition to discussing justifiable grounds for the
upholding of human rights, the second intention of this chapter is to argue that
the two aspects – intrinsic and instrumental – should be seen as part of a single
process. The upholding of human rights in practice in educational experiences
provides significant opportunities for learning. In turn, the learning gained may
ensure that those rights will be more effectively upheld. However, even though
existing studies do support claims of positive learning effects, for example the
recent study on rights-respecting schools in the United Kingdom (Sebba and
Robinson 2010), this virtuous cycle is far from being an automatic process. The
learning of human rights – like all learning – is highly unpredictable and we
cannot assume that living in a rights-respecting environment will necessarily
lead to respect for human rights. (Just as emancipated thinkers through
history – Julius Nyerere, Mary Wollstonecraft, etc. – have emerged from largely
authoritarian and constraining educational and value systems.) Furthermore, it
is important to acknowledge the significant differences in country contexts and
their effects on experiences of learning human rights. This unpredictability needs
to be acknowledged, but it does not cast doubt on the validity of rights-based
approaches, since, while there are likely learning benefits, human rights should be
upheld in educational institutions whether or not there are these consequences.

   This point brings us to questions of the relationship between ends and
means. As discussed in the previous chapter, a 'separation' between the ends
of upholding human rights and the educational means adopted is a source of
concern. ('Separation' here refers to a relationship based solely on empirical
causality, without an integration of the fundamental principles contained in
the ends – i.e. 'harmony'.) From the perspective of the effectiveness of means,
a tension between undemocratic school practices – in Jerome and Bhargava's
(2009: 356) terms, 'authoritarian and unequal classrooms' – and the stated
rights-respecting aims will be problematic for a number of reasons. Learners are
likely to perceive the tensions and this will inevitably affect the learning process
(Morris and Cogan 2001). In a *harmony* approach, in contrast, the human rights

that are the end are embodied within the educational processes. This is true not only in a negative sense of avoiding abuses of human rights within schools (as outlined in Harber 2004, etc.) but also incorporating the values in a positive way, such as embodying inclusiveness. This embodiment may lead to enhanced effectiveness for learning, but it is not dependent on it, since it is also seen as intrinsically valuable.

A separation of ends and means in this way can be seen as something of an illusion. As argued by Dewey (1966 [1916]), ends do not lie 'outside' means in the way that we commonly perceive them to. This idea is expressed eloquently by Emma Goldman (1970 [1923]: 260):

> All human experience teaches that methods and means cannot be separated from the ultimate aim. The means employed become, through individual habit, and social practice, part and parcel of the final purpose; they influence it, modify it, and presently the aims and means become identical.

Human rights within education, therefore, are justified neither solely through the intrinsic importance of upholding rights, nor solely through their instrumental benefits. Instead, the frontier between the two starts to dissolve as we move into a space in which the learning of human rights and the expression of human rights are fused.

6

Is there a Universal Right to Higher Education?

The protests surrounding the recent reforms to higher education (HE) in countries such as Chile and the United Kingdom – and the associated media debate – are underpinned by the central question of whether access to university is a right or a privilege. While often reduced to the matter of fee levels, the reforms have deeper implications in terms of reframing HE study as a predominantly private good leading to an economic return, and for which individuals should consequently bear the cost. Defenders of free HE, in contrast, argue that it is a public good and that it should be a universal entitlement in the same way as primary and secondary education.

Enrolment in HE has increased rapidly over the past half century, rising to a total of 150 million students worldwide in 2007 (Altbach et al. 2009). Yet net rates of access remain low in the majority of countries – while the global gross enrolment rate for the tertiary[1] level is 26 per cent, low-income countries enrol an average of 7 per cent of the age cohort – with significant numbers unable to obtain a place. Given the considerable resource implications for states, the question of whether HE study can be justifiably restricted to a few or should be made generally available becomes of paramount importance worldwide. This chapter assesses the validity of claims that access to HE might be a right, and explores the nature and scope of such a right. This form of clarification is particularly important in light of the conceptual vagueness characterizing current debates on the topic.

In some high-income countries, HE has expanded to the extent that there are almost universal opportunities for this level of study, whether or not it is considered a right and enshrined in law. However, this chapter does not aim to assess the extent to which HE in this way is, or is becoming, a de facto right in some countries. Its task is a normative, in debating whether or not we are justified in asserting a right to HE. Establishing the validity of a moral right is of fundamental importance since it affects our positionings on questions relating to conditions of access, institutional diversity, investment of resources and the nature of provision.

General justifications and international law on the right to education have been discussed in Chapters 2 and 3, and will not be covered in full here. This chapter will assume – as is generally accepted in law – that all people have a right to elementary education, and assess if this right should extend to HE. As argued in Chapter 4, there are problems with confining the right to education to the primary level, both in terms of the coherence of the right and its effects on socio-economic equality. This chapter will assess the extent to which we can include HE within the remit of the universal right.

The chapter will focus primarily on the question of access to HE, rather than broader issues of justice in universities' relations to current students and the wider society. In Brennan and Naidoo's (2008) terms, therefore, it focuses on the 'import' rather than the 'export' role in relation to social justice – although, as the authors emphasize, the two are strongly linked. In terms of what is meant by 'higher education', there are some challenges in providing a satisfactory definition. It is hard to disentangle the concept of HE from the particular conceptions or normative visions put forward by theorists, or from the specific models appearing at different points in history in different parts of the world. In a descriptive sense, HE today refers to a range of institutions, most important of which is the 'university', but including other forms of college with distinct characteristics.[2] In recent years there has also been a proliferation of different forms of course making it hard to establish a criterion in relation to subject area.

Nevertheless, some conceptual boundaries must be placed on the notion of HE. We would not, for example, call a short beginner's course in Spanish language 'higher education', even if it were for people who had completed their school education. The first necessary aspect of HE is that it depends on earlier study, in that students entering HE are building on substantial previous learning (normally through schooling, though not necessarily). For that reason, HE is normally undertaken by adults. The second necessary aspect is that it involves in-depth and sustained study. Normally it would involve specialization in a particular area of knowledge, although a breadth of subjects is also possible, particularly in the early stages. We might like to add to this condition that HE should be 'emancipatory' (Barnett 1990), a 'conversation' (Oakeshott 1989) or that it be 'rationally defensible' (MacIntyre 1990). However, despite the desirability of these conditions, we could not exclude from the concept of HE examples that did not always display these characteristics.

A final point is that the question of whether HE is a right should not be identified entirely with that of whether it should be state-funded. There are a number of aspects of the university – including research and public engagement – that might justify state funding even if HE study were not considered to be a right. Likewise, although a debatable point, there might be circumstances in which some fees might be charged even if HE is considered a right – as long as they did not represent an impediment to access.

Legal basis

The purpose of this chapter is not to analyse the content of the right to HE as it exists in international law. Nevertheless, a brief look at its formulation in law will be helpful in relation to later discussions. HE has appeared as part of the general right to education since the 1948 UDHR, and in subsequent legally binding instruments such as the ICESCR of 1966, and the CRC of 1989. Article 26 of the UDHR states that, 'higher education shall be equally accessible to all on the basis of merit'. When taken in the context of the guarantees earlier in the Article about compulsory and free-of-charge elementary education, the notable element here is that there is no mention of the level of overall access for the population. The right guarantees that HE be *accessible*, but not *generally available* (Beiter 2006: 97). The requirement put forward – a very important one – is that no one should be barred from HE for any reason other than 'merit', that is not through financial disadvantage, etc. However, it is possible to successfully apply this condition to a university system that had places for only 1 per cent of the population – and with a very large number of people competing for a small number of places. It is, therefore, essential to consider the procedural requirement for fair access along with attention to the total number of places available (McCowan 2004, 2007). In this respect, the Charter of the Organization of American States of 1948 represents an improvement, stating that 'Higher education shall be available to all, provided that, in order to maintain its high level, the corresponding regulatory or academic standards are met'. The condition for particular academic standards raised here – understood as a minimum requirement – is preferable to a competition for a fixed number of places – as will be discussed in the sections that follow.

Some developments in the expression of the right to HE can be observed in the Convention against Discrimination in Education (1960) with its undertaking to 'make higher education equally accessible to all on the basis of individual capacity', and in the ICESC, which states that, 'Higher education shall be made equally accessible to all, on the basis of capacity, by every appropriate means, and in particular by the progressive introduction of free education'. 'Capacity' is distinct from 'merit' in that it relates to future potential rather than 'students' past academic achievements' (Beiter 2006: 97), and therefore is clearly a step forward in terms of facilitating access for students from disadvantaged backgrounds who may have had poor quality previous schooling. There is also in the ICESC an (albeit tentative) mention of free-of-charge provision. However, the later CRC removes the clause about free provision, requiring states to 'Make higher education accessible to all on the basis of capacity by every appropriate means.' In fact, the practice of national governments has not indicated a movement towards introduction of HE that is free at the point of delivery: quite the opposite in fact, as in the United Kingdom, there has been a tendency in many countries towards the charging of fees even in public institutions. These have been introduced on the basis of the costs of expanding access to HE, constraints on public funds and the disproportionately privileged backgrounds of the majority of HE students and their consequent ability to fund themselves. As stated above, it is not absolutely impossible for a right to carry some financial charge, if not an impediment to access – although the fee levels in public and private universities in many countries certainly go beyond this, and undermine the universal entitlement. Student loans can mitigate the negative effects of fees, but do not completely remove them, and even in countries in which they are generally available, can still represent a disproportionate disincentive to students from low-income backgrounds on account of fear of debt or lack of confidence in the benefits of HE study (Altbach et al. 2009). Differential fee levels (relating to differences of quality or prestige) also undermine the requirement for access on the basis of merit or capacity.

The right to HE in international law, therefore, is partially deficient in its formulation since in determining a possible right, attention must be paid not only to procedural aspects of access to those places available, but also of the extent of availability of provision. Furthermore, even the limited requirements have not been met in the majority of states.

Justifications for the general right to education

Hodgson (1998) acknowledges in relation to the justifications he puts forward for the right to education that while children are the main beneficiaries, it has a lifelong application. This point is acknowledged in UNESCO recommendations, in the Jomtien Declaration and Dakar Framework. Adult education specifically has been broadly claimed as a right (e.g. Gadotti 2011) as has early childhood education (e.g. Committee on the Rights of the Child 2005[3]). Nevertheless, despite these endorsements, in practice it has been primary and in some cases secondary education that has been recognized as an absolute right for all people.

Philosophical justifications of the right to education often follow existing law in seeing it as applying primarily during childhood – the right being one to acquire particular attributes (corresponding to aims such as socialization autonomy, economic self-sufficiency) that will enable a full adult life. Haydon (1977) labels as *optional* education those forms which – however desirable they may be – go beyond this basic entitlement.

However, it is not clear from these discussions why the right to education should apply only to children, or only to particular forms of formal education. As discussed in Chapter 4, the restriction of the absolute right to education to the 'elementary' level is justified neither on the basis of education's intrinsic and instrumental value, nor on the basis of positional advantages conferred. So, it is impossible to determine a particular level of literacy necessary for employment and recreation: very often as a person's skill and sensitivity in reading and writing develops through life, her work opportunities and engagement in cultural activities are progressively enhanced. It is quite arbitrary to determine that the learning provided in primary school is a right and at subsequent levels is simply a good. In relation to the autonomy proposed by Haydon, and to Curren's 'initiation into practices that express human flourishing', it is hard to see how the development of these qualities has an end point – they are not tasks that can be completed. Any threshold of educational development established to mark the ending of the entitlement would be arbitrary.

Taking the positional aspect, a restriction of the absolute right to education to the primary level is also inadequate, particularly in light of the qualifications inflation that has rendered primary school leaving certificates almost worthless in the employment market in most countries. Of course, the positional dimension of education is complex from the perspective of universal rights given that we cannot universalize positional advantage, although we can guard against unfair disadvantage.

The right to education – if it is a right at all – must apply in some way throughout life. Education in this sense would be no different from other rights like health, for which it would be strange to question its lifelong applicability. This is not to deny the importance of childhood as a phase of life in relation to education, and it is clear that the most intensive forms of education should occur in the stages of rapid development during childhood and adolescence. If it can be shown that some learning can only take place at particular phases of life, there may be justifications for compulsory education. Yet this is different from restricting the *right* to these phases. The right to education should not have a beginning and end point.

The right to HE, therefore, should be seen in the context of a general right to education that runs through life. HE in this way is one of a number of options for organized learning available to people in adulthood, along with various forms of vocational education, job specific training, creative and artistic pursuits, personal development and so forth.

Specific characteristics of a right to HE

However, it could be seen as insufficient to argue for a right to HE purely on the basis of a right to lifelong education. It could rightly be asked whether there was anything in particular about HE that gave it value. As argued by Barnett (1990: 6), HE is not just 'more of what has gone before', it indicates 'a special level of personal development'. Some elements can be seen as specific to the right to HE, among the range of other educational options. The first and most prominent of these is that HE – in most societies – provides unparalleled access to the best paid and most rewarding forms of employment. In part this stems from knowledge and skills gained (instrumental benefits), but also to the positional dimension of degree diplomas. These provide advantage over those people without HE level study, but there is also divergence between different diplomas, given the hierarchies of institutions within and between countries. As Brighouse (2009: 6) states, the credential provides 'enhanced competitiveness for the unequally distributed desirable positions and the unequally distributed goods that attach to them'.

Exclusion from these opportunities is clearly unjust and can be seen as an argument for a right to HE. However, as stated above, this form of justification is not sufficient, as instrumental reasons on their own cannot form the basis of a right. (Conversely the phenomenon of graduate unemployment and other obstacles in converting HE into opportunities in contemporary societies cannot be used as an argument against a right.) One of the limitations of current academic debates on HE is their often exclusive focus on this aspect. Bou-Habib (2010), for example, assesses arguments for and against state funding of HE, concluding from a Rawlsian difference principle perspective that public subsidies are justifiable in so far as they promote the interests of the worst off in society. The author asserts that 'we should not automatically assume that tax-funded HE is a 'basic right' and neither should we assume that it is a privilege for which graduates alone should pay' (p. 493). As pointed out by Kotzee and Martin (2011), one problem with the account is that Bou-Habib (and others) address HE purely in its 'external' role in achieving other social goods. In this sense alone, it may be that there is not a right to HE – particularly as the advantages pointed to (primarily economic) could be provided by other means. Furthermore, if we primarily consider the positional benefits of HE –and we assume that the HE is necessarily positional in its benefits – then it becomes incoherent to assert a universal right (given that not everyone can have positional advantage over everyone else). The positional benefits in fact are contingent on a restricted and unequal system, and would no longer apply in a universal and horizontal system. It is important, therefore, to consider not only the instrumental and positional benefits accrued from HE study, but also its intrinsic value and students' experiences within the period of study. Like Kotzee and Martin (2011), this chapter considers that it is the non-instrumental value of HE – the experience of learning, and the individual and collective process of intellectual development – that people have a right to. HE is not the only means of engaging in this form of intellectual development, but it is an important one.

The intrinsic value of HE study can be understood in different ways. The acquisition of knowledge in specific fields can be seen to have intrinsic value, leading to an enhanced appreciation of, say, mathematical proofs, Islamic architecture or fourteenth-century poetry – an appreciation enabled by sustained and in-depth study of a type not normally possible in other forms of education. In a broader sense, we can see HE as providing initiation into a form of 'culture' in the Humboldtian sense of 'the sum of all knowledge that is studied, as well as the cultivation and development of one's character as a result of that study' (Readings 1996: 15). Clearly, universities are guardians of just a part of what we would normally consider to be culture, but are no less valuable for that. In terms of widening participation, this aspect takes on particular importance, as certain groups in society have been marginalized historically on account of their restricted access to this store of culture. Furthermore, the deep enquiry and critical reflection enabled by HE study can be seen to have intrinsic value. This view is put forward by Nussbaum (1997: 30), drawing on the Stoics' idea that 'higher education is a part of every human being's self-realization' on account of its role in developing criticality.

In those fields of study linked directly to professions, there can also be intrinsic value, in terms of the dexterity acquired at say graphic design or mastery of legal procedure. There are of course a range of other instrumental benefits of HE study (see Bynner et al. 2003; McMahon 2009), not least of which is the development of political awareness and the ability to function as an informed and active citizen in a democratic society (Ahier et al. 2003; Arthur and Bohlin 2005). Added to these is the enjoyment of the experience of HE study, the value of interaction with other students and staff, the making of friends and so forth. Universities, therefore, contribute to both qualities identified in Chapter 3: *understanding* – through sustained and in-depth enquiry into areas of knowledge, and *agency* – through ethical professional development and heightened capacity for action as a citizen.

HE, in this way, has specific characteristics that provide a foundation for the right in addition to the characteristics shared with all education discussed in the previous section. There remain, however, some common objections to the assertion of a right to HE: four of these will be addressed in the sections that follow. The first is whether HE – as an often resource intensive and highly specialized activity, and one that has historically been restricted to the elites – is in fact a privilege and not a right. The second is whether it is appropriate to assert a universal right to HE given that not all people may have the capacity or desire to study at this level. Third, that movement towards a universal HE system leads to an intolerable degradation of quality; and fourth, that the right is unviable given the inability of states to fund universal access. The response provided here to these issues will in part be that the questions themselves are based on misunderstandings of and ambiguities in the idea of a right.

A right or a privilege?

'Education: a right, not a privilege!' can be found on placards in student protests around the world, from Santiago and Bogotá to London. The idea of education as a right has had enduring popular appeal around the world, particularly in contexts in which large proportions of the population are systematically excluded from education of adequate quality. The idea of HE specifically as a right has also had significant rhetorical appeal among certain groups, especially as a response to the introduction of fees in public institutions. On the other hand, proponents of 'cost-sharing' for HE have emphasized that university study is extremely expensive, that it benefits the few but is paid for through general taxation, and that it brings significant private advantages. In the latter sense, it is certainly a privilege for those people.

I will argue that both of these perspectives are valid, but that there is a use of the term 'right' that can to some extent accommodate itself to both. A good deal of the popular opposition to human rights generally speaking is based on concern that a rights culture encourages people to think about what they can 'get' rather than what they can 'give' to society. This criticism is based on a misunderstanding of the notion of human rights, in that accepting that a right pertains to all human beings entails extensive responsibilities in upholding that right for all others. While the increasingly individualistic nature of society and a lack of commitment to the welfare of others may be a valid concern, this trend is not one that can be attributed to rights.

Concerns for a culture of 'getting' can certainly be observed in the sphere of HE. Brighouse and McAvoy (2009) provide a compelling account of HE as a 'privilege', in the sense that in our unequal contemporary societies, advantaged groups have disproportionate access to prestigious university courses, which in turn can offer further positional advantage. The response to this situation – in the absence of a radically more equal social organization – is that institutions and the students emerging from them should contribute much more to society, and its most disadvantaged members, that they currently do.

HE is certainly a privilege in this sense, and there are good reasons to believe that many students from advantaged backgrounds both take university study for granted and pay insufficient attention to their debt to the rest of society subsequently. It can be argued that this casualness with regard to the precious opportunity for HE study is the fruit of a sense that it has in some way 'fallen into people's laps'; there is stronger appreciation of educational opportunities in countries in which the right has been won through struggle in recent history.

Nevertheless, there is another sense of 'privilege' used in relation to HE. The idea of privilege questioned by the Chilean students is one that is controlled and conferred by those in power, and may be conditional in particular ways. In this way, HE has historically been a 'privilege', in the sense that it has only been available to particular segments of society (on the basis of gender, social class, racial/ethnic group, etc.), or to a very tiny intellectual elite (i.e. a small proportion of those people with the capacity for HE study). Elites have a vested interest in maintaining the restricted size of the university system, and given the prominent role of universities as sites of critique of government, there have also been disincentives for states to expand access to 'the masses', except in the form of demand-absorbing private institutions offering narrow vocational training.

Of course, in this sense we are really talking about HE being 'for the privileged', rather than being 'a privilege', but it is important to highlight this aspect since it is often the meaning attached to the term when contrasted with a right.

HE should be considered a right in the sense that it should be made available to all, but it should also be considered a privilege in the sense that it is a precious opportunity that must be taken advantage of as fully as possible and then used for the benefit of society. Nevertheless, being a right, its availability cannot be conditional on any particular use that it is subsequently put to, or indeed any previous performance (apart from adequate preparation). We may very much want students to go on to contribute to society after studying, and pay back their debt so to speak, and we may do our best to encourage them to do so, but they should be free to decide for themselves how to utilize the opportunity given. In any event, as stated above, enjoying the right to HE study entails upholding the right for all other members of society – and indeed – given that we are talking of a *human* right – for all members of the human community.

University for all?

The second point relates to the proportion of the population that should study at university. Famously, the New Labour government in the United Kingdom set a goal of 50 per cent of 18–30-year-olds.[4] The arbitrariness of this figure is shown when it is disaggregated. In spite of the increase in the rates of young people going to university in recent years, the high proportion of the top socio-economic groups and low proportion of the bottom groups has changed little. UK government statistics (BIS 2011) show a very small improvement in the progression of students with free school meals (a proxy for socio-economic level), with the gap between these students and others still at 18 percentage points. Measures based on socio-economic class (BIS 2009) also show only a small improvement in the gap between the classes 1 and 3, and 4 and 7 in recent years (27.8 per cent as opposed to 13.7 per cent progression for 18-year-olds). This phenomenon is evident around the world, with in some cases the proportion of lower-income students actually going down in the context of expansion of the system. Any justification of the target of 50 per cent on the basis that half of the population might have the desire and capacity to benefit from HE is, therefore, clearly false (unless one considers that higher socio-economic groups have more inherent aptitude for HE study). The places available in HE in most countries correspond more to perceived needs of the national economy than any notion of individuals' learning interests.

Yet while most HE systems unfairly restrict the numbers of students entering, it is not necessarily the case in an ideal scenario that all people should study at university. The idea that HE is not suitable for all people could be proposed as an objection to a universal right. In fact, upholding HE as a right is entirely consistent with recognizing that not all people will want or be suitable to taking up the opportunity. Rights are freedoms and not obligations (although they will entail duties towards others). It is important that we protect the right to worship in society, even if only a tiny minority have any religious belief. A significant proportion of the population – even with the opportunity of free-of-charge HE study – may decide not to take it up, or will opt for another form of education. This proportion would be larger in a society in which university diplomas – independent of actual learning acquired – were not essential for most forms of well-paid employment: as Trow (2006) points out, in contemporary systems with near universal access, for the upper and middle classes HE has become almost an 'obligation'.

However, individual desire to study is not the only factor that might justifiably restrict access – there is also the question of selection procedures adopted by institutions and the system as a whole. The principal implication of HE being a right is that no person should be unfairly barred from having access to it. The most obvious barriers are economic in nature, and if considered a right, university study should be either free or at such a low cost that it would not provide an obstacle to any segment of society. An associated point relating to fees is that higher quality provision should not carry a higher price – a characteristic of markets in most products, and one that is implied by the current reforms in the United Kingdom, and already seen in countries such as Brazil in which the process of privatization is highly developed (McCowan 2004).

However, some entrance restrictions on the part of institutions are justified. A minimum level of academic preparation is necessary in order to gain meaningful access to the study made available in universities. (This chapter cannot address the question of which specific requirements there might be.) Restrictions on entry to those who have this level of preparation are not justified by protection of academic standards relating to the institution, but by the interests of the individual students, who will be at best wasting their time by pursuing a course that they are not yet able to engage with. In conjunction with this point, students should be able to return to HE study at a later stage in life, and be supported in obtaining the necessary preparation. The forms of selection adopted must be criterion-referenced and not norm-referenced in the sense that the university system must be able to expand (and contract) in relation to the numbers of students wishing to study at that level and with the required level of capacity.

There is no justification for a fixed number of places for which the highest performing students are selected.

A universal right to HE does not, therefore, require, or even encourage, all people to attend university. It may well be that only a small proportion of the population will opt for it. Furthermore, a right to HE is consistent with entry requirements that ensure the prospective students will be able to engage meaningfully with the course in question.

Massification and quality

One issue of relevance here is concern over quality of provision in the context of massification or universalization of HE. The question of the right to education inevitably involves quality, since we can only consider the right to have been realized if quality is of an acceptable level. There is little gain in ensuring access for 100 per cent of the population to universities with inadequate provision for learning.

Concerns over quality are, therefore, entirely legitimate, and cannot be dismissed simply as entrenched elitism or belief in the inevitability of loss of standards when education is extended to all. Recent history has shown substantial problems of quality in the context of a rapid expansion of the university system, and in operating open access admission procedures. Some countries in continental Europe and Latin America, for example, have operated systems of entry that are not restrictive, and are controlled only by the possession of a secondary leaving certificate. While enabling greater enrolment, these systems have been characterized by overly large class sizes and very high rates of dropout. Argentina, for example, has a completion rate of less than 24 per cent and Italy of approximately 45 per cent (Altbach et al. 2009; European Commission 2010).

Trow's (1974, 2006) well-known analysis of the movement from elite to mass and universal systems is of relevance here. There are problems that will naturally be faced in the transition of the HE system, just as they have been faced in the universalization of primary and secondary education (and are still being faced in most LMICs). These challenges stem from the rate of growth, changes to the absolute size of systems and institutions, and changes in the proportion of the relevant age group enrolled (Trow 1974). However, it is important to distinguish between problems of implementation and issues of principle. The argument put forward in this chapter is that there is a moral right to HE, and not that there are no challenges in putting this vision into practice. The problems faced in countries such as Argentina and Italy are those of expanding enrolments without sufficient allocation of resources, and not therefore problems inherent in the universalization of HE, any more than they are at primary and secondary levels.

Similar issues can be seen in relation to individual institutions. Rapid expansion or an open access system in a single university may well lead at least in the short term to a loss of quality or of a specific ethos that characterized it. In fact, a universal right to education does not necessarily mean expansion of existing institutions, but merely expansion of overall places which may involve a large number of small institutions – if it is true that maintaining a small size can ensure a higher level of quality. What is clear, however, is that small institutions cannot unfairly restrict access to a specific portion of the population.

Limits on available resources

An obvious objection to an assertion of the right to education is lack of funds. Some of what might correspond to a right to HE is of non-interference kind – that is, being free to pursue one's intellectual development – but there is also a significant amount of provision that needs to be made by society. Clearly, the amount of time and resources that individuals and groups can call on from others in pursuing their educational interests is finite, and contingent on the particular conditions of a society at a particular point in time. Decisions have to be made in relation to the length of time it is justifiable for an individual to remain in HE, and the distribution of resources between HE and other educational levels and options.

One objection that can be made to a right to HE in this way is that it leads us on a slippery slope of unending educational consumption, akin to saying that if there is a right to food then there is a right to lobster and caviar.[5] Of course, there cannot be a universal right to the educational equivalent of lobster and caviar: for example, something luxurious and scarce, which could not be made available for everybody at the same time. HE does not necessarily come into this category – the learning (if not the positional) aspects at least are non-rivalrous and non-expendable – although it has to be accepted that some current forms of HE are extremely costly and may go beyond what would be possible in a universal entitlement.

Even a 'no frills' HE system may seem beyond the possibilities of many countries today. Yet we should not veto a moral right to HE on the basis that there are insufficient funds in the present moment. In a general sense, as argued by Sen (2004), we should not reign in our deliberation on rights by only considering what might now be practically possible in a particular country. The right to be free from murder or arbitrary imprisonment applies equally to people who happen to live in countries currently lacking the funds to support an adequate police force and legal system. When we think more specifically about HE, current rates of expenditure on HE students would indeed be hard for most societies to cope with for 100 per cent, or even 50 per cent, of the population. Yet as Bou-Habib (2010) argues, we cannot assume from the start an upper limit on expenditure on HE, until we have discussed the demands of the various priorities that governments might have. This is particularly so in cases of countries in which the 'lack' of public funds to expand HE systems has been caused or at least exacerbated by corruption, mismanagement and tax evasion. In addition, there are different ways in which HE can be provided, not all of which are so resource intensive. To take some current examples, Cuba and Venezuela have achieved 95 and 78 per cent gross enrolment rates[6] respectively on moderate budgets (UIS 2011). Having said this, there will of course always be some limits on funds available, and – as is the case with the realization of every human right – decisions have to be made in practice about where to employ and how to distribute resources.

*

This chapter has put forward two main arguments in response to the question posed.

1. HE is a right of all people, but only as one of a range of educational experiences available to adults.
2. Non-discriminatory access procedures are important, but not adequate in themselves; sufficient places must be available for all those desiring to study and with a minimum level of preparation.

In relation to the first point, it is recognised that general claims for education as a right are contested, given the difficulties common to all welfare rights in identifying the duty-bearer, in determining which forms of education might correspond to the right and whether these are universal or specific to a given context. Yet if we uphold a general right to education it is arbitrary to create cut-off points (say 5–16); the entitlement must exist in some form throughout life. There is no implication, in asserting this right, that all or even most people should take it up, although there should be easy re-entry points so that people can choose to come to HE at later stages in life.

HE as a right rests on the non-instrumental value of university study – in fact, as argued in previous chapters, while education has instrumental and positional value, it is only possible for there to be a right to education if there is some intrinsic value (otherwise the rights would be to the other goods – e.g. viable livelihood, political participation – with education just a means of supporting them). The extraordinary positional advantage conferred by a university degree is specific to our contemporary age, and yet the other benefits of university study pertain even when societies have developed other forms of sorting and selection. This chapter has focused on the question of access to HE for students: in addition, it is important to remember that there are other forms of public interest in the university, and even possible rights pertaining, for example, to the access of local communities to services provided, or the access of society as a whole to the knowledge developed.

The implications of this argument for policy are clear: HE systems as a whole need to expand, and furthermore elite institutions should either increase the number of places they offer, or if they wish to maintain their small size for educational reasons, should substantially democratize access. Tuition fees – other than small matriculation charges – should not be charged. As argued above, HE should be one of a range of options for post-school education available for the population, and occurring in formal institutions, but also in the workplace, trades unions, religious groups, social movements, political campaigns, community associations and so forth. Lawson's (1979) concern was that establishing HE for all might place an intolerable burden on the curriculum, forcing it to diversify to the extent that it was no longer recognizable. In fact, this outcome is not necessary if we retain the idea that HE is only one of a range of options of adult education. Furthermore, a right to HE does not necessarily imply access to an institution corresponding to our current 'university': the latter is but an institutional manifestation of higher learning that is dominant in the temporary age, while the sustained and in-depth enquiry characteristic of HE can take place in other forms of setting.

There is also a time element to the question, in that an 18-year-old may not choose to pursue HE (or be sufficiently equipped to undertake that study), yet the option should remain for entry at a later stage of life. (In fact, considerable progress in facilitating entry of 'mature' students has been made in many countries in recent years). Given the inequalities at the lower levels of the education system, substantial resources should be allocated to enabling people after leaving school to obtain the necessary preparation for entering HE (in addition to addressing the inequalities at primary and secondary levels directly). Beyond access, ensuring a right to HE would also involve a range of other considerations such as retention, quality of experience during study and subsequent transitions. In fact, an adequate gauge of the fulfilment of the right to HE would involve something akin to Tomaševski's (2006a) 4 As scheme: that is, availability (existence of sufficient places), accessibility (non-discrimination in access to those places), acceptability (meaningful and respectful curriculum) and adaptability (institutional flexibility in accordance with student needs).

In relation to the second principle above, there has been considerable debate over questions of justice in university admissions. However, these debates have been predicated on the situation of limited places that characterizes HE in many (though not all) countries today. A right to HE would require the system to expand and contract in relation to the number of students desiring and able to study. In saying that HE should be accessible to all on the basis of capacity, it should not be a competition in which the highest performing students get access to a limited number of places, but a requirement for fulfilling a minimal level of preparation. The ongoing debates over affirmative action policies in a number of countries, therefore, become immaterial: the meritocratic versus positive discrimination debate is predicated on an artificially restricted number of places. A just system would require there to be sufficient places for all who have the desire and ability for HE study.

Even with universal access, there remain questions of diversity of institutions and potential disparities of prestige between them that would need to be addressed. Attention to non-discrimination in the UDHR needs to be applied not only to access to the system as a whole, but to the institutions themselves, meaning that applicants should not be unfairly barred from accessing universities and courses of quality. This requirement would not preclude diversity in the system in terms of ethos, range of courses and other aspects, but it would entail consistently high quality across all institutions – that is, horizontal rather than vertical differentiation (Brennan and Naidoo 2008). This task is highly challenging in contemporary societies given the entrenched inequalities stemming from educational experiences prior to university entry: as argued by Grover (2004), access to post-secondary education depends on the upholding of a universal right to secondary education, not currently a reality in the vast majority of countries.

Students from wealthy backgrounds in our current unequal societies do not have a 'right' to HE in the sense of obtaining added economic benefits at the expense of the general taxpayer, while access to low-income students is severely restricted. Yet engagement in meaningful educational experiences – of which HE is an example – can indeed be seen as a right, one that should be upheld universally and throughout the life course.

Notes

1 Tertiary is a broader category than higher education, including non-university and technical post-school institutions.
2 In discussing access, this chapter will at times refer to 'higher education' and at times to 'university', but without denoting a specific technical distinction between them.
3 In this General Comment it is stated that, 'The Committee interprets the right to education during early childhood as beginning at birth and closely linked to young children's right to maximum development.'
4 Figures for HE access are not always comparable between countries, as they include a range of different forms of study, not all of which would be considered HE in all contexts.
5 This point was made by my colleague Paul Temple in a personal communication.
6 The net rate for each age cohort would be lower.

7

Contributions of the Capabilities Approach

Imagine the case of two children of a Quechua-speaking family in the Urubamba Valley, stretching out from the historic town of Cuzco, Peru. Chaska and Arturo are seven and eight years old and study in the second and third grades in the local school, located a few hundred metres from their house. Given that there is a school in the vicinity of the children's home and places are available, it would appear that – compared to the 61 million children out of school around the world (UNESCO 2012) – these are the lucky ones. And yet, if we look more closely, problems emerge. In the first place, the school teaches through the medium of Spanish, a language in which the children are not fully proficient. Speakers of Quechua – the language of the Incas – make up approximately 13 per cent of the population of Peru, but along with Aymara and other indigenous groups in the country, have historically been marginalized by the Spanish descendant and mestizo population. There is some provision for bilingual and intercultural education in Peru since reforms in the 1990s, but it has not been universalized, and the practice is still distant from the rhetoric (García 2004). Second, the curriculum still has some vestiges of the historical project of assimilation, with the absence of the culture of the local population within the school serving to reinforce a sense of inferiority and inadequacy.

Furthermore, the basic provision in the school is of questionable quality, with outdated textbooks, frequently absent teachers and meagre school facilities. The poverty of the children's family means they struggle even to take advantage of the learning opportunities that are there, given the lack of space at home to study, and the need to work in the fields after school. Chaska's opportunities for study are even more limited than her brother's, given her extra responsibility for the care of younger siblings and household duties. These factors – exacerbated by the parents' own lack of formal education and consequently restricted ability to support their children – may well lead them to repeat the academic year, and to early dropout (Balarin and Cueto 2007). Indigenous children in the Andean region will commonly complete only four or five years of elementary education. Even if they do survive in the system, there will be little use for their primary school diplomas in the rural environment in which they live, and even in the nearby town opportunities are severely limited.

Has the right to education been fulfilled in the case of Chaska and Arturo? On the surface at least, they are fully guaranteed their right to formal education. They have a legal entitlement to full-time education and live in reasonable proximity to a school that can offer them a place free-of-charge. In a statistical sense, the government has fulfilled its obligations. However, there is a serious risk of what Robeyns (2006: 70) describes as:

> policymakers ... being contented when they have strictly followed the rules that a limited interpretation of the rights imposes on them, even when additional efforts are necessary to meet the goal that underlies the right.

The poverty of a rights-based approach that is inattentive to people's ability to exercise the right in practice can be clearly seen in the educational field. In neighbouring country Brazil, for example, there is a constitutional right for all people to be in compulsory, free-of-charge education from the ages of 4–17.[1] With its strong state guarantee for education, and near universal coverage in terms of primary schools, Brazil is in a privileged position in relation to EFA: the infringement of the right is far more blatant in the low-income countries of Africa and Asia. Nevertheless, 6 per cent of children of primary age are not enrolled in school (UNESCO 2011), many drop out before completion, and of those still in school a significant proportion cannot meaningfully engage in learning because of socio-economic disadvantage or the poor quality of provision. At secondary and higher levels the disparities between the privileged and the disadvantaged are starker still. There are also general concerns over quality, with a recent World Bank study estimating that 78 per cent of 15-year-olds in Brazil have not attained minimal competencies in mathematics (Filmer et al. 2006).

How is it possible to build consideration for the substantial limitations in the opportunities for Chaska and Arturo and the millions of others like them around the world into our understandings of EFA? As argued in previous chapters, it is clear that a conceptualization of the right to education as access to school is insufficient. This chapter assesses the contribution that the capabilities approach can make to an alternative conceptualization, one that can more satisfactorily provide a normative orientation for EFA. The chapter will progress through three stages. First, there will be a brief recap of the current right to education, and a closer look at some of the problematic aspects raised by the above example. Second, consideration will be made of the proposal that the rights-based approach should be abandoned altogether in favour of an alternative framework such as capabilities. The capabilities approach, developed initially by Amartya Sen and Martha Nussbaum, has in recent years become influential in international development. The approach posits that development should be understood not as increases in income or access to resources, or even satisfaction of subjective preferences, but as the enhancement of people's freedoms to do and be what they have reason to value. Capabilities have been applied to education by various researchers and theorists (e.g. Saito 2003; Terzi 2008; Unterhalter 2007; Vaughan 2007; Walker and Unterhalter 2007), providing distinctive perspectives on social justice in education, particularly in relation to gender. While a capabilities approach to education has much in common with a human rights-based approach, there are differences of emphasis and some potential tensions.

Having presented a partial defence of rights, this chapter makes an assessment of the contribution that the capabilities approach can make to providing a fuller conceptualization of the right to education. The argument put forward here is that capabilities are not a substitute for rights, but that they enrich a rights framework by providing a more comprehensive view of the content of the right and of the conditions necessary for people to exercise their rights.

Questioning the right to education

As explored in previous chapters, the legal expression of the universal right to education, while containing valuable guarantees, is deficient in terms of its detail. The absolute right is confined to the primary level, with insufficient attention to other levels and to lifelong learning. Moreover, the right assumes that school is the most appropriate vehicle for the delivery of the right, without adequate discussion of the multiple forms that education can take, and the valuable forms of learning in informal and non-formal contexts. Perhaps most importantly, there is little acknowledgement that schooling can infringe as much as promote rights, through indoctrination, corporal punishment, humiliating treatment or exposure to sexual violence (though the Convention on the Rights of the Child [Article 28] goes further than previous rights instruments in guarding against these). In addition to the need for emphasis on meaningful learning, the right to education also needs to acknowledge *positional* aspects, relating to certification and the disparity of prestige between different educational institutions. One of the potentially negative roles of formal education is to reproduce or even magnify initial socio-economic inequalities. If disadvantaged communities are given access to formal education, but confined to low prestige institutions that cannot confer opportunities for further study and valuable employment, then the right to education has been inadequately fulfilled.

Unterhalter shows one of the difficulties with the formal right to education with illustrations from her research:

> At a school in Durban, South Africa, in 2005, children described hunger and social isolation as aspects of poverty. One girl graphically recounted the months in which she had no money for soap or water, could not wash herself or her clothes, and was unable to come to school because of shame. (Unterhalter 2007: 64).

There are, in this way, multiple obstacles that may prevent uptake of the right, even when schools provide places. To this we can add problems with the quality of education in terms of teaching, the learning environment and the broader experience of school. Unterhalter also highlights another form of obstacle to a rights-based approach, in this case where the bringing of the duty-bearer to account is made difficult or impossible due to social conditions:

> Representatives of women's organizations in a state in Northern India in 1999 were thinking about legal action to demand their constitutional rights to education. But they faced the threat that whoever brought the action would be in grave danger and would have to live in fear of his or her life. (Unterhalter 2007: 64)

The difficulties of operationalizing a rights-based approach to education in practice is also shown in Greany (2008) in relation to girls' education in Niger, given the difficulties of legal recourse and holding the government to account. The uptake and defence of the right in this way depend on the possession of particular capacities and social conditions. The existence of a citizen's right to education, therefore, is inadequate if citizens are viewed as disembodied political subjects: factors of gender, social class, race/ethnicity amongst others have a strong impact on the ability to construct, exercise and defend rights.

These limitations of rights have led some to reject the framework altogether. Robeyns (2006), in her influential analysis, acknowledges the advantages of a rights-based approach over human capital theory, but critiques it on the basis of four features: for being overly rhetorical; for overemphasizing the legal aspect; for inducing policy makers to be contented with a limited interpretation of the right; and for being too government focused. While Nussbaum does not view rights and capabilities as rivals (stating that 'it seems best to regard the capabilities approach as one species of a human rights approach' [Nussbaum 2006: 291]), she shares Robeyns's reservations about rights frameworks, seeing them as deficient in their emphasis on formal rather than effective entitlements:

> Women in many nations have the nominal right of political participation without having the right in the sense of capability: for example, they may be threatened with violence if they leave the home. (Nussbaum 2000: 98)

Robeyns's conclusion is that the real end of our efforts is expanding capabilities, with rights one of a number of possible strategies for obtaining the end. She states:

> [A]t the theoretical level, rights always need a prior moral criterion. Rights are always rights *to something*. Capabilities, on the other hand, are always things that must matter intrinsically, whether or not they additionally also matter instrumentally. (Robeyns 2006: 82)

In this way, a progression is seen between human capital theory, rights and capabilities, with capabilities being the preferred framework, drawing on some of the insights and opportunities presented by the former two. To what extent is this a justified position?

An initial point is that while these critiques of the ineffective actualization of rights *in practice* are justified, they cannot be considered faults inherent in the concept of 'human right'. If implemented in the appropriate way, the four problems raised by Robeyns can be resolved – with the possible exception of the final point about being too government focused. While, as argued by Pogge (2002), all individuals are responsible for human rights, the mechanism of accountability works primarily via states, and this may in some circumstances be problematic. The capabilities approach may indeed make a valuable contribution in this respect, as will be discussed below.

The distinction between capabilities as intrinsically important and rights as instrumentally so, however, is problematic. It is true that 'rights' as such (in the sense of a mechanism for enforcing justified claims) are not ends in themselves. However, the *objects* of rights are. Capabilities are as much related 'to something' as rights are. If Robeyns is asserting that the objects of rights should be capabilities, then this is a plausible claim (one that will be discussed below). Yet it is problematic to reduce rights to a strategy. Affirming that something is a right is to give a moral claim a certain *status*. It is to say that it is a claim that in most cases trumps competing considerations, such that it cannot be infringed, whatever the benefits for others. Rights language may be used rhetorically to achieve a particular effect, and the associated legal mechanisms may be used instrumentally, but this is different from asserting that the right itself is a strategy.

Nussbaum's version of the capabilities approach does incorporate an account of positive welfare rights, including educational rights. Nussbaum proposes for the ten central capabilities she enumerates that:

> If people are systematically falling below the threshold in any of these core areas, this should be seen as a situation both unjust and tragic, in need of urgent attention – even if in other respects things are going well. (Nussbaum 2000: 71)

Assertions of a threshold for all human beings are significant in their expression of not an aspiration but a moral requirement. A rights framework takes as the 'default' position a situation of upholding of rights, and views infringements as an aberration – thus distinguishing it from charity-based approaches, in which the transfer of resources to the disadvantaged is seen as a 'special' act of kindness.

While Nussbaum (2006) does assign duty for the realization of these entitlements to both nation-states and the international community, the notion of a duty-bearer and culpability in the case of infringement is stronger in a rights-based approach than generally is the case in capabilities. As will be discussed below, there are problems with an overemphasis on the nation-state as the duty-bearer for rights, and restrictions on populations holding duty-bearers to account in practice; nevertheless the assertion of human responsibility for the immediate removal of rights infringements is of fundamental importance.

The notion of 'human right', therefore, can and should be retained, principally because of its indication of the status and urgency of a moral claim, and its specification of corresponding duties. For these reasons, the arguments put forward by Robeyns and others do not constitute a basis for *replacing* a rights framework (although they do alert us to the need to guard against minimal interpretations and ineffective realization). The remainder of this section will assess two further reasons for retaining the notion of right: the procedural aspect of rights, and recent developments within human rights theory and practice that have responded to the critiques outlined above.

One argument for retaining the notion of rights relates to procedural aspects of justice. This position is put forward by Sen (2004, 2005), who argues that capabilities, while providing a comprehensive metric for gauging human development, cannot capture all important aspects of social justice. The capabilities need to be supplemented with consideration for just *procedures*:

> While the idea of capability has considerable merit in the assessment of the opportunity aspect of freedom, it cannot possibly deal adequately with the process aspect of freedom, since capabilities are characteristics of individual advantages, and they fall short of telling us enough about the fairness or equity of the processes involved, or about the freedom of citizens to invoke and utilise procedures that are equitable. (Sen 2005: 155–6)

In this sense, in addition to rights to capabilities, there might be others relating to procedures, such as the right to a fair trial, even if the result of that trial is to deprive one of liberty. There are procedural aspects of education of this sort – although there will not be space in this chapter to address them in full. Examples include the criteria for entry into selective educational institutions, and the question of the justice of 'levelling down' those students who have attained high educational achievement on account of socio-economic advantage.

A further reason for retaining a rights framework is that conceptual tools have been developed in recent years within human rights theory and practice that allow us to address some of the limitations. One important element of the Vienna Declaration and Programme of Action emerging from the World Conference on human rights in 1993 was to affirm three principles of human rights: their indivisibility, interrelatedness and interdependence. This affirmation served to challenge the distinction between civil and political rights on the one hand, and economic, social and cultural rights on the other, a division that had characterized the Cold War period. As discussed in previous chapters, these principles have been applied to education in the need to address the right *to* education, along with rights *within* education, and rights *through* education.

If the right to education is taken in conjunction with other established rights, then there are protections against some of the concerns raised in the Peru example above. For example, the UN Declaration on the Rights of Indigenous Peoples of 2007 states:

> Indigenous peoples have the right to establish and control their educational systems and institutions providing education in their own languages, in a manner appropriate to their cultural methods of teaching and learning. (Article 14)

In this way, the Quechua community would not be forced to choose between an education that threatened its language and cultural integrity, and no education at all. This example has highlighted indigenous rights, but we could take many others. Unterhalter's (2003) research on South Africa shows how the fulfilment of the right to 'education' (schooling) incurs infringement of other rights, given the prevalence of sexual abuse and risk of contracting HIV/AIDS. Other infringements of rights within schools – such as indoctrination, humiliation and corporal punishment – can to a large extent be addressed by viewing the right to education in conjunction with other rights. The notions of the indivisibility, interrelatedness and interdependence of human rights, therefore, provide a much firmer basis for viewing educational rights, but difficulties remain, even with this expanded conception.

Critiques of rights based on their ineffective implementation in practice are descriptively valid, given the widespread infringements of all rights, including that to education all around the world. However, it is not the case that rights-based approaches focus purely on distant legal frameworks and are inattentive to the challenges of exercising those rights in everyday life. One significant area that will be addressed in chapter 8 is attempts through human rights education to empower people to understand their rights, to take advantage of available legal mechanisms and keep governments and other authorities to account. In response to Robeyns's (2006: 70) concern over 'policymakers being contented when they have strictly followed the rules that a limited interpretation of the rights imposes on them', schemes have emerged to monitor a much fuller upholding of the right – such as Tomaševski's '4 As'.

If we apply this scheme to the schools in the Urubamba Valley, we come some way towards addressing the concerns raised at the start of the chapter. The limited conception of the right relates primarily to 'availability', but if we incorporate the other three 'As' a much fuller conception is provided. The 'accessibility' requirement would ensure that Chaska's household duties, along with other constraints stemming from her gender, would not bar her from access to the school. The 'acceptability' criterion would ensure that Quechua language and culture would be present within the school context, while also equipping students to function effectively in the dominant language, Spanish. 'Adaptability' would ensure that the school was flexible enough to allow students to undertake seasonal agricultural duties and still complete the year's academic work.

There are, therefore, resources from within rights-based approaches that can respond to some of the critiques of rights – and for the reasons outlined above, there are compelling arguments for not abandoning the notion of 'right'. Nevertheless, there are important ways in which capabilities may still be able to enhance our conceptualization and practice of upholding the right to education. The following section will assess these contributions of capabilities to a rights framework.

The contribution of capabilities

The capabilities approach emerged in response to perceived inadequacies in gauges of human well-being. Instead of income or preference satisfaction, Sen (e.g. 1992, 1999a) proposed that the focus should be on *freedoms*. A distinction is drawn between functionings – 'beings and doings' such as ' being adequately nourished, being in good health ... having self-respect, taking part in the life of the community, and so on' (Sen 1992: 39) – and the capability to achieve those functionings. This distinction is significant since it allows us to discriminate between the woman who decides to spend an evening at home and the woman who is prevented from leaving the house by social mores, and between the man who is starving and the man who is fasting. There is, therefore, a 'counterfactual' aspect to capabilities, by acknowledging the importance of things people can do but decide not to.

These ideas have also been developed by Nussbaum, drawing on the thought of Aristotle and Marx concerning the constituents of a truly human life. Nussbaum (2000) introduced the idea of *combined* capabilities, emphasizing the need for both *internal* capabilities (developed states of the 'basic' capabilities that are innate to individuals) and external social conditions. So, political participation, for example, would require both knowledge and skills such as literacy and communication, but also conducive political institutions and an unrestrictive social climate (McCowan and Unterhalter 2009). The capabilities approach has been influential in international development in recent years and underpinned the creation of the Human Development Index, as well as a broader embrace of 'human development' approaches by the UN and other agencies.

There are some significant overlaps between rights and capabilities in a general sense. First, both take the individual as the primary reference point – in an ethical if not an ontological sense (Robeyns 2005). Second, both notions are grounded in the central importance of freedoms (Osmani 2005; Sen 2009; UNDP 2000). A right to something is an entitlement and not an obligation (although there are exceptions, such as the stipulation for compulsory primary education in international right instruments). As with capabilities, there is a counterfactual aspect to rights, in the sense that it is important that one has the right to freedom of religious worship, even if one does not actually exercise it. At the same time, it is argued (although not accepted by all) that human rights are inalienable: for example, that one cannot voluntarily give oneself up into slavery. Nevertheless, even if one cannot voluntarily give up the right to, say, healthcare, one can choose not to exercise that right in a particular moment. In both frameworks, these freedoms are constitutive of a valuable life. Furthermore,

Sen's (1985) insistence that attention be paid to both well-being and agency is echoed in rights frameworks.

As encountered above, a divergence between rights and capabilities approaches is that the former contains a more explicit specification of a duty-bearer – although there is considerable variation between proponents of capabilities in relation to this and other questions. There are also differences in relation to the universality of the frameworks. Controversially, Nussbaum (2000) has proposed a list of ten central human functionings as an underpinning scheme for national constitutions around the world. A canonical list, however, is resisted by Sen, who argues that valued functionings should be decided through debate at the local level, and it is this emphasis on establishing norms through public deliberation that characterizes the approach as a whole. Human rights, at least in their legal manifestation, appear to present a more rigid universal framework, since the objects of the rights are the same regardless of locality (even though they are expressed at a very general level, and can be interpreted differently in different contexts). There are, however, distinct positions on this question amongst proponents of human rights, as discussed in the introduction. Despite the apparent universality, and the fact that human rights are frequently designated as 'Western', Sen (2004) argues that they resonate with and draw on ideas from intellectual and political traditions from around the world. Furthermore, he argues that human rights should be subject to the same form of scrutiny as proposed in relation to capabilities:

> Indeed, the role of public reasoning in the formulation and vindication of human rights is extremely important to understand. Any general plausibility that these ethical claims – or their denials – have is, on this theory, dependent on their ability to survive and flourish when they encounter unobstructed discussion and scrutiny (along with adequately wide informational availability). (Sen 2005: 160)

Nevertheless, despite Sen's proposals, this form of public discussion is given more attention in capabilities than in human rights frameworks, not because the latter concept is conceptually incompatible with local decision making, but because grassroots approaches are marginal within the human rights field as a whole.

Rights and capability approaches share a great deal in terms of their fundamental moral and political tenets, but differ on certain aspects of scope and focus. Both affirm the value of human freedom and equality, although the equality of all human beings that they seek is located in different spaces

(Sen 1992) – for rights an identical set of fundamental entitlements, and for capabilities, equal ability to achieve a range of valued functionings (ones that will differ across individuals and groups). Can the two frameworks work in conjunction, and if so how?

There has been substantial interest in the relationship between rights and capabilities in general terms in recent years (e.g. UNDP 2000; Van Hees 2012; Vizard et al. 2011), as well as concerted efforts to work with the two frameworks in international development in mutually reinforcing ways. One way in which this relationship can be viewed is for the *objects* or *subject-matter* of rights to be understood as capabilities. That is to say, the right would not be to a resource, such as a health clinic, but to the ability to enjoy good health and longevity, an ability that depends on having the information and the economic and social conditions necessary to take advantage of this and other resources and convert them into good health. Viewing rights as rights to capabilities, therefore, guards against the dangers identified by Nussbaum and Robeyns of assuming that the holding of formal entitlements is sufficient for them to be exercised in practice. There are clear implications for education here that will be drawn out below.

While both Sen and Nussbaum endorse this view, the ways in which rights and capabilities are brought together differ between the two major proponents. Sen holds to a notion of 'goal rights' relating to basic capabilities – a response to the perceived inadequacies of both deontological and consequentialist approaches, allowing the realization of rights to be part of our evaluation of states of affairs, with rights understood as having both intrinsic and instrumental value (Alexander 2004; Osmani 2005; Sen 1982). As discussed above in relation to thresholds, in contrast to Sen's 'broad consequentialism', Nussbaum (2000: 14) considers that 'Central capabilities may not be infringed upon to pursue other types of social advantage'. Alexander characterizes Nussbaum's view as 'deontological eudaimonism', an ethical theory:

> that asserts the inviolability of a set of capabilities considered to be fundamental for the good life and yet accommodating within it the possibility of a consequential reasoning in contexts where different components … could conflict with one another. (Alexander 2004: 452)

According to Nussbaum, there are not supposed to be trade-offs between the basic capabilities, but in certain 'tragic' situations there may have to be, when some rights require more urgent attention than others (Nussbaum 2000).

Yet, despite differences, both Sen and Nussbaum see capabilities as constituting the fundamental entitlements that must be guaranteed to individuals and groups through the organization of society. Through this conception, they provide a coherent justification for welfare rights and their essential connection to civil and political rights – with the exercising of the latter being dependent on economic and social conditions, and the securing of economic and social guarantees being largely dependent on civil and political freedoms (Alexander 2004; Vizard 2005).

There are further potential benefits that a capability perspective can bring to a rights-based approach. Nussbaum (2006: 291) refers to its role in promoting affirmative action in the public sphere, in providing a firmer position on the basis of rights claims (simply that of a person's membership of the human community); and clarifying that entitlements are not dependent on current laws and institutions. Alexander (2004) discusses the capability approach's contribution in attending to issues such as domestic violence, sexual harassment and bodily integrity.

A capabilities framework is, therefore, well-equipped to address the factors which in subtle, and not so subtle, ways prevent individuals from fully exercising a right, due to obstacles to meaningful uptake, a restrictive experience of exercising the right, and in converting it into other valuable opportunities. There are three areas in particular in which capabilities can make a significant contribution in the field of education:

1. Providing a fuller conception of the realization of the right
2. Directing attention to the heterogeneity of learners
3. Guarding against an overly state-facing approach.

These three points relate to different aspects of the right to education: the first, the criteria by which we gauge whether the right has been upheld; the second, the constraints and facilitators on individuals and groups exercising the right, and variations in the values attached to it; and third, the responsibility for the upholding of the right.

A fuller conception of the realization of the right

The capabilities approach is significant in its insistence that the enjoyment of education involves not just a formal entitlement to schooling, but all the conditions (economic, cultural and so forth) necessary for having access, being able to engage meaningfully in learning and converting that learning into opportunities. As Nussbaum (2006: 287) states: 'To secure a right to citizens in these areas is to put them in a position of capability to function in that area'. This emphasis stems from the central insight of the capabilities approach, namely that resources are not a guarantee of real opportunities. Chaska and Arturo, in this way, require a school promoting quality education in a language they can understand, with a curriculum that respects their culture; it also involves ensuring that work requirements do not lead to absence and dropout from school, or that adaptive preferences – particularly for Chaska – do not lead to a 'choice' to give up education and thereby restrict future opportunities.

It is a simple point – though one in need of constant reaffirmation – that a formal entitlement is insufficient without the conditions in place to exercise it effectively – in Nussbaum's (2000) terms, combined capabilities involving both 'internal' abilities and 'external' social conditions. As seen above, recent work from human rights advocates – such as the 4 As scheme – has developed a much fuller account of the conditions for fulfilling the legal right. Nevertheless, the capabilities approach provides a powerful conceptual tool for understanding real as opposed to formal opportunities.

A further important aspect is the ability to convert education into meaningful opportunities in the wider society. As stated above, in addition to engagement in experiences of meaningful learning, the right to education needs to acknowledge the *positional* aspect of schooling in terms of the prestige attached to particular institutions and qualifications. The notion of capabilities acknowledges this feature, but also the forms of discrimination against individuals and groups in accessing opportunities in society, even when in possession of appropriate knowledge and skills (Unterhalter and Brighouse 2007). Restrictions on rural indigenous Peruvians exercising the opportunities in employment and elsewhere that should be conferred on them by education, therefore, also need to be taken into account.

An associated point is that as well as providing a conception of equality of opportunity in education, a further contribution that the capabilities approach can make – one that cannot be discussed in full in this chapter – is to the conceptualization of the aims of education. Education in this conception would be oriented primarily to the enhancement of people's capabilities, involving first the development of specific abilities and skills, and second, a reasoned understanding of one's actions and values, with an enhanced capacity for making choices (Vaughan 2007). Attention must be paid to the capability to have access to education of quality, but also to education as a conversion factor for other capabilities (the former corresponding to rights *to* and *within*, and the latter to rights *through* education).

Attention to the heterogeneity of learners

The second contribution – one closely linked to the above – is the sensitivity of the capabilities approach to human heterogeneity, and the need to look beyond gauges of equal inputs or outcomes (Unterhalter 2009). Welfare rights can be interpreted in terms of equal distributions of resources, but as seen in the above examples, acknowledgement must be made of individual and group characteristics that affect the conversion of resources into freedoms. One example commonly observed is that the 'equal' treatment of boys and girls in terms of inadequate toilet facilities in schools affects the latter disproportionately, leading to absences during menstruation, for instance. Children who are undernourished, who do not have the space at home to study or who lack adequate facilities within the school are not in a position to enjoy the right to education, and further provision must be made. As stated above, the notion of 'rights within education' goes some way towards responding to the need to ensure the prerequisites of learning are in place. Yet capabilities provide a more cogent critique and response to the problems of providing equal treatment for all. As Unterhalter states:

> [W]e should look not just at inputs like teachers, hours in class, or learning materials or outputs, earning from a particular level of education ... or preference satisfaction – what is best for the family as assumed in human capital theory. Evaluations should look at the condition of being educated, the negative and positive freedoms that sustain this condition and the ways in which being educated support what each and every individual has reason to value. (2007: 75)

One relevant aspect here is that the capabilities approach is sensitive to the private sphere. Some approaches to rights are characterized by a distinction between public and private spheres, with the latter being outside state influence (though this is not the case of all rights theories – see Curren 2009). Yet emphasis on the public sphere can render invisible the discrimination and obstacles to the exercising of rights faced by particular groups on account of ascribed roles – the most prominent example being gender inequalities in the home. This feature can be seen in the above example in Peru, where despite the full public entitlements, the children are severely disadvantaged by a poor home environment for study, and Chaska especially so on account of responsibilities for domestic work.

Equally, it is necessary to be attentive to differences between students obtaining the same 'results' from school. As Unterhalter (2007) points out, we cannot judge two students who have failed their school leaving exams in the same way if one has freely chosen to go out with friends instead of revising, and the other has dedicated herself fully but has been unable to succeed due to the poor quality of her school. Furthermore, students may have reason to attach value to different areas of the curriculum, including forms of learning that are not formally assessed. In this way we can distinguish between two aspects of heterogeneity that must be acknowledged: first, differing needs that entail different resources (the welfare aspect), and second, differing values attached to education and its outcomes (the agency aspect).

Guarding against an overly state-facing approach

Even with a more nuanced notion of indivisibility of rights, there are still problems relating to the identification of the responsible party for upholding those rights. Robeyns (2006) is right to critique the overemphasis on government in rights. It is not that within a rights framework only governments are responsible, as even from a legal perspective, citizens are at times directly responsible, and at others indirectly so through their influence on the state. If we take a moral rights perspective, the importance of developing a human rights 'culture' becomes clear (Osler and Starkey 2010). Nevertheless, there is a temptation in a rights approach to focus attention on state action. Capabilities can guard against this by emphasizing how these issues need to be discussed and enacted at different levels from the top to the grass roots. It is important to clarify here that guarding against a state-facing approach does not imply a justification for private providers in education (particularly those whose primary interest is profit); it is to emphasize a broader societal involvement than that of formal state institutions.

Tikly and Barrett (2009, 2011) present a modified version of Robeyns's position. While they acknowledge that rights-based approaches do not always have a purely legal orientation, they point to the limitations of an overemphasis on the state, asserting in contrast that:

> a capabilities approach draws attention to the importance of the wider moral imperative for providing a quality education, and the importance of communities, as well as the state, in developing and realising this imperative through their own commitments and actions.... (pp. 10–11)

Institutional approaches to rights will always fall short if there is not a simultaneous attention to practices and values embedded in society. The element of public discussion emphasized by Sen takes on essential importance for this reason. In addition to intrinsic and instrumental value, Sen identifies what he calls the 'constructive' value of democracy in that it 'gives citizens an opportunity to learn from one another, and helps society to form its values and priorities' (Sen 1999: 10). Respect for human rights in this way emerges from debate and interaction between people, and the notion of human rights and the specific rights that are upheld are constantly reformulated in the process. The problems of ignoring the private sphere raised above can also be addressed by this broader conception of endorsement of human rights.

Rights, therefore, should not be reduced to a formulation engraved on the stone of the law, but conceived as a set of fundamental moral and political values that are constructed and reconstructed through argument and debate in the public sphere. Law is important, of course, as a means of fulfilling positive welfare rights and rectifying rights abuses, but it cannot be the only means by which the fundamental moral framework is enacted and sustained. This approach also ensures that rights frameworks are more sensitive to local contexts and provide space for the diversity of values amongst groups and individuals, while at the same time providing universal guarantees of agency and well-being.

*

In summary, the EFA movement should retain an underpinning of education as a fundamental human right: while there are a number of valid and pressing critiques of rights frameworks, there is a baby in the bathwater to be saved. A right is not just a legal entitlement involving a mechanism of claim between citizen and government. In a more fundamental sense, it can be regarded as a threshold of individual well-being and agency that must honoured universally. It is, therefore, not just a 'strategy' for achieving certain goals, but a marker of the pre-eminent status of those goals. Furthermore, a rights framework demands that 'normality' involves the upholding of all these rights for all human beings, and that infringement shows culpability and requires urgent and concerted action.

Nevertheless, it must be recognized that the practice of rights is in many cases reduced to the bare minimum of fulfilment of legal obligations (and in many cases not even that, as evidenced by the very large numbers of children out of school altogether). These problems are not inherent in the concept of rights, but they are highly intractable, and are still present more than 60 years after the proclamation of the Universal Declaration of Human Rights. The capabilities approach is potentially a key force for reviving and refocusing the framework of rights.

The educational rights of Chaska and Arturo are clearly not being upheld if we take the broader conception of rights informed by the capabilities approach.

First, attention is needed to the subtle barriers – including self-exclusion through adaptive preferences – that may lead to non-enrolment and drop-out even when places are available. Second, the right needs to acknowledge experiences within the school, and how these nurture or endanger students. Last, the outcomes need to be included in our evaluations, thinking not only of the learning gained by students (learning in its broadest sense, as well as the basic skills that characterize the calculations of the dominant development agencies), but also the conditions of society that determine how this learning is converted into opportunities.

Note

1   This age range was established by a constitutional amendment in November 2009.

8

Learning Human Rights

Is it indeed significant that education is or is not a human right? If we can agree that education is good for many different reasons, and can muster up the resources to give widespread access to education, is it just a matter of philosophical curiosity whether or not it is an absolute right? Indeed, this is the approach taken by EFA, which has involved a range of different agencies, including some such as the World Bank that is ambiguous in its endorsement of the idea of education as a fundamental right, but nevertheless supports the expansion of school systems. Research on EFA has consequently focused on the complexities of implementation, the challenges of actually getting children into school and keeping them there, rather than questions of why we would want education or schools in the first place. Given that we can all agree that education is a good thing without agreeing *why* it is a good thing, a focus on implementation would seem like an excellent strategy at first sight. This book, however, has argued that this is not the case. It is significant why we value education and it is significant whether we consider education is a human right.

As discussed in Chapter 1, the first reason is one of the fragility of instrumental justifications. If access to school is justified only on a cost-benefit basis, that the rate of return to school justifies the investment, there is likely to be wide access to schooling, but not universal access, leading to the exclusion of certain populations around the world.

The second reason it is important why we value education – far from an esoteric point, but surprisingly often forgotten – is that there is not one thing called education. Education expresses itself in multiple and often contradictory forms, with much of what happens in schools in all regions of the world being largely meaningless, and some positively harmful to students. Even in generally positive environments in which some learning is taking place, there are competing visions of what education is aiming at and how it is organized. It is this second point that I will address in this chapter. The position taken by agencies in much multilateral educational work in the international context is that, while we cannot agree on everything, we can press ahead with conventional schools delivering the basic skills of literacy and numeracy. Instead, I will argue that there are much more substantial contours of the aims and processes of education that we need to commit to internationally. These aspects relate essentially to the ethical dimension in education. As outlined in Chapter 4, the diversity of educational provision is underpinned by the criterion of providing meaningful learning processes that uphold the full set of human rights. But does this requirement entail education about human rights? What is the relationship between justifications for education and the content of education, or between the human right to learning and the learning of human rights?

The purpose of this chapter then is to draw out the implications of the arguments formed in the earlier sections of the book for addressing the question of whether there might be a right to human rights education (HRE), and how it should be conducted. Controversially perhaps, I will argue against the conventional logic associated with HRE:

1. To have human rights we need to know what they are and have the capacity to claim and exercise them.
2. Education can provide the required knowledge, skills and values.
3. Therefore, there is a right to education.

As I will argue in greater detail below, this logic creates too much of a division between education and human rights, casting education as a treatment that leads to a particular result. An alternative view sees there to be a more porous boundary between education and human rights.

This chapter starts by mapping the notion of HRE. Drawing on the justifications for the general right to education presented in previous chapters, implications are drawn out for the question of whether there is a right specifically to HRE. Following that, the chapter addresses the question of the forms HRE might take within that conception. There are important questions that cannot be covered here, such as issues of effectiveness of implementation, programme evaluation and global policy convergence. Instead the focus will be on the fundamental justifications and conceptualizations of HRE.

Mapping HRE

Monisha Bajaj's book *Schooling and Social Change* provides a fascinating account of experiences of HRE in India. Here we see in vivid detail the extent of oppression and discrimination faced by certain groups, the transformative potential of HRE as well as some of the risks and potential backlash. The book assesses the experience of the Institute of Human Rights Education (IHRE), which has a large programme involving nearly 4,000 government schools across the country. The programme is working in the context of the severe marginalization of the *adivasis* or tribal groups in India, and the *dalits* (formerly known as untouchable caste), the latter, while officially illegal, still confined to menial jobs and excluded from religious sites and contact with other castes. These groups have all the characteristics of disempowerment, combining lack of formal education and the consequent restricted access to both information and opportunities, with a deeply ingrained sense of the naturalness of their inferiority. Within schools, students also face corporal punishment, lack of basic amenities and discrimination on the basis of caste.

The HRE programme run over three years in many cases brought significant changes to this situation. Children began to take action over issues of discrimination in the community, dropout of students from school, female infanticide, and early marriage that was preventing girls from continuing their studies. However, they also faced significant opposition from their own families, and from those whose power and privileges were being disrupted. Take these two examples:

> A Dalit student in seventh standard discussed using the tap to wash his plate one day and getting yelled at by a village elder from a higher caste. He defended his right, but he and his family were threatened with violence. (p. 84)

> One sixth standard student, learning about human rights for the first time, went to the headmaster to complain that he had not received a uniform to which he was entitled; as punishment, he was caned and threatened with expulsion. (p. 84)

These examples show the courage that is needed to rectify the injustices that the students face. It also showed the need for judgement and discretion, to distinguish between courageous action and foolhardiness that will endanger themselves and others. Another important area of learning through action was a movement from individual interventions to collective ones, given the fragility and increased dangers of the former. A highly significant feature identified by the study was the role of *coalitional agents*, relatively more privileged students who develop solidarity for and take action on behalf of, or together with, more disadvantaged peers. Despite the challenges of implementation in a curriculum oriented towards exams and basic skills, HRE had found a place and was bringing real change.

Holding this vivid illustration of the realities of HRE in practice in mind, we turn to the concept of HRE. The characteristic of the English language – in which nouns can be strung together in adjectival fashion, that is 'human rights education', rather than having to specify 'education for human rights' or 'education in human rights' etc. – allows for greater ambiguity, and is both a strength and a weakness. It leaves room for confusion, uncertainty and contradiction, but at the same time enables a multifaceted interpretation – one that certainly is in keeping with a multifaceted nature of the relationship between the two concepts.

In fact, there is considerable diversity of interpretation and practice in HRE. There are national HRE initiatives in more than 100 countries (Bajaj 2011), although with widespread evidence of 'decoupling', where the content is sanitized so as not to prove too challenging to existing power structures or pushed to the periphery of school experience. There are also long traditions of HRE in the work of NGOs, adult education and professional training. There will first be a brief view of the treatment of HRE in international law before turning to conceptual interpretations and examples in practice.

Legal status

It is a frequently heard point that the seminal statement of the right to education in the UDHR incorporates HRE within it. The second part of Article 26 states:

> Education shall be directed to the full development of the human personality and to the strengthening of respect for human rights and fundamental freedoms. It shall promote understanding, tolerance and friendship among all nations, racial or religious groups, and shall further the activities of the United Nations for the maintenance of peace.

As discussed in Chapter 2, these points are expanded in Article 29 of the CRC, which proposes that the aims of education should also include the development of respect for a child's own culture and that of others, and equality of the sexes.

These are statements of broad aims, incorporating a clear purpose for education in underpinning a world human rights culture. The statements do not give any indication as to how education might go about doing this – too much to ask of a human rights instrument perhaps, but nonetheless a significant omission as far as schools and educators are concerned, since they are left with a grand responsibility based on little more than faith. What is it about schools that means they will be able to simply 'strengthen respect for human rights'? (And it is largely schools that are being referred to, although non-formal education is acknowledged in subsequent interpretations of the right). Such faith in the potential of schools, if not blind then certainly rose-tinted, runs the risk of either an overestimation of the role of knowledge in determining action, an oversimplification of the process of value formation in the young, or naiveté as regards the character and environment of educational institutions in practice. Schools can in fact strengthen respect for human rights, but the relationship is far more complex than acknowledged here.

Having said that, it is of course of fundamental importance that the UDHR and subsequent right instruments refer to these overarching aims, and give education a role in fostering human rights. This role has been further affirmed in a range of other declarations and documents of the UN and other agencies. The Council of Europe Charter on Education for Democratic Citizenship and Human Rights Education of 2010 provides the following definition:

> 'Human rights education' means education, training, awareness raising, information, practices and activities which aim, by equipping learners with knowledge, skills and understanding and developing their attitudes and behaviour, to empower learners to contribute to the building and defence of a universal culture of human rights in society, with a view to the promotion and protection of human rights and fundamental freedoms.

Here we have a comprehensive and precise definition that serves us well in mapping the range of practices associated with HRE. It is inclusive of different approaches, but is distinctive in its reference to the building of a human rights culture (this reference was echoed in the subsequent *UN Declaration on Human Rights Education and Training*) – indicating that beyond the mechanisms of legal recourse, we need an environment of endorsement of and respect for human rights. This vision is certainly one shared by this book. The question remains of how best to form and support this culture, particularly given our inauspicious starting point.

Categorizations of HRE

Approaches to HRE have been categorized in different ways. Tibbitts (2002) presents a scheme based closely on observation of practice, leading to the identification of three dominant models: values and awareness; accountability; and transformational. The 'values and awareness' approach aims to transmit basic knowledge about human rights and engage interest in them, and characterizes HRE in schools and public awareness campaigns. The accountability model on the other hand focuses on the law, monitoring of human rights violations, advocacy and lobbying. In this model:

> Personal change is not an explicit goal, since it assumes that professional responsibility is sufficient for the individual having an interest in applying a human rights framework. (Tibbitts 2002: 166)

This aspect distinguishes it from the third model, the *transformational*, in which individuals and groups undergo a process of development, empowering them to more effectively defend their own rights. This third model is associated with community development, women's groups and minority rights. These three forms are distinguished by their different target groups as well as different understandings of HRE, but Tibbitts also points out how HRE expresses itself in different ways in different contexts: for example, in developing countries; post-totalitarian countries; older democracies; and post-conflict situations. HRE also manifests itself in different ways at the diverse levels of education, whether early years, school, university, adult education or professional training.

Bajaj (2011), on the other hand, distinguishes between three ideological orientations of HRE: global citizenship, coexistence and transformative action. The former:

> seeks to provide learners with membership to an international community through fostering knowledge and skills related to universal values and standards. *Human Rights Education for Coexistence* focuses on the interpersonal and intergroup aspects of rights and is usually a strategy for tolerance utilized where conflict emerges not from absolute deprivation, but from ethnic or civil strife. The third approach, *Human Rights Education for Transformative Action*, usually involves learners who are marginalized from economic and political power and for whom HRE includes a significant process of understanding their own realities. (pp. 23–4)

The third of these links closely with Tibbitts's 'transformational' model, while the first two provide us with fresh insights into the distinct values underpinning HRE in different environments.

One of the most common schemes for understanding HRE is that of education *about* human rights and education *for* human rights (e.g. Lohrenscheit 2002).

The former focuses primarily on knowledge, with students gaining awareness of human rights law, mechanisms for legal recourse, monitoring and accountability systems and so forth. It also addresses the historical development of human rights – in Starkey's (1991: 16) phrase 'human rights education looks at the past to prepare the future'. It is not necessarily restricted to factual knowledge, and can also involve an appreciation of controversies relating to human rights and the development of awareness and values. Education *for* human rights, on the other hand, aims to equip leaners with the attributes needed to effectively defend and promote their own and others' rights in practice. The latter will involve knowledge, but also skills and dispositions, such as effective communication and interpretation of media, and development of global solidarity. In some interpretations (e.g. Lohrenscheit 2002) this form is synonymous with Freirean *conscientisation*, leading to social transformation through praxis.

This distinction mirrors that observable in other curricular areas, such as the move from 'civics', involving transmission of knowledge relating to constitution and government, to 'citizenship education', in which there is a broader understanding of democracy, attempt to foster relevant skills and values and adopt participatory methods. Proponents are keen to point out, however, that there is not a clear hierarchy between education *for* and education *about* human rights, with the knowledge component also playing an important role.

To these two, a third is often added, education *through* (or *as*) human rights. In this case, learning takes place through actual experiences of upholding of human rights: an example being the rights-respecting schools in the United Kingdom, in which the transformation of school disciplinary policy in line with principles of the Convention on the Rights of the Child enables a particular kinds of learning and moral development in the students (Sebba and Robinson 2010).

Amnesty International (2009) places this distinction at the heart of its Guidelines for Human Rights Friendly Schools:

- For human rights – Learning in order to be able to practice human rights in one's daily life
- About human rights – Learning important knowledge about human rights principles, issues, and debates
- Through human rights – Learning must take place using inclusive, participatory and democratic methods.

The categorization was also utilized in the *UN Declaration on Human Rights Education and Training* of 2011. Similar schemes had previously been adopted for comparable areas of study such as citizenship (Kerr 1999) as mentioned above, and sustainable development (Sauvé 1996).

As can be seen, this three-way frame (about, for and through) is reminiscent of another used in this book: rights *to*, *within* and *through* education. In fact there are strong parallels between them, the difference being that the former assesses the place of rights within education and the curriculum, and the latter the place of education within the set of rights. Confusingly the *through* in the latter scheme relates to the *for* in the former scheme (both relating to the acquisition of knowledge, skills and values for defending rights in the broader society) and the *within* in the latter to the *through* in the former (both relating to the incorporation of human rights in the educational practices themselves).

While the education *about* and education *for* human rights is a useful distinction in practice, the difference between them is not as straightforward as it first appears. In fact, both of these approaches are education for human rights, in the sense that both are employing educational means to attain the end of enhanced upholding of human rights. The difference is one of educational strategy adopted: in the *about*, the focus is on knowledge, frequently based on a commitment to existing human rights law, to existing institutions that uphold that law and the need for individuals to understand established rights and the mechanisms for recourse. As Starkey (1991: 15) states, 'For texts to have any force whatsoever requires that they be known'; moreover, 'Action, in this sense, presupposes knowledge, and knowledge, education.' In the education *for*, the means adopted are different, seeing a need for individuals to have much broader range of attributes in order to defend and uphold rights, involving particular skills and dispositions that underpin their use. There are differences, therefore, in the means adopted, and there are also subtle differences in the ends, since while they both uphold human rights there are distinct understandings of those rights – with differing emphasis on the law and popular action. Again, the third form, education 'through' rights, is also for human rights, although distinctively it sees that experiences of upholding human rights are an effective means of promoting learning about them.

The field of practice of HRE is therefore unified by the aim of using education to promote and defend human rights in the broader society, but differs markedly in relation to the understandings of human rights underpinning them and in the strategies adopted to achieve them. We now turn to the central question of why we might want to engage in HRE in the first place.

Why human rights education?

General justifications

The value of HRE rests on the value of human rights themselves. It is not within the remit of this chapter to provide a general assessment of human rights, and I will assume here that human rights are of value, and turn attention to the question of whether human rights *education* is desirable or necessary. The movement from the former to the latter may seem simple and straightforward, but in fact there are a range of pathways we can take.

First, we can see HRE as having both societal and individual benefits. HRE can be seen as a means of achieving a change in people's attitudes and behaviour in ways that will be beneficial to the whole of society. So, an individual can develop respect for others' views, acknowledge the interests of those outside their immediate community, ethnic or national group, and refrain from subjecting others for example, to physical aggression or psychological humiliation. (As will be discussed in the next section, there are difficulties in using these societal benefits as a justification for a *right* to HRE, but they are nevertheless a justification.) HRE can also be seen as a means to the upholding the human rights of the learner herself: gaining information about international rights instruments, developing communication skills for negotiating with relevant authorities and the dispositions to act courageously in defence of one's rights. We would normally think of the latter form as particularly relevant to those groups who are significantly disempowered, and because of economic disadvantage, discrimination or lack of voice currently unable to claim their legally recognized rights.

Education can also be seen to have diverse value in relation to the specific attributes to be developed in human beings and the conditions to be developed in society. As discussed in the previous section, it can fulfil a range of functions in relation to human rights, such as: informing people of them; equipping people to exercise them; instilling their value; and enabling people to participate in their construction. These different roles for education can be seen to vary in relation to three factors:

1. The underpinning conception of human rights
2. The process of realization of human rights in practice
3. Understandings of education

So, seeing human rights to derive their existence from their formulation in law (1) will lead to a different treatment in schools from a view that they are established through popular struggle, or public discussion. The skills and knowledge with which learners are equipped to uphold rights will differ depending on whether the process of realization (2) is a purely legal one, or based also on advocacy, protest, day-to-day interactions and the work of civil society organizations. Last (3), there will be differences depending on whether education is understood as a process of knowledge transmission, or one of emergence of joint understanding and collective construction of knowledge.

In fact, justifications for HRE appear strong in all of these scenarios, whether we adopt a fixed or malleable conception of human rights, or a transmission or construction conception of education. From a top–down human rights perspective people need to be informed and adopt relevant values, and from a bottom–up perspective people need to be empowered to participate – both involving education (though of different types).

We can see clearly that HRE is desirable, but is it actually essential for the upholding of human rights? The question of whether education is an absolutely necessary condition depends on how we understand rights. If we focus on what is provided by the state for the individual, such as the provision of services such as health care, guarantees of security and freedom from religious persecution, in one sense all of these can be guaranteed in the absence of education. However, this is a very passive treatment of the fulfilment of rights, and ignores the active elements of the rights-holder as somebody who makes a claim on others, struggles collectively for the recognition of a demand, and makes the choice of whether to exercise that right or not. In this active sense of the rights-holder as somebody who holds states accountable rather than simply receiving a service, then education *is* a necessary part, since it is impossible to play an active role without the necessary information, analytical capacities, communication etc.

Justifications for a right

There are strong reasons, therefore, for supporting the practice of HRE. But is in fact a *right*? There are two ways in which HRE could be classified as such:

1. There is an independent justification for HRE as a right
2. HRE is an inseparable part of general education

As discussed in the previous section, the benefits of HRE can be to society or to the individual. In this case it is better to say *rights-holder* than individual, as in many cases we may be speaking of a group (such as indigenous community) rather than an individual person. There are strong reasons for considering HRE a right for those individuals or groups who are suffering human rights abuses. If HRE is seen from the perspective of empowering people to defend and exercise their own rights, then there is a strong justification on the basis of the general right to freedom from subjugation (with its basis in human agency) and associated oppression and exploitation.

Societal benefits are a cause for concern in terms of justifying a *right*, since rights exist at least in part precisely to protect individuals against the kinds of calculations that sacrifice some to an aggregated societal interest. In this way, children's rights and HRE programmes in schools can be based on an intention to improve student behaviour and consequently make the school more attractive to prospective parents. Negative ways in which HRE programmes can manifest themselves according to this logic are discussed by Osler and Starkey (2010: 17):

> What passes for human rights education in many policy documents and schools
> is, at best, inadequate, and may be little more than a mechanism for managing
> young people's behaviour. Some of what is designated human rights education
> is designed to encourage compliance amongst learners, rather than to promote
> critical thinking. Young children may be taught simply to be nice to each other,
> rather than to stand up for justice.

On the other hand, there may be entirely valid societal or global interests derived from HRE, such as encouraging learners to develop solidarity and act for global justice. We are then faced with two different forms of HRE: a space for empowerment of populations whose human rights are being infringed; and a space for developing values of global justice for those whose human rights are for the most part upheld.

There are compelling reasons to consider the empowerment aspect of HRE as a right. Yet what about the second aspect identified, the development of values of global justice and commitment to upholding the rights of others? Is this a right? The best way to approach this question is in fact to acknowledge the inseparable nature of the two aspects. Human rights do not consist separately of some things that I can claim for myself and other things that I need to do for others. Endorsing universal rights is in and of itself a substantial responsibility and commitment to upholding and defending those rights for all others as well as oneself. (Hence the redundancy of asserting that young people should think about their responsibilities as well as their rights – this is only necessary if we misunderstand the notion of right.) So the empowerment and solidarity aspects are inseparable.

Unavoidably HRE would involve both having capacities to defend and exercise one's own rights, and respect and act for the rights of others. (Bajaj's study indicated a way in which these can come together through the coalition of the relatively more privileged students working in solidarity to rectify abuses against those who suffered most discrimination.) In this integrated sense, HRE becomes a right for all and not only the most marginalized (even though the need of the latter may appear more immediately pressing). Building a human rights culture entails the involvement of all in the endorsement of rights. Magendzo (2005: 138) reflects thus on the era of the Pinochet regime in Chile:

> This led me to ask myself why the only ones who were reflecting on human rights education were those who had suffered the most during the repression. I came to the conclusion that when democracy was recovered, human rights education should be the centre of education. It should be the main objective.

A further point relates to intrinsic value. As discussed in Chapter 3, it is only possible to affirm that something is the object of a right if there is some intrinsic value in the object. As we have seen, much of the justification for HRE regards it as an 'enabling right', one that supports other rights that do have intrinsic value. Yet the objects of rights cannot be purely instrumental in this way. Take the example of education as a means of enabling people to have access to information about healthcare. While this educational component is essential, the *right* is to healthcare, with education simply part of the strategy for realizing the right in practice. Viewing HRE simply as an enabler, therefore, is a restricted view. If HRE does consist of simply informing people about existing rights and providing them with the skills to access them, then we cannot justify it as a right in itself. Yet, as seen above there is an active sense of a rights-holder that necessarily involves awareness, understanding and agency, and these in turn require education. A broader vision of HRE sees it, in addition to the above, as a process of critical reflection, deliberation and formation of human rights. In this sense, there is intrinsic value to the process as it is an engagement of the individual in the creation of the social unit of which she is a part.

Starkey (1991: 16) emphasizes the 'unfinished nature of the work of human rights' and expresses this need for learners to be involved debate around them:

> Human rights is not a rigid and static system, it is a dynamic concept implying on the one hand the preservation of freedoms and on the other an impulse towards justice. Armed with the principles of human rights and a knowledge of

the struggles involved in their achievement, citizens of all ages can debate what it is they want to hold on to and what it is that needs changing. The past and the future are in creative tension around the notion of human rights.

The children in Tamil Nadu in this way, armed with the principles of human rights, applied them to their specific context and collectively developed strategies for addressing discrimination (Bajaj 2011). Debate, therefore, enables more effective action against human rights abuses, working collectively rather than individually. Yet there is a further role for debate, one that represents its intrinsic value. Deliberation is in this latter sense *constitutive* of rather than instrumental in upholding human rights. Human rights are formed and maintained through public discussion itself, and that deliberation is an instantiation of human rights.

An alternative route into this question is to consider whether HRE is an essential part of education generally speaking (taking as a given that we have a human right to education). My justification for the right to education in general has resisted the specification of subjects, such as geography or chemistry, given their particularity in relation to time and place. Given the need for the right to education to adapt itself to different cultures, times and individuals, it must necessarily be open in relation to content. But is there a way in which the whole curriculum might be imbued with HRE?

Some authors have argued that HRE has become necessary in light of the changing nature of societies and schools. Hornberg (2002: 190), for example, asserts that globalization has made HRE an essential part of general education:

> Human rights education is, by its very nature, a topic which has the potential to help students transcend national, social, cultural and economic and other boundaries. It is a good vehicle to make them become aware of global interdependencies.

In relation to one of the manifestations of globalization – multi-ethnic societies and schools – Osler and Starkey (2010: 18) argue that human rights serves the role of forming the basis of dialogue between people of different cultures and perspectives. Another way in which general education might be seen necessarily to involve HRE is in relation to empowerment of marginalized groups – much of this process may entail acquisition of literacy and general forms of knowledge (rather than any explicit HRE) so as to participate in politics, defend one's interests and thereby avoid exploitation (Wringe 1988). Spring (2000) puts forward a view of this type, seeing the right to education generally speaking as being justified by the need for people to defend their human rights, and to 'creat[e] a moral duty to actively protect the human rights of others'.

If we take an expansive view of HRE, beyond its appearance as a school subject, we can see how it might comprise an integral part of education generally speaking in the ways alluded to by the above authors. Two characteristics of education are fundamental here: first, that it involves some form of collective reflection, in observing, considering and trying to understand the nature of the universe through communication; second, that it is inherently moral. By moral, I do not mean that it is always morally *good* (at least not in practice), only that it always has significance in the moral realm, and in the political. This idea follows Paulo Freire's view of the impossibility of neutrality in education:

> There never is, nor has ever been, an educational practice in zero space-time – neutral in the sense of being committed only to preponderantly abstract, intangible ideas. To try to get people to believe that there is such a thing as this... is indisputably a political practice ... (Freire 1994, p. 65)

From these points we can see that general education will always involve reflection on society and the individual, the formation of personalities and the creation of ideas that are morally and politically significant. This point applies to all levels of education, including universities (Boothe and Dunne 1999). The moral and political domain for sure is wider than human rights, but there must necessarily be some consideration of the fundamental entitlements that might be guaranteed for all human beings. Education will therefore always move learners (and teachers) towards or away from the human rights culture aspired for by advocates. Beyond the specific curriculum subject of 'human rights', or associated area like 'citizenship', all curricular domains thereby take on relevance, including arts and literature.

Added to these points is the principle of indivisibility of rights referred to above – that the right to education must necessarily be consistent with the full set of human rights, and therefore the processes will both positively embody and refrain from infringing other human rights. The experience of living in this rights-respecting environment is in itself a significant source of human rights learning, as will be explored further in the section that follows.

There is therefore a basis on which to justify HRE as a right, both in an independent sense, and as an integral part of education as a whole. The following section will draw out the implications of these arguments for the approaches, methods and practices of HRE.

How human rights education?

Proximity

In order to understand the different forms of HRE, I will draw on a framework previously used in relation to citizenship education (McCowan 2009). As discussed in Chapter 4, the notion of *proximity* is a way of understanding the relationship between ends and means in education, between the overarching aims and the activities organized to achieve them. For the most part we understand the relationship between the former and the latter in a causal sense: we select the methods that will give us the greatest chance of achieving our goals. This relationship is termed *separation*. While it appears a logical approach, it has limitations as the most effective means may not be morally valid (as in the saying 'the ends justify the means'). A macabre example here would be the use of corporal punishment and fear of humiliation in class as a means of motivating students to more effectively memorize the articles of the Convention on the Rights of the Child.

An alternative approach to the formation of means is termed *harmony*. In this case the means must conform to the principles of value contained in the ends. So, educational activities designed to foster understanding of human rights must themselves be imbued with the principles of human rights. This form will also involve the exemplification of human rights in teachers' own practice, in the management of the school and will characterize what is often referred to as the 'hidden curriculum'. This mode is emphasized in Amnesty International (2009):

> The concept of an education through human rights offers clear support for an approach that goes beyond teaching human rights in classrooms to modelling human rights in everyday policies and practices. (p. 12)

There are, therefore, significant implications for the role of teachers in HRE. According to the Bajaj study, much of the success of the programme was connected with the modelling of human rights in the teachers' behaviour, their assistance in interventions and persuasion of the community of the legitimacy of the action. Teachers also described their own development as a result of their teaching of HRE programmes, an indication of the dynamic nature of the process.

Participatory pedagogy is often justified on the basis of its effectiveness for learning. As Tibbetts (2002) states, the 'interactive pedagogical approach' is 'linked more strongly with attitudinal or behavioural change that with a pure lecturing approach'. While important, this is not the only reason why participatory methods should be adopted in the classroom. They should be adopted primarily because they embody the principle of participation that is itself a human right.

Harmony is supported in the Council of Europe Charter:

> Teaching and learning practices and activities should follow and promote democratic and human rights values and principles; in particular, the governance of educational institutions, including schools, should reflect and promote human rights values and foster the empowerment and active participation of learners, educational staff and stakeholders, including parents.

Important aspects emphasized here are the incorporation of human rights into pedagogy and management, and broad community involvement in educational decision-making, seen itself to have an empowering role. Elsewhere in the Charter, the significance of participation for learning is further emphasized:

> Member states should promote democratic governance in all educational institutions both as a desirable and beneficial method of governance in its own right and as a practical means of learning and experiencing democracy and respect for human rights.

As discussed in Chapter 5, there is abundant evidence of this learning through democratic governance in rights-respecting schools (e.g. Covell 2010; Covell and Howe 2001). Harmony also manifests itself in the access policies of schools and systems, whether fostering inclusion of all social groups or discriminating on the basis of gender, race/ethnicity, ability and a range of other factors, leading either to complete exclusion from the school system or relegation to provision of poor quality.

After separation and harmony comes *unification*. In this third mode, educational processes are no longer distinct from the practices themselves. In this way, the act of exercising human rights – claiming, constructing and defending – is itself a source of learning. The children in the Bajaj study learn not only from the HRE programme in terms of acquiring useful knowledge and skills (separation), but also experience the modelling of human rights within the school (harmony) and through the process of campaigning and intervening for rights outside school (unification) learn about collective action, strategies of change and negotiation. There is not a clear hierarchy between these three. However, as outlined above, in HRE – and in any form of education involving values – the *separation* mode on its own is highly problematic.

This scheme allows us to understand the frame of 'about, for and through' more clearly. Education through human rights is an example of *harmony* if occurring within the school setting, and of *unification* if outside an educational institution or experience. Both education 'about' and 'for' are forward-looking, in that they aim to equip students with the skills to exercise and defend human rights at a subsequent point in time, and therefore risk falling into separation mode. Yet they can still incorporate principles of human rights into their processes and thereby represent *harmony* (and this incorporation is strongly evident in discussions of 'for human rights'). So in these cases, attention must be paid to the teacher–student relationship, the forms of pedagogy and the process of construction of the curriculum, as well as the broader backdrop of decision-making in institution and system. In practice, we will need all of these three. Learners need some propositional knowledge of human rights (*about*), to develop certain skills (*for*) and to have real experiences of rights-respecting environments (*through*).

Malleable versus fixed

Education about human rights of course needs to be a critical reflection on knowledge, rather than a simple absorption. As Spring (2000: 104–5) states, we must beware 'the potential danger of human rights education's repeating the traditions of indoctrinating-nationalistic education and ignoring cultural differences'. The transmission/construction binary in fact has two components: the conception of human rights and the pedagogical approach for communicating that conception. Both of these can be more or less critical or conformist, open or closed, malleable or fixed. (The associations of these terms in each case makes the former appear more desirable, but I am not suggesting that rejection of current conceptions is always preferable.) So there is a continuum of conceptions of human rights from on the one hand, a fixed universal list that derives its legitimacy from existing enshrining in law, and that cannot be added to or subtracted from, to, on the other hand, an entirely bottom–up process of struggle and claiming of rights, locally defined. In the pedagogical sphere, the continuum is from a pure transmission model, where the teacher transmits objectively valid knowledge and the students absorb the knowledge faithfully, to, on the other hand, a learning process starting with a blank page and constructing the set of rights collectively during the educational process.

Again, we should not impose a strict hierarchy on these, nor suggest that there is value in encouraging students to reject international rights instruments out of hand. Neither is it being suggested that teachers should never transmit knowledge to students. Yet HRE must consider the learner as a *subject* in the Freirean sense, someone who is an agent in their own learning, and correspondingly an agent in political processes. Ultimately, human rights only have value if they are endorsed by human beings, and true endorsement (rather than unreflective absorption) depends on open discussion and critical reflection.

Process

The importance of consonance between human rights and the teaching styles, decision-making and the broader environment within the educational institution, leads us to a consideration of process. This book has argued that the right to education is a right to meaningful learning processes, rather than a right to educational inputs or specific levels of learning achievement. This approach goes against the dominant understanding of the educational entitlement proposed by international organizations, particularly the World Bank, such as the proposal for a Millennium Learning Goal of attainment on maths, language and science tests (Filmer et al. 2006). Given the need to protect the openness and spontaneity of education, and to value a broad range of outcomes beyond narrow cognitive ones, we need to embrace a conception of learning experiences as being valuable in themselves. These processes of course lead to subsequent benefit for learners, but ones that are open and perhaps unexpected, rather than being universally stipulated or predefined.

This emphasis on learning process is one that resonates with the above discussion of HRE. Focusing on harmony and unification entails attention to the quality of the experience itself – protecting students' freedom of expression, physical integrity, dignity and so forth – rather than simply subordinating (or in some cases sacrificing) the moment of learning for a supposed future moment of benefit. Furthermore, the process of discussing human rights in the classroom is not only significant in so far as it may enhance political action subsequently outside the school, it is valuable in itself, as an instantiation of open and ethical enquiry in the collective.

*

How we see HRE depends on our understanding of what human rights are. If human rights are granted from above, or derive their validity from their legal formulation, then the most appropriate response is to view, analyse and internalize the law. Yet if we understand human rights as being constructed, debated and revised through deliberation, then a very different educational approach emerges. From this latter perspective, education serves as a space for developing the skills, knowledge and dispositions to participate in the formation of human rights, and to claim and defend them in the broader society (as proposed by Spring [2000] and others). But this is only one way of viewing the educational process. Educational spaces are not just sites of preparation for the broader society, but are arenas of society in their own right. In this way, human rights are actually constructed and played out within the deliberations and broader experiences in school.

As argued above, education necessarily involves human rights, in that it will always have ethical implications, and either uphold or infringe those rights and liberties. Education is an inherently moral and political undertaking, and will involve questions of our relationship with others and how we behave towards them, with significant consequences for the development of a human rights culture. The right to education – a right to exploration of reality – is a right to HRE – an exploration of lived morality and politics. Conversely, the exercising and defending of human rights will always entail learning. This dialectic is an incarnation of the reflection-action duad outlined in previous chapters.

9

Principles and Implications

All people have the right to education because the capacity to understand the world, and act in it, is fundamental to human life. Education underpins the human qualities of understanding and agency, opening spaces for diverse forms of learning including the development of specific abilities, the acquisition of new knowledge, reflecting on self and context, expanding moral sensibility and reimagining society. Understanding and agency are mutually reinforcing. Developing a profound vision of reality enhances our capacity for ethical action, while acting in the world is itself a key source of learning. Education, therefore, at its best is a cycle of ever deeper and broader understanding, and enhanced agency.

These two elements correspond to Freire's dialectic of reflection and action within the concept of praxis:

> In problem-posing education, people develop their power to perceive critically the way they exist in the world with which and in which they find themselves; they come to see the world not as a static reality, but as a reality in process, in transformation ... Hence, the teacher–student and the students–teachers reflect simultaneously on themselves and the world without dichotomizing this reflection from action, and thus establish an authentic form of thought and action. (Freire 1972: 83)

Freire is here addressing a situation of extreme objectification of rural peasants, and the need to bring a radical transformation of society; yet the idea applies also to the less dramatic ways in which every day we learn and act, and are faced with and respond to the challenges of injustices and unknowns. Similar ideas, although with a distinct political orientation, are expressed in Schön's (1983) notion of the 'reflective practitioner'. What we have is a pendulum moving ever more quickly between two poles (reflection and action), with no ultimate distinction between them. There is a parallel between these two qualities and the *wisdom* and *compassion* at the heart of Buddhist thought – neither can exist without the other, and each reinforces and refines the other. A true feeling of solidarity for others, and action consonant with that feeling, is bound up with the realization that ultimately we are not separate from them.

However, the above is one among many ways of framing the educational venture, and the right to education permits a rich diversity of conceptions of education. This diversity is not arbitrary, but must cohere around certain principles, relating to the types of education that might be considered a right, and the ways in which education should be conducted. Four criteria have been identified in the preceding chapters: (1) intrinsic value, (2) engagement in educational processes, (3) lifelong application and (4) consonance with the full set of human rights.

1. If education is considered a right, then it must have intrinsic value. If education is only instrumentally valuable, then it is not right in itself, merely an accessory to other rights. Most discussions of the right to education – and advocacy work of development agencies – point to its role in supporting other aspects of well-being (health, family planning, employment, etc.). In this sense it is an *enabling* right, underpinning all others (Waldron and Ruane 2011). While education does in fact serve this function (and it is a valid function), for it to be right in itself it also needs to have intrinsic value.
2. The right to education is a right to educational *processes*, rather than inputs or outputs. In particular, there are problems with associating the right with access to schooling. Furthermore, a right to education cannot stipulate universal learning outcomes, given the diverse values attached to it, the unpredictability of education and the need for spontaneity and freedom in learning. People have a right to engage in meaningful processes of learning.
3. The right to education cannot be confined to a particular period of life. While childhood is of critical importance for learning, the right includes all levels of education and has a lifelong application.
4. A right to education must be consonant with other human rights. It must be conducted in a manner that does not infringe learners' physical integrity, freedom of thought and so forth (indivisibility of rights). Following R. S. Peters, there are moral constraints on what counts as education. It must be both *witting* and *willing*, in other words, learners must be aware that they are engaged in an intentional process of learning, and have some desire to be engaged in such a process (i.e. excluding brainwashing, conditioning, etc.).

Given the above, we can express the right to education in the following manner:

> All people have a right throughout life to engage in educational processes that are intrinsically as well as instrumentally valuable, and that embody respect for human rights.

Instrumental value in addition to intrinsic value is of course desirable, but, as argued in Chapter 5, only in relation to external purposes that are consistent with the full set of human rights.

It is not being suggested that this kind of formulation should be adopted in identical fashion in rights instruments. The task of drafting international law has specific challenges, given the need to define obligations that can be justiciable, and to settle on a text that is both acceptable to defenders of the right but will not alienate nation-states. Yet as argued by this book, rights are moral as well as legal, and it is as important to infuse a sense of these rights within culture as it is to establish them in law. Educators, learners and policy-makers need to grapple with the principles of the right to inform the expression of universal educational entitlements within their daily work.

While critiques of rights, such as that of Robeyns (2006) reviewed in Chapter 7, do not constitute a reason for abandoning a rights approach, they do highlight the need to redefine the right to education, emphasizing the centrality of engagement in educational processes that are meaningful, attentive to human heterogeneity and that respect human rights. According to the conception outlined above, the right to education should be at the same time more specific and less specific than commonly expressed in international rights instruments. Its character and nature need more careful outlining than is commonly observed, but there is no need to identify education with formal education, let alone restrict it to the primary level. This book has argued that the focus on schools in both international law and the EFA initiative is understandable in the short term, but ultimately limited. Much of what occurs in schools around the world is little more than time-wasting for all involved, and some is actually harmful. Much meaningful and effective education takes place outside schools, even when not carrying certification. Attention is needed to the learning opportunities themselves – while these are often best provided by structured programmes of instruction in formal institutions, they are not always.

This book has also argued that it is incoherent to restrict the absolute right to education to the primary level. While some countries may currently consider that they only have resources for universal primary education, this should not be confused with a limitation of the justified claim to this level. The only coherent conceptualization of the right is one that applies throughout life. This is not to say that full-time education needs to be provided to every individual from birth to grave. It is likely that even with a fully implemented lifelong right to education most full-time provision would indeed be during childhood. Yet opportunities for study must be available at all times in life. It is important in this respect to remember that the right to education involves 'welfare' and 'non-interference' elements. In part, protecting the right to education involves others actively creating and resourcing educational institutions and opportunities. But it also involves refraining from limiting people in their pursuit of learning, that is, through censoring information, obliging them to work very long hours without leisure time, attaching costs to learning, thereby placing them out of reach, and so forth. There are also more subtle forms of 'interference' that need to be avoided, such as the denigration of indigenous knowledge, or the marginalization of minority cultures and languages. Spring (2000) points to testing regimes that limit the content of the curriculum and prevent students from imaginative engagement with knowledge and alternative visions of society as infringements of liberty rights in education. As Freire (1972: ch. 2) states:

> Any situation in which some individuals prevent others from engaging in the process of inquiry is one of violence. The means used are not important; to alienate human beings from their own decision-making is to change them into objects.

Just as the provision of education must be open, allowing for those engaging in the process of learning to establish their own grasp of reality, so our vision of development must be open, allowing people to create and sustain their own vision of society.

Positional advantage

However, there is an element of fundamental importance that is not captured in the expression of the right outlined above. As discussed in Chapter 4, whatever the actual learning going on in schools, they remain fundamental conduits to desirable opportunities in life. Certification remains indispensable for valued employment, continuing study and many other opportunities. Any consideration of justice and education needs to acknowledge the positional dimension, of one's opportunities in relation to others in society. In a stratified system – and all education systems in the world are to some extent stratified – some people, by virtue of the wealth of their parents, their gender, race/ethnicity and other background factors, will have access to institutions that confer positional advantage over others.

In part, the positional dimension is addressed by the Convention against Discrimination in Education of 1960, discussed in Chapter 3. Through this Convention, States-Parties are obliged to develop policy:

> To ensure that the standards of education are equivalent in all public educational
> institutions of the same level, and that the conditions relating to the quality of
> the education provided are also equivalent. (Article 4(b))

If fully implemented, the Convention would bind states to ensure that no group is confined to an education of lesser quality than others – within the public sector at least. This would certainly deal with many of the gross forms of inequalities in education. Yet even with a maximalist reading of the Convention it would be hard to eradicate the subtle ways in which groups obtain positional advantage through education, through the prestige attached to private schools, and even some state schools, and the social networks enabled by them, even when there are not gross differences in quality.

As discussed in Chapter 4, positional advantage is hard to capture in a right, since we cannot grant all people an entitlement to advantage over others at the same time. Two other things might be possible: first, granting people a right not to suffer unfair disadvantage; or granting the right to access to those opportunities for gaining the advantage (rather than the advantage itself). Neither of these is entirely satisfactory, since they present challenges in determining which kinds of differences in outcome (if any) are justified and what might constitute equal opportunities.

Ultimately, it must be acknowledged that it is not possible to fully capture the equality requirements of the education system within this kind of right. This should not be the source of concern. As discussed in the introduction, human rights are not a complete scheme of justice: they provide minimum protections for all human beings – one of the few legitimate means of protecting people against an unbridled market economy (Ife 2009) – but should function together with other principles and mechanisms of justice in society. These other mechanisms would include procedural justice (e.g. fair selection procedures), redistribution, historical redress and so forth. As discussed in Chapter 7, the capabilities approach is one of the complementary lenses for conceptualizing justice in the opportunities accruing from education.

The Diploma Disease study as far back as 1976 showed how the positional role of schools led to qualification escalation and could compromise its core function of fostering learning, and in fact was increasingly doing so, particularly in newly developing education systems (Dore 1976). This danger leaves us with three alternatives for the development of educational opportunities in society. First, procedures for entry into employment and further study could be changed so that formal education certification was no longer necessary (as proposed by Dore). These changes would make the positional concerns unnecessary, allowing efforts to be focused on meaningful learning. However, despite qualifications inflation and the pernicious effects of the diploma disease, this type of change is highly unlikely anywhere in the world, and indications are that the reverse is taking place.

Second, formal education could be reformed so that in addition to the desired certification, it provided the necessary experiences of meaningful learning, and was in harmony with other human rights. There are considerable efforts in this direction around the world, many associated with the very welcome emphasis on quality by international agencies after initial enthusiasm focusing predominantly on enrolment. Nevertheless, while there are significant exceptions (see Farrell and Hartwell 2008) the institution of school proves highly resistant to reform.

Last, an alternative strategy is to accept that formal education is both highly desired in terms of its certification and often flawed in terms of the provision of learning experiences. The response, therefore, would be to ensure that people have access both to formal education and to high-quality non-formal education. This may not be an ideal solution, and presents significant challenges in terms of provision, but is perhaps the most viable option at the present moment.

An example of successful combination of both meaningful learning and positional elements is the Landless Movement in Brazil (see McCowan 2009). This social movement has created a large network of primary schools in its rural communities, as well as early years provision, adult education and teacher education courses. In all its educational work, it aims to promote positive valuing of the rural environment, equip people for productive work (principally in agriculture), and develop political awareness so that community members can defend their own rights and engage in campaigns for social justice more broadly. Whether or not we endorse these particular aims, the Landless Movement has certainly been successful in combining the learning element of the right to education with the positional considerations. In relation to the latter, it has a network of primary schools within the state system that allow children in the communities access to the formal qualifications that will allow them to progress to secondary and higher education and employment opportunities. Yet it has also undertaken a fundamental reworking of the school environment, involving management, pedagogy and curriculum, with the aim of providing meaningful and empowering learning experiences. In addition to formal education there are also a range of non-formal opportunities available, of a vocational, political and cultural nature.

The Landless Movement is, of course, not alone in finding innovative ways of resolving the tension between intrinsic, instrumental and positional aspects of schooling. A research agenda that emerges from this study is the need to provide a much more extensive documentation of these experiences around the world.

Further implications for policy and practice

It will be clear to the reader by now that this is not the kind of book that offers convenient and concrete solutions to policy-makers. The aim has been to provide a revisioning of the kinds of education that all human beings should have a right to, rather than taking our current situation as a starting point and identifying the best path along which steps might be taken. Indeed, where we want to go is a very long way from where we are now, and while education can transform society, many of the educational changes we would like to make are predicated on fundamental societal changes. In this sense, the book deals in the currency of 'ideal theory', or what Sen (2009) calls *transcendental* approaches to justice – although it is only certain fundamental criteria that are stipulated universally, leaving the substance of education open to diverse and contextualized understandings.

However, the fact that the book proposes a normative vision and expresses an ideal does not mean that it is detached from current reality or irrelevant to policy and practice. Visions are needed to guide our work, even in the smallest of actions. If we do decide that regular primary schools are the best way to pursue universal educational entitlements at the current moment, it makes a difference whether we see them as an end in themselves, or as one of a number of forms of expressing the fundamental experience of education – one that must be constantly revitalized and ultimately transcended.

Shaking up and reorienting the right to education is important for educators as well as policy-making. In their daily work, teachers are constantly working to aspirations, whether noble and solidaristic, or narrow and self-serving. The task of defining the right to education cannot be left to a small group of formulators of law, it is a conversation between all those involved in the educational endeavour. This book is contribution to that debate, a set of ideas to be chewed over, to disturb the unwarranted complacency of current educational discussions.

There are some immediate implications that arise from this vision. Both international development and education policy currently favour evidence-based policy-making, developing a rational approach based on scientific evidence of social phenomena and the impact of previous interventions, rather than adherence to historical priorities or ideological positions. This trend has been charcterized by the seductive label of 'What works...?'. While attention to evidence and rigorous research is certainly desirable, there are some dangers in this approach. First, attention to the forms of intervention that have greatest impact assumes that we are agreed on what kind of impact we want. Neither in relation to development nor education is there such a high level of consensus that would warrant this assumption. A 'non-ideological' approach to policy-making of this sort merely shuts down debate and closes off the possibility of other ends.

The second danger relates to the framework of proximity outlined in the previous chapter. *Separation* models are charcterized by an emphasis on an empirically observed link between a particular intervention and a particular result. This model leaves itself open to an 'ends justifying the means' approach, rather than incorporating the values of the ends within the means. In this way, education and development goals may be reached through strategies that ignore the principles of participation of local communities, may not respect their views or dignity, and may restrict other freedoms.

In addition to evidence-based policy, a second dominant current in international education is the increasing presence of the private sector. In addition to private involvement in government education systems, this phenomenon has manifested itself in the growth of low-cost private schools in poor communities. Advocates such as James Tooley (e.g. 2009) claim that these schools hold the answer to EFA, in expanding access at low cost and providing education of a higher quality than that available in the state system. Countries such as India, Nigeria and Kenya have seen a proliferation of these schools. (Tooley is personally involved in this sector as co-founder of the education company Omega Schools, running ten schools in Ghana.) Private schools are also receiving a boost from the emergence of 'new philanthropy' and influential bodies such as the Bill and Melinda Gates Foundation, which are 'doing' development while bypassing the normal channels of the state (Ball 2012). A number of these foundations see the private sector as the answer to effective and efficient development, and an increased role for the private sector in EFA is also supported by the recent World Bank (2011) education strategy.

Recent research (e.g. CREATE 2011) questions whether these schools are actually expanding access in the first place, or merely absorbing slightly wealthier students from government schools. Even if they were to be increasing enrolment, there are still substantial problems with involvement of the private sector in fulfilling the right to education. Concerns about private schools frequently focus on the element of positional advantage. Attendance at elite private schools, and even to a smaller degree the low-cost private institutions, is a marker of social standing and frequently leads to enhanced opportunities through the prestige attached to the diploma, as well as inserting the young person into a network that will facilitate employment and other opportunities. These pernicious effects on social equality have been debated at great length elsewhere (e.g. Brighouse 2004; Swift 2004), and as discussed above are part of the range of requirements of social justice that are complementary to the human right to education. Yet there are aspects of the private sector that are problematic from a different perspective, that of meaningful learning.

As outlined above, the framework of proximity has highlighted the importance of embodiment of the values of human rights in the institution, and their exemplification in teachers' practice. This requirement makes problematic any kind of commercial interest in education. If the primary motive of institutions is profit and not the educational values and the well-being of the students, then this embodiment cannot take place. The for-profit lobby claims that it is possible simultaneously to make profit and ensure the well-being of children, but inevitably is faced with situations of conflict between the two. If it is possible to market a low quality product and with the right pricing and advertising still gain customers (as it is in other areas such as food, clothing, transport, etc.), what hope for universal entitlements to meaningful and valuable learning? A purely private system could deliver high-quality learning experiences, but will do so only for some, and will naturally veer towards stratification of quality. This point does not in any way imply that the public systems functioning today in most countries are not stratified, or are not flawed in other ways. They certainly are, but at least in a system free of commercial interests there is the possibility of the universal right being upheld. Furthermore, it is not being argued here that centrally planned, standardized state systems are the answer – there is much of value in an untidy but richly diverse offering. Within this scattered landscape, non-profit private institutions with a genuine commitment to educational values and social justice can also make a valuable contribution – indeed, the line between these and non-state public initiatives and grassroots movements is thin.

Beyond questions of public and private, the clear implication for schools is that all should become rights-respecting institutions. This model involves the integration of human rights principles into teaching and learning, and the running of the institution. It thereby addresses rights to, within and through education. With the vision of HRE put forward in the last chapter we can see how these three forms are intimately linked: learning of human rights and the development of the ability to exercise and defend those rights (rights through education) are inherent in the rights to and within education. We have some blueprints for this form of institution: Amnesty's Human Rights Friendly Schools, UNICEF'S Rights-Respecting Schools as well as initiatives such as the Citizen School in Porto Alegre and many others, express respect for and commitment to learners' and communities' agency and welfare through all aspects of their work. These are inspiring models, but as yet islands in an ocean of 'rights ignoring' schools or at worse 'rights infringing' schools. Of course, there are also many other schools and teachers who express this commitment as part of their everyday educational work, without going under the label.

The rights-respecting school without doubt presents a significant challenge to teachers. It requires that teachers embody the values of respect for human rights within their own lives and in their teaching. Yet equally, it accords teachers full respect within the educational system; in contrast to the denigration of teachers through 'teacher proof' policies, they are fully involved in the conceptualization as well as the delivery of initiatives. As proposed in the concept of *seamless enactment* outlined in a previous book (McCowan 2009), not only is there consonance between ends and means, but all the participants in the educational process – students as well – are involved at every stage of curricular transposition, from ideals, to ideal curriculum, implementation and effects. As Lechner (2001: 280–1) states: 'Pupils should be enabled to co-author the document that describes the education they are going to have.' Teachers and students are no longer vessels tamely conveying and receiving the policies, messages and knowledge forms stipulated on high.

Another point of importance relates to indivisibility, interrelatedness and interdependence of rights. This point in fact is broadly acknowledged in the literature and at least in the rhetoric of international development agencies (e.g. World Bank 2011). It is accepted that education is fundamental to the upholding of rights, but also importantly that other rights – such as health, nutrition, security – are needed in order to meaningfully access education. There are a number of preconditions that must be in place for people to engage fully in educational processes, for example, 'freedom from harassment, freedom to concentrate … freedom to access information about education, engage in discussion …' (Unterhalter and Brighouse 2007: 81), highlighting interdependence between different human rights.

What we need ultimately is a rights-based approach to development, but one that does not fall prey to the risks of dressing up existing development practice in human rights rhetoric, ignoring the impracticality of local communities pursuing legal recourse, and presenting rights as a fait accompli, insensitive to local understandings and traditions. One way forward is the fusion of human rights and community development put forward by Ife (2009), leading to the emergence of what he terms 'contextualized human rights' (p. 152). In this view, human rights are needed to provide a framework for community development, to ensure that the interests of those outside the community are also respected, that diversity is acknowledged. This is an essential point: while deliberation at the local level is of value in itself, even decisions that have been reached democratically need to conform to certain principles of respect for all people. (So as to avoid a situation, for example, of a majority democratically deciding to exclude a minority.) Conversely, community development contributes to human rights by balancing the local with the universal, and providing a site for bottom–up discussion of and construction of rights.

What implications might there be for the post-2015 agenda, once the target date for the MDGs has been reached, and the targets mostly missed? The Lancet review (Waage et al. 2010) of the MDGs, while acknowledging the positive effects of the goals in providing a focus for advocacy and aid, and improving monitoring, has highlighted a number of limitations, recommending in any future formulation the principles of 'holism, equity, sustainability, ownership, and global obligation' (p. 21). Certainly, the principles of indivisibility, interrelatedness and interdependence of human rights respond to one of the critiques, that of the sectoral silo-based nature of the goals, and entail a much more holistic vision of development. The involvement of teachers, students and communities in the conceptualization as well as the implementation of education policy corresponds to the *ownership* element. Another problem highlighted in the review is the danger associated with indicators:

Targets and indicators frequently fall short of being meaningful measures of MDG achievement … This criticism might seem rather severe – specific targets and indicators were never meant to measure all progress against a complex goal. Rather they were meant to be indicative of progress. The risk, however, is that once targets and indicators become established, their indicative function is forgotten, and they become the end, not the means, of the MDGs. (p. 11)

The focus on processes put forward in this book represents an even greater wariness of targets and indicators than that expressed above. In fact, the kind of education argued for here is one that by definition resists predefined and universally stipulated objectives, given the need for a rich spontaneity in educational interactions. Nevertheless, indicators and targets – and the broader MDGs they are attached to – do have a role to play, particularly if they are attentive to the general principles outlined by Waage et al. (2010). Transcendental approaches to justice can provide us with a vision to orient our work, but in day-to-day practice we need to adopt something akin to Sen's (2009) comparative approach – 'making some things a bit better rather than waiting for the best resolution' (Waage et al. 2010: 19). By way of an example, whatever the limitations of the Human Development Index, it is better than relying solely on GDP per capita – as long as we remain conscious of the fact that this is a provisional stage and we must move towards a fuller representation of capabilities.

Towards a culture of human rights

In the introduction, a vignette was presented of an indigenous community in Amazonas state, recently coming into contact with mainstream Brazilian society. How have the discussions in the ensuing chapters coloured our view of this dilemma? Should the children from the community go to school? The first point to make here (one that should be obvious, but sadly is all too rarely acknowledged) is that the children are not moving from a state of *no* education to *some* education, they are transitioning between different forms of education. So the question is, should the community move from their traditional educational forms to mainstream schools?

This is a question indigenous communities are grappling with around the world from Ecuador to India, balancing the need to acquire the tools to compete in the global paradigms of development with the need to maintain their cultural and educational traditions. Joel Spring (2000), primarily with reference to Native American communities, argues for a universal right to education primarily on this basis, that indigenous communities need to be able to negotiate globalization on their own terms, neither shielding themselves from it, nor yielding completely and surrendering their own culture. Whether school or another form, education should in this way not present the learner with a stark choice between opportunities for material wealth on the one hand and cultural and spiritual wealth on the other, or between education that is relevant to one's locale and education that opens up new horizons. It should, of course, do both. These dilemmas are by no means confined to indigenous communities.

EFA is not (necessarily) a plot to entrap the global poor permanently in a subservient position in the capitalist order, and to control and discipline their minds to an externally defined order (Lechner 2001). It could be, if is reduced to a restricted menu of basic skills, with little by way of critical reflection and terminating abruptly at the end of primary school. EFA is a justified goal if that education can both adhere to universal values of human dignity, solidarity and freedom, and also be populated by the interests and desires of the inhabitants of the diverse globe. Currently the thirst for formal education worldwide is unquenchable, but it is a thirst driven largely by the necessities of survival and a quest for career success, given the centrality of school systems to accreditation that in turn leads to employment opportunities. Survival and employment should be available for all, and they should not be dependent on the tenacity of individuals to maintain themselves in a meaningless and unfriendly school system. It is not this kind of education that we want for all, but an education that opens one's vision and imagination, and equips one to follow the deep course of one's chosen trajectory.

The previous chapter put forward the idea that the right to education is necessarily a right to HRE. In the first place, this connection is due to HRE's role in allowing people to defend and exercise their rights, and importantly to deliberate on and construct them. Second, it can be seen that HRE is an inevitable part of a general education fully expressed, given the latter's inherently political and moral nature. So education involves human rights, but conversely human rights are inherently educational: the experience of living and interacting in a rights-respecting environment is itself an invaluable form of learning.

So does this make planned education irrelevant? If we learn from doing, why have schools, workshops and classes? In the language of *proximity*, why does all harmony not become unification? The answer lies in the need to move from a vicious to a virtuous cycle. Formal and non-formal education – any form of intentional learning – are still necessary to address and break the patterns of hostility, fragmentation and lack of awareness that too often charcterize our societies and relations. Interventions are needed to foster a spiral towards understanding and ethical action, and away from narrow-mindedness and violence.

Organized education becomes increasingly unnecessary in so far as society supports learning in all its spaces, and embodies ethical action. Human rights activists and educators in this way all work towards the creation of a human rights culture, which is itself a learning culture. This, therefore, is the way in which the human right to learning and the learning of human rights become unified. Life lived to its full is characterized by constant learning, and learning in turn opens the door to life.

References

Ahier, J., Beck, J. and Moore, R. (2003) *Graduate Citizens? Issues of Citizenship and Higher Education*. London: RoutledgeFalmer.

Alexander, J. (2004) 'Capabilities, human rights and moral pluralism', *International Journal of Human Rights*, 8(3), 451–69.

Alexander, R. (2008) 'Education for All, the quality imperative and the problem of pedagogy. CREATE pathways to access, Research Monograph no. 20'. Brighton: Centre for International Education, University of Sussex.

Altbach, P., Reisberg, L. and Rumbley, L. (2009) *Trends in Global Higher Education: Tracking an Academic Revolution*. Paris: UNESCO.

Amnesty International (2009) *Guidelines for Human Rights Friendly Schools*. London: Amnesty International Publications.

Arthur, J. with Bohlin, K. (eds) (2005). *Citizenship and Higher Education: The Role of Universities in Communities and Society*. London: Routledge.

Bajaj, M. (2011) *Schooling for Social Change: The Rise and Impact of Human Rights Education in India*. New York: Continuum.

Balarin, M. and Cueto, S. (2007) 'The quality of parental participation and student achievement in Peruvian government schools', *Young Lives, Working Paper No. 35*. Available at: http://economics.ouls.ox.ac.uk/13652/1/WP35_final%20version.pdf (accessed 25 April 2011).

Ball, S. (2012) *Global Education Inc: New Policy Networks and the Neo-liberal Imaginary*. London: Routledge.

Barber, M. and Mourshed, M. (2007) *How the World's Best-Performing School Systems Came Out on Top*. London: McKinsey&Co.

Barnett, R. (1990) *The Idea of Higher Education*. Buckingham: Open University Press.

Barrett, A. M. (2009) *The Education Millennium Development Goal beyond 2015: Prospects for Quality and Learners*. Bristol: EdQual RPC.

— (2011) 'A Millennium Learning Goal for education post-2015: a question of outcomes or processes', *Comparative Education*, 47, 123–37.

Barrón Pastor, J. (2010) 'Globalisation perspectives and cultural exclusion in Mexican higher education', in E. Unterhalter and V. Carpentier (eds), *Global Inequalities and Higher Education: Whose Interests Are We Serving?* (London: Palgrave Macmillan), pp. 197–218.

Becker, Gary S. (1964, 1993, 3rd edn) *Human Capital: A Theoretical and Empirical Analysis, with Special Reference to Education*. Chicago: University of Chicago Press.

Beiter, K. (2006) *The Protection of the Right to Education by International Law*. Leiden: Martinus Nijhoff.

Beitz, C. (2009) *The Idea of Human Rights*. Oxford: Oxford University Press.

Bhana, D. (2005) 'What matters to girls and boys in a black primary school in South Africa', *Early Child Development and Care*, 175(2), 99–111.

BIS (2009) *Full-time Young Participation by Socio-Economic Class (FYPSEC)*, 2009 Update. London: Department for Business, Innovation and Skills.

— (2011) Widening Participation in Higher Education: Analysis of Progression Rates for Young People in England by Free School Meal Receipt and School Type. London: Department for Business, Innovation and Skills.

Bobbio, N. (1996) *The Age of Rights*. Cambridge: Polity Press.

Boothe, K. and Dunne, T. (1999) 'Learning beyond frontiers', in T. Dunne and N. J. Wheeler (eds), *Human Rights in Global Perspectives*. Cambridge: Cambridge University Press, pp. 303–28.

Bou-Habib, H. (2010). 'Who should pay for higher education?' *Journal of Philosophy of Education,* 44(4), 479–95.

Bourdieu, P. and Passeron, J. (1977) *Reproduction in Education, Society and Culture*. London: Sage.

Bowles, S. and Gintis, H. (1976) *Schooling in Capitalist America: Educational Reform and the Contradictions of Economic Life*. New York: Basic Books.

Bowring, B. (2012) 'Human rights and public education', *Cambridge Journal of Education*, 42(1), 53–65.

Bramall, S. and White, J. (2000) 'Will the New National Curriculum live up to its aims?' *IMPACT Paper No. 6.* London: Philosophy of Education Society of Great Britain.

Brandford, S. and Rocha, J. (2002) *Cutting the Wire*. London: Latin American Bureau.

Brennan, J. and Naidoo, R. (2008) 'Higher education and the achievement (and/or prevention) of equity and social justice', *Higher Education,* 56(3), 287–302.

Brighouse, H. (2002) 'What rights (if any) do children have?', in D. Archard and C. Macleod (eds), *The Moral and Political Status of Children*. Oxford: Oxford University Press, pp. 31–52.

— (2004), 'What's wrong with privatising schools?' *Journal of Philosophy of Education,* 38, 617–31.

— (2006) *On Education*. London: Routledge

— (2009) 'Justice in higher education: an odd view'. Paper presented at the Society of Applied Philosophy meeting at the Eastern American Philosophical Association, 29 December.

Brighouse, H. and McAvoy, P. (2009) 'Privilege, wellbeing, and participation in higher education', in Y. Raley and G. Preyer (eds), *Philosophy of Education in the Era of Globalization*. New York: Routledge, pp. 165–80.

Bynner, J., Dolton, P., Feinstein L., Makepiece, G., Malmberg, L. and Woods, L. (2003) *Revisiting the Benefits of Higher Education: A Report by the Bedford Group for Lifecourse and Statistical Studies, Institute of Education*. Bristol: HEFCE.

Callan, E. (1997) *Creating Citizens*. Oxford: Clarendon Press.

Carr-Hill, R. (2012) 'Finding and then counting out-of-school children', *Compare*, 42(2), 187–212.

Committee on the Rights of the Child (2001), http://daccess-dds-ny.un.org/doc/ UNDOC/GEN/G01/412/53/PDF/G0141253.pdf?OpenElement/.

Coomans, F. (2007) 'Content and scope of the right to education as a human right and obstacles to its realization', in Y. Donders and V. Volodin (eds), *Human Rights in Education, Science and Culture – Legal Development and Challenges*. Paris and Aldershot: UNESCO Publishing/Ashgate, pp. 183–230.

Cornwall, A. and Molyneux, M. (eds) (2007) *The Politics of Rights: Dilemmas for Feminist Praxis*. London: Routledge.

Cornwall, A. and Nyamu-Musembi, C. (2004) 'Putting the "rights-based approach" to development into perspective', *Third World Quarterly*, 25(8), 1415–37.

Covell, K. (2010) 'School engagement and rights-respecting schools', *Cambridge Journal of Education*, 40(1), 39–51.

Covell, K. and Howe, B. (2001) 'Moral education through the 3 Rs: rights, respect and responsibility', *Journal of Moral Education*, 30(1), 29–41.

Cox, S., Robinson-Pant, A., Dyer, C. and Schweisfurth, M. (eds) (2010) *Children as Decision Makers in Education: Sharing Experiences across Cultures*. London: Continuum.

CRC/GC/2001/1 (2001) Committee on the Rights of the Child, 'General Comment No. 7: Implementing child rights in early childhood', CRC/C/GC7, 2005.

CREATE (2011) *Making Rights Realities: Researching Educational Access, Transitions and Equity*. Brighton: University of Sussex.

Curren, R. (2009) 'Education as a social right in a diverse society', *Journal of Philosophy of Education*, 43(1), 45–56.

Currie, J. (2001). 'Early childhood education programmes', *Journal of Economic Perspectives*, 15(2), 213–38.

Davies, L. (2004). *Education and Conflict: Complexity and Chaos*. London: Routledge/ Falmer.

De Beco, G., Hyll-Larsen, P. and Ron Balsera, M. (2009) 'The right to education: human rights indicators and the right to education of Roma children in Slovakia'. Background paper prepared for the *Education for All Global Monitoring Report 2010*.

Dewey, J. (1955 [1916]) *Democracy and Education: An Introduction to the Philosophy of Education*. New York: Macmillan.

— (1964) 'The continuum of ends-means', in R. Archambault (ed.), *John Dewey on Education: Selected Writings*. Chicago: University of Chicago Press, pp. 97–107.

— (1966 [1916]) *Democracy and Education*. London: Collier-Macmillan.

Dore, R. (1976) *The Diploma Disease: Education, Qualification and Development*. London: George Allen & Unwin.

Dubey, M. (2010) 'The Right of Children to Free and Compulsory Education Act, 2009: the story of a missed opportunity', *Social Change*, 40(1), 1–13.

Dyer, C. (2000) '"Education for All" and the Rabaris of Kachchh, Western India', *International Journal of Educational Research*, 33(3), 241–51.

Enslin, P. and Tjiattas, M. (2009), 'Philosophy of education and the gigantic affront of universalism', *Journal of Philosophy of Education*, 43, 2–17.

European Commission (2010) 'Efficiency and effectiveness of public expenditure on tertiary education in the EU', *European Economy Occasional Papers No. 70*. Brussels: Publications office of the European Union.

Farrell, J. and Hartwell, A. (2008) 'Planning for successful alternative schooling: a possible route to Education for All'. *Research Papers IIEP*. Paris: IIEP.

Filmer, D., Hasan, A. and Pritchett, L. (2006) 'A Millennium Learning Goal: measuring real progress in education'. *Working Paper No. 97*. Washington, DC: Center for Global Development.

Flutter, J. and Ruddock, J. (2004) *Consulting Pupils: What's in it for Schools?* London: RoutledgeFalmer.

Frank, A. G. (1967) *Capitalism and Underdevelopment in Latin America*. New York: Monthly Review Press.

Freire, P. (1972) *Pedagogy of the Oppressed*. London: Sheed and Ward.

— (1994) *Pedagogy of Hope: Reliving Pedagogy of the Oppressed*. New York: Continuum.

Friboulet, J.-J. Niameogo, A., Liechti, V., Dalbera, C. and Meyer-Bisch, P. (2006) *Measuring the Right to Education*. Fribourg: Schulthess.

Gadotti, M. (2011) 'Adult education as a human right: the Latin American context and the ecopedagogic perspective', *International Review of Education*, 57(1/2), 9.

Gamarnikow, E. (2011) 'The right to education in human rights governance and politics: reporting and monitoring intercultural education', *Revista Iberoamericana sobre Calidad, Eficacia y Cambio en Educación*, 9(4), 44–62.

García, M. E. (2004) 'Rethinking bilingual education in Peru: intercultural politics, state policy and indigenous rights', *International Journal of Bilingual Education and Bilingualism*, 7(5), 348–67.

Gereluk, D. (2008) *Symbolic Clothing in Schools*. London: Continuum.

Global Initiative to End All Corporal Punishment of Children (2010) *Global Report 2010: Ending Legalised Violence against Children*. Global Initiative to End All Corporal Punishment of Children/Save the Children Sweden.

Goldman, E. (1970 [1923]) *My Disillusionment in Russia*. New York: Thomas Y. Crowell.

Gready, P. and Ensor, J. (eds) (2005) *Reinventing Development? Translating Rights-Based Approaches from Theory into Practice*. London: Zed Books.

Greany, K. (2008). 'Rhetoric versus reality: exploring the rights-based approach to girls' education in rural Niger', *Compare*, 38, 555–68.

Green, A. (1990) *Education and State Formation: The Rise of Education Systems in England, France and the USA*. London: Macmillan.

Gregory, I. M. M. (1973) 'The right to education', *Proceedings of the Philosophy of Education Society of Great Britain*, 7(1), 85–102.

Griffin, J. (2008) *On Human Rights*. Oxford: Oxford University Press.

Grover, S. (2004) 'Secondary education as a universal human right', *Education and the Law*, 16(1), 21–31.

Guardian (2012) 'Russia overtakes UK and France in global arms spending league table'. Available at: www.guardian.co.uk/world/2012/apr/17/russia-overtakes-uk-france-arms (accessed 17 April 2012).

Hahn, C. (1987) 'The right to a political education', in N. Tarrow (ed.), *Human Rights and Education*. Oxford: Pergamon, pp. 173–87.

Halvorsen, K. (1990) 'Notes on the realization of the human right to education', *Human Rights Quarterly*, 12(3), 341–64.

Hanushek, E. and Woessmann, L. (2007) *Education Quality and Economic Growth*. Washington, DC: World Bank.

Harber, C. (2004) *Schooling as Violence: How Schools Harm Pupils and Societies*. London: RoutledgeFalmer.

Hart, R. (1992) *Children's Participation: From Tokenism to Citizenship* (Innocenti Essays, 4). Florence: UNICEF.

Hart, S., Cohen, C., Erickson, M. and Fekkoy, M. (eds) (2001) *Children's Rights in Education*. London: Jessica Kingsley.

Haydon, G. (1977) 'The right to education and compulsory schooling', *Educational Philosophy and Theory*, 9(1), 1–15.

Heyneman, S. P. (2003) 'The history and problems in the making of education policy at the World Bank 1960–2000', *International Journal of Educational Development*, 23, 315–37.

Hirst, P. H. (1974) *Knowledge and the Curriculum*. London: Routledge & Kegan Paul.

Hodgson, D. (1998) *The Human Right to Education*. Dartmouth: Ashgate.

Hoppers, W. (2007) 'Meeting the learning needs of all young people and adults: an exploration of successful policies and strategies in non-formal education'. Background paper prepared for the *GMR 2008*. Paris: UNESCO.

Hornberg, S. (2002) 'Human rights education as an integral part of general education', *International Review of Education*, 48(3–4), 187–98.

Howard, R. (2009) 'Education reform, indigenous politics, and decolonisation in the Bolivia of Evo Morales', *International Journal of Educational Development*, 29(6), 583–93.

Howe, R. B. and Covell, K. (2005) *Empowering Children: Children's Rights Education as a Pathway to Citizenship*. Toronto: University of Toronto Press.

Ife, J. (2009) *Human Rights from Below. Achieving Rights through Community Development*. Cambridge: Cambridge University Press.

Illich, I. (1973) *Deschooling Society*. Harmondsworth: Penguin.

Inkeles, A. and Smith D. (1975) *Becoming Modern: Individual Change in Six Developing Countries*. Cambridge, MA: Harvard University Press.

Jansen, J. (1998) 'Curriculum reform in South Africa: a critical analysis of outcomes-based education', *Cambridge Journal of Education*, 28(3), 321–31.

Jerome, L. and Bhargava, M. (2009) 'Establishing a rights respecting initial teacher education programme', in A. Ross (ed.), *Human Rights and Citizenship Education*. London: CiCe, pp. 353–8.

Kane, L. (2001) *Popular Education and Social Change in Latin America*. London: Latin American Bureau.

Karmel, J. (2009) *The Right to Education*. Saarbrücken: VDM Publishing.

Kerr, D. (1999) 'Citizenship education in the curriculum: an international review', *The School Field*, X(3/4), 5–32.

King-Calnek, J. (2006) 'Education for citizenship: interethnic pedagogy and formal education at Escola Criativa Olodum', *Urban Review,* 38(2), 145–64.

Knowles, D. (2001) *Political Philosophy*. London: Routledge.

Kotzee, B. and Martin, C. (2011) *Who Should Go to University?* Paper presented at the Annual Conference of the British Educational Research Association, 7 September.

Kymlicka, W. (2002) *Contemporary Political Philosophy: An Introduction*, 2nd edn. Oxford: Clarendon Press.

La Belle, T. J. (1987) 'From consciousness raising to popular education in Latin America and the Caribbean', *Comparative Education Review*, 31(2), 201–17.

Leach, F. M. and Mitchell, C. (2006) *Combating Gender Violence in and around Schools*. Michigan: Trentham.

Leadbetter, C. and Wong, A. (2010) *Learning from the Extremes*. San Jose: Cisco.

Lawson, K. (1979) 'The concept of higher education for all explored', in G. Roderick and M. Stephens (eds), *Higher Education for All?* Barcombe, Lewes, Sussex: Falmer Press, pp. 27–66.

Lansdown, G. (2001) 'Progress in implementing the rights in the convention', in S. Hart, C. P. Cohen, M. F. Erickson and M. Fekkoy (eds), *Children's Rights in Education*. London: Jessica Kingsley, pp. 37–59.

Lechner, D. (2001) 'The dangerous human right to education: factors helping and hindering the process', *Studies in Philosophy and Education*, 20, 279–81.

Levinson, M. (1999) *The Demands of Liberal Education*. Oxford: Oxford University Press.

Little, A. (1999) 'Development and education: cultural and economic analysis', in F. Leach and A. Little (eds), *Education, Cultures and Economics: Dilemmas for Development*. London: Garland, pp. 3–32.

— (2008) *EFA Politics, Policies and Progress*. CREATE Pathways to Access Research Monograph No. 13. London: Institute of Education.

Lohrenscheit, C. (2002) 'International approaches in human rights education', *International Review of Education* 48(3–4): 173–85.

Macbeath, J. and Moos, L. (2004) *Democratic Learning: The Challenge of School Effectiveness*. London: RoutledgeFalmer.

MacIntyre, A. (1990) *Three Rival Versions of Moral Enquiry*. London: Duckworth.

Magendzo, A. (2005) 'Pedagogy of human rights education: a Latin American perspective', *Intercultural Education*, 16(2), 137–43.

Marshall, T. H. (1950) *Citizenship and Social Class and Other Essays*. Cambridge: Cambridge University Press.

Massey, I. (2003) 'The case for RRR'. Available at: www3.hants.gov.uk/education/hias/childrensrights/rrr-general/rrrthecase.htm (accessed 5 November 2010).

Mazrui, A. A. (1975) 'The African University as a multinational corporation: problems of penetration and dependency', *Harvard Educational Review*, 45, 191–210.

McClelland, D. C. (1961) *The Achieving Society*. New York: Van Nostrand.

McClure, K. R. (2009) 'Madrasas and Pakistan's education agenda: Western media misrepresentation and policy recommendations', *International Journal of Educational Development*, 29(4), 334–41.

McCowan, T. (2004) 'The growth of private higher education in Brazil: implications for equity and quality', *Journal of Education Policy*, 19(4), 453–72.

— (2007) 'Expansion without equity: an analysis of current policy on access to higher education in Brazil', *Higher Education*, 53(5), 579–98.

— (2008) 'Curricular transposition in citizenship education', *Theory and Research in Education*, 6(2), 153–72.

— (2009) *Rethinking Citizenship Education: A Curriculum for Participatory Democracy*. London: Continuum.

— (2010) 'Reframing the universal right to education', *Comparative Education*, 46(4), 509–25.

McCowan, T. and Unterhalter, E. (2009) 'Education for democratic citizenship: a capabilities perspective'. Background paper to the *Brazil Human Development Report*. Brasília: UNDP.

McEvoy, L. and Lundy, L. (2007) 'E-consultation with pupils: a rights-based approach to the integration of citizenship education and ICT', *Technology, Pedagogy and Education*, 16(3), 305–19.

McMahon, W. (2009) *Higher Learning, Greater Good: The Private and Social Benefits of Higher Education*. Baltimore, MD: Johns Hopkins University Press.

McMillan, L. K. (2010): 'What's in a right? Two variations for interpreting the right to education', *International Review of Education*, 56, 5–6.

Melchiorre, A. (2004). 'At what age … are school-children employed, married and taken to court?', *The Right to Education Project*. Available at: www.right-to-education.org/sites/r2e.gn.apc.org/files/age_new.pdf.

Melchiorre, A. and Atkins, E. (2011) *At what Age … Are School-Children Employed, Married and Taken to Court? Trends over Time*. London: Right to Education Project. Available at: www.right-to-education.org/node.

Morris, P. and Cogan, J. (2001) 'A comparative overview: civic education across six societies', *International Journal of Educational Research*, 35, 109–23.

Mundy, K. (2006) 'Education for all and the new development compact', *International Review of Education*, 52(1), 23–48.

Noddings, N. and Slote, M. (1996) 'Changing notions of the moral and of moral education', in J. J. Chambliss (ed.), *The Philosophy of Education: An Encyclopedia*. London: Garland, pp. 341–55.

Nussbaum, M. (1997) *Cultivating Humanity: A Classical Defense of Reform in Liberal Education*. Cambridge, MA: Harvard University Press.

— (2000) *Women and Human Development: The Capabilities Approach*. Cambridge: Cambridge University Press.

— (2006) *Frontiers of Justice*. Cambridge, MA: Harvard University Press.

Oakeshott, M. (1989) 'The idea of a university', in T. Fuller (ed.), *The Voice of Liberal Learning: Michael Oakeshott on Education*. New Haven and London: Yale University Press, pp. 95–104.

Olafson, F. (1973) 'Rights and duties in education', in J. Doyle (ed.), *Educational Judgments*. London: Routledge and Kegan Paul, pp. 173–95.

Orend, B. (2002) *Human Rights: Concept and Context*. Peterborough: Broadview.

Osler, A. and Starkey, H. (2005) *Changing Citizenship: Democracy and Inclusion in Education*. Maidenhead: Open University Press.

Osler, A. and Starkey, H. (2010) *Teachers and Human Rights Education*. Stoke-on-Trent: Trentham.

Osmani, S. (2005) 'Poverty and human rights: building on the capability approach', *Journal of Human Development and Capabilities*, 6(2), 205–19.

Packer, S. (2007) 'International EFA architecture: lessons and prospects; a preliminary assessment'. Background paper for the *Education for All Global Monitoring Report 2008*, 2008/ED/EFA/MRT P1/57, Paris: UNESCO.

Palme, M. (1999) 'Cultural ambiguity and the primary school teacher: lessons from rural Mozambique', in F. Leach and A. Little (eds), *Education, Cultures, and Economics: Dilemmas for Development*. New York: Falmer Press, pp. 261–82.

Parkes, J. and Heslop, J. (2011) 'Stop violence against girls in school: a cross-country analysis of baseline research from Ghana, Kenya and Mozambique', *ActionAid International*. Available at: www.ungei.org/files/svags_a_cross_country_analysis_of_baseline_research_from_ghana_kenya_and_mozambique.pdf (accessed 13 December 2012).

Peters, M. (2002) 'Re-thinking education as a welfare right', *School Field*, 13(5), 79–96.

Peters, R. S. (1966) *Ethics and Education*. London: Allen and Unwin.

— (1967) 'What is an educational process?' in R. S. Peters (ed.), *The Concept of Education*. London: Routledge and Kegan Paul, pp. 1–23.

Pinnock, H. (2009) *Language and Education: The Missing Link*. London: Save the Children.

Pogge, T. (2002) *World Poverty and Human Rights: Cosmopolitan Responsibilities and Reforms*. Cambridge: Polity.

Pollis, A. and Schwab, P. (1980) 'Human rights: A Western construct with limited applicability', in A. Pollis and P. Schwab (eds), *Human Rights: Cultural and Ideological Perspectives*. New York: Praeger Publishers, pp. 1–18.

Psacharopoulos, G. (1985) 'Returns to education: a further international update and implications', *The Journal of Human Resources*, 20, 583–604.

Readings, B. (1996) *The University in Ruins*. Cambridge, MA: Harvard University Press.

Reimer, E. (1971) *School is Dead. An essay on alternatives in education*. Harmondsworth: Penguin.

Right to Education Project (2009) *Right to Education Indicators based on the 4 A framework: Concept Paper*. Available at: www.right-to-education.org/sites/r2e.gn.apc.org/files/Concept%20Paper.pdf (accessed 23 February 2012).

— (2011) *Right to Education Project: Promoting Mobilisation and Legal Accountability.* Available at: www.right-to-education.org/ (accessed 25 April 2011).

Rioux, M. H. and Pinto, P. C. (2010) 'A time for the universal right to education: back to basics', *British Journal of Sociology of Education*, 31(5), 621–42.

Robeyns, I. (2005) 'The capability approach: a theoretical survey', *Journal of Human Development and Capabilities*, 6(1), 93–114.

— (2006) 'Three models of education: rights, capabilities and human capital', *Theory and Research in Education*, 4(1), 69–84.

Robinson, C. (2005) 'Promoting literacy: what is the record of education for all?' *International Journal of Educational Development*, 25(4), 436–44.

Rogers, A. (2004) *Non-Formal Education: Flexible Schooling or Participatory Education?* Hong Kong: CERC, University of Hong Kong.

Rose, P. (2007) 'NGO provision of basic education: alternative or complementary service delivery to support access to the excluded?' *CREATE Pathways to Access, Research Monograph No. 3.* Brighton: Centre for International Education, University of Sussex.

Rostow, W. W. (1960) *The Stages of Economic Growth: A Non-Communist Manifesto.* London: Cambridge University Press.

Saito, M. (2003) 'Amartya Sen's capability approach to education: a critical exploration', *Journal of Philosophy of Education*, 37(1), 17–33.

Santos, T. dos (1970) 'The structure of dependence', *American Economic Review*, 60, 231–6.

Sauvé, L. (1996) 'Environmental education and sustainable development', *Canadian Journal of Environmental Education*, 1, 7–35.

Scanlon, T. (2003) 'Rights, goals and fairness', in T. Scanlon (ed.), *The Difficulty of Tolerance: Essays in Political Philosophy.* Cambridge: Cambridge University Press, pp. 26–41.

Schön, D. (1983) *The Reflective Practitioner. How Professionals Think in Action.* London: Temple Smith.

Schultz, T. W. (1961) 'Investment in human capital', *American Economic Review*, 51(1), 1–16.

Sebba, J. and Robinson, C. (2010) *Evaluation of UNICEF UK's Rights Respecting Schools Award (Final Report).* London: UNICEF UK.

Sen, A. (1982) 'Rights and agency', *Philosophy and Public Affairs*, 11, 3–38.

— (1985) 'Well-being, agency and freedom: the Dewey lectures 1984', *The Journal of Philosophy*, 82(4), 169–221.

— (1992) *Inequality Re-examined.* Oxford: Clarendon Press.

— (1999) 'Democracy as a universal value', *Journal of Democracy*, 10(3), 3–17.

— (2004) 'Elements of a theory of human rights', *Philosophy and Public Affairs*, 32(4), 315–56.

— (2005) 'Human rights and capabilities', *Journal of Human Development*, 6(2), 151–66.

— (2009) *The Idea of Justice.* London: Allen Lane.

Serpell, R. (1999) 'Local accountability to rural communities: a challenge for educational planning in Africa', in F. Leach and A. Little (eds), *Education, Cultures, and Economics: Dilemmas for Development*. New York: Falmer Press, pp. 111–42.

Smith, M. K. (2000) 'Curriculum theory and practice', in *The Encyclopaedia of Informal Education*. Available at: www.infed.org/biblio/b-curric.htm.

— (1997–2011) 'Ivan Illich: deschooling, conviviality and the possibilities for informal education and lifelong learning', in *The Encyclopedia of Informal Education*. Available at: www.infed.org/thinkers/et-illic.htm.

Snook, I. and Lankshear, C. (1979) *Education and Rights*. Melbourne: Melbourne University Press.

Somerset, A. (2009) 'Universalising primary education in Kenya: the elusive goal', *Comparative Education*, 45(2), 233–50.

Spring, J. (2000) *The Universal Right to Education: Justification, Definition, and Guidelines*. New Jersey: Lawrence Erlbaum.

Starkey, H. (ed.) (1991) *The Challenge of Human Rights Education*. London: Cassell.

Stenhouse, L. (1975) *An Introduction to Curriculum Research and Development*. London: Heinemann Educational.

Subrahmanian, R. (2005) 'Gender equality in education: definitions and measurements', *International Journal of Educational Development*, 25(4), 395–407.

Swift, A. (2004) 'The morality of school choice', *Theory and Research in Education*, 2(1), 7–21.

Tao, S. (2012) 'Why are teachers absent? Utilising the capability approach and critical realism to explain teacher performance in Tanzania', *International Journal of Educational Development*, 33, 2–14.

Terzi, L. (2008) *Justice and Equality in Education: A Capability Perspective on Disability and Special Educational Needs*. London: Continuum.

Tibbitts, F. (2002) 'Understanding what we do: emerging models for human rights education', *International Review of Education*, 48(3–4), 159–71.

Tikly, L. and Barrett, A. M. (2007) 'Education quality – research priorities and approaches in the global era'. *EdQual Working Paper No. 1*. Bristol: Edqual.

— (2009) 'Social justice, capabilities and the quality of education in low income countries'. *EdQual Working Paper, Quality No. 8*. Bristol: Edqual.

— (2011) 'Towards a framework for researching the quality of education in low-income countries', *Comparative Education*, 47(1), 1–23.

Tomaševski, K. (2001a) 'Human rights obligations: making education available, accessible, acceptable and adaptable'. *Right to Education Primers No. 3*. Gothenburg: Novum Grafiska.

— (2001b) 'Human rights in education as prerequisite for human rights education'. *Right to Education Primer No. 4*. Lund and Stockholm: Raoul Wallenberg Institute and SIDA.

— (2003) *Education Denied: Costs and Remedies*. London: Zed Books.

— (2004) 'Annual report of the Special Rapporteur on the right to education'. *Sixtieth Session of the Commission on Human Rights*, 15 January, E/CN.4/2004/45.

— (2006a) *Human Rights Obligations in Education: The 4-A Scheme*. Nijmegen: Wolf Legal Publishers.

— (2006b) *The State of the Right to Education Worldwide: Free or Fee: 2006 Global Report*. Copenhagen. Available at: www.katarinatomasevski.com/images/Global_Report.pdf.

Tooley, J. (2009) *The Beautiful Tree: A Personal Journey into How the World's Poorest People Are Educating Themselves*. Washington, DC: Cato Institute.

Trow, M. (1974) 'Problems in the transition from elite to mass higher education', in OECD (ed.), *Policies for Higher Education*. Paris: OECD, pp. 51–101.

— (2006) 'Reflections on the transition from elite to mass to universal access: forms and phases of higher education in modern societies since WWII', in J. J. F. Forest and P. G. Altbach (eds), *International Handbook of Higher Education*. Dordrecht, The Netherlands: Springer, pp. 243–80.

UNDP (2000) *Human Development Report 2000: Human Rights and Human Development*. Oxford: Oxford University Press.

UNESCO Institute for Statistics (UIS) (2011) 'Statistical tables'. Available at http://stats.uis.unesco.org/unesco/TableViewer/tableView.aspx?ReportId=3345andIF_Language=eng (accessed 21 November 2011).

UNESCO (2005) *Challenges of Implementing Free Primary Education in Kenya*. Assessment Report. Nairobi: UNESCO Nairobi Office.

— (2006) *Strong Foundations: Early Childhood Care and Education*. EFA Global Monitoring Report 2007. Paris: UNESCO.

— (2008) *The Right to Education: Monitoring Standard-Setting Instruments of UNESCO*. Paris: UNESCO.

— (2011) *The Hidden Crisis: Armed Conflict and Education*. EFA Global Monitoring Report 2011. Paris: UNESCO.

— (2012) *Reaching Out-of-School Children is Crucial for Development*. Education for All Global Monitoring Report Policy Paper 04. Paris: UNESCO.

UNICEF (2000) *Defining Quality in Education*. New York: UNICEF. Available at: www.unicef.org/education/files/QualityEducation.PDF.

UNICEF/UNESCO (2007) *A Human Rights-based Approach to Education for All*. New York: UNICEF/UNESCO. Available at: http://unesdoc.unesco.org/images/0015/001548/154861e.pdf.

United Nations (1948) *Universal Declaration of Human Rights*. Available at: www.un.org/en/documents/udhr/index.shtml (accessed 22 February 2011).

— (1989) *Convention on the Rights of the Child*. Available at: www2.ohchr.org/english/law/crc.htm (accessed 22 February 2011).

— (2001) *The Aims of Education – Convention on the Rights of the Child, General Comment 1*. Office of the United Nations High Commissioner for Human Rights.

— (2003) *The Human Rights Based Approach to Development Cooperation: Towards a Common Understanding among UN Agencies*. Interagency Workshop on Human

Rights Based Approach, Stamford, Connecticut. Available at: http://hrbaportal.org/?page_id=2127) (accessed 19 July 2012).

Unterhalter, E. (2003) 'The capabilities approach and gendered education: an examination of South African complexities', *Theory and Research in Education*, 1(1), 7–22.

— (2007) *Gender, Schooling and Global Social Justice*. London: Routledge.

—(2009) 'Translations and transversal dialogues: an examination of mobilities associated with gender, education and global poverty reduction', *Comparative Education*, 45(3), 329–45.

Unterhalter, E. and Brighouse, H. (2007) 'Distribution of what for social justice in education? The case of Education for All by 2015', in M. Walker and E. Unterhalter (eds), *Amartya Sen's Capability Approach and Social Justice in Education*. New York: Palgrave Macmillan, pp. 67–86.

Vandenberg, D. (1990) *Education as a Human Right: A Theory of Curriculum and Pedagogy*. New York: Teachers College Press.

Van Hees, M. (2012) 'Rights, goals and capabilities', *Politics Philosophy & Economics*, forthcoming.

Vaughan, R. (2007) 'Freedom through education: measuring capabilities in girls' schooling', in M. Walker and E. Unterhalter (eds), *Amartya Sen's Capability Approach and Social Justice in Education*. Basingstoke: Palgrave Macmillan. Association Conference, Amman, Jordan, 21–23 September.

Vegas, E. and Petrow, J. (2008) *Raising Student Learning in Latin America: The Challenge for the 21st Century*. Washington, DC: World Bank.

Verhellen, E. (1993) 'Children's rights and education: a three track legally binding imperative', *School Psychology International*, 14, 199–208.

Verheyde, M. (2006) *Article 28: The Right to Education*. Leiden: Martinus Nijhoff.

Vizard, P. (2005) 'The contributions of Professor Amartya Sen in the field of human rights'. *CASE Paper 91*. Available at: http://sticerd.lse.ac.uk/dps/case/cp/CASEpaper91.pdf (accessed 6 January 2010).

Vizard, P., Fukuda-Parr, S. and Elson, D. (2011) 'Introduction: the capability approach and human rights', *Journal of Human Development and Capabilities*, 12(1), 1–22.

Waage, J., Banerji, R., Campbell, O., et al. (2010) 'The Millennium Development Goals: a cross-sectoral analysis and principles for goal setting after 2015', *Lancet*, 376, 991–1023.

Waldron, F. and Ruane, B. (2010) *Human Rights Education: Reflection on Theory and Practice*. Dublin: The Liffey Press.

Walker, M. and Unterhalter, E. (eds) (2007) *Amartya Sen's Capability Approach and Social Justice in Education*. Basingstoke: Palgrave Macmillan.

Watkins, K. (2000) *The Oxfam Education Report*. Oxford: Oxfam.

Wellman, C. (1998) *The Proliferation of Rights: Moral Progress or Empty Rhetoric?* Oxford: Westview.

Wenar, L. (2005) 'The value of rights', in J. K. Campbell, M. O'Rourke and D. Shier (eds), *Law and Social Justice*. Cambridge, MA: MIT Press, pp. 179–209.

— (2010) 'Rights', in E. N. Zalta (ed.), *The Stanford Encyclopedia of Philosophy* (Fall 2010 edn). Available at: http://plato.stanford.edu/archives/fall2010/entries/rights/.

White, J. (1990) *Education and the Good Life: Beyond the National Curriculum.* London: Kogan Page.

— (2007) 'What schools are for and why'. *IMPACT Paper No. 14.* London: Philosophy of Education Society of Great Britain.

Willis, P. (1978) *Learning to Labour: How Working Class Kids Get Working Class Jobs.* Aldershot Gower: Saxon House/Teakfield Ltd.

Wilson, D. (2004) 'A Human Rights contribution to defining quality education'. Background paper prepared for the *Education for All Global Monitoring Report 2005.* Paris: UNESCO.

World Bank (2006) *From Schooling Access to Learning Outcomes: An Unfinished Agenda.* An analysis by the Independent Evaluation Group of the World Bank. Washington, DC: World Bank.

— (2011) *Learning for All: Investing in People's Knowledge and Skills to Promote Development.* World Bank Education Strategy 2020. Washington, DC: World Bank.

World Conference on Education for All (1990) *World Declaration on Education for All: Meeting Basic Learning Needs.* Available at: www.unesco.org/education/efa/ed_for_ all/background/jomtien_declaration.shtml (accessed 22 February 2011).

Wringe, C. (1986) 'The human right to education', *Educational Philosophy and Theory,* 18(2), 23–33.

Yates, C. (2012) 'Reflections on Masters teaching at the IOE EID 1985–2010: From better understanding social change to promoting improved social justice'. Paper presented at the 85th Anniversary of International Education, Institute of Education, University of London.

Young, M. (2008) *Bringing Knowledge Back In.* London: Routledge.

Index